THE UNFORTUNATE FALL

THE UNFORTUNATE FALL

*Theodicy and the Moral Imagination
of Andrew Marvell*

John Klause

ARCHON BOOKS
1983

© 1983 John Klause. All rights reserved.
First published 1983 as an Archon Book,
an imprint of The Shoe String Press, Inc.,
Hamden, Connecticut 06514
Printed in the United States of America

The paper in this book meets the guidelines for permanence and durability
of the Committee on Production Guidelines for Book Longevity
of the Council on Library Resources.

Library of Congress Cataloging in Publication Data

Klause, John 1943–
    The unfortunate fall.

    Bibliography: p.
    Includes index
    1. Marvell, Andrew, 1621-1678—Religion and ethics.
2. Theodicy in literature.   3. Good and evil in literature.   4. Theology in literature.   I. Title.
PR3546.K55   1983   821'.4   83-13521
ISBN 0-208-02026-8

To my parents, in deepest gratitude;
and to Youree and his Company,
"who by their learning and good life,
seem'd to me iustly to claime
an interest for the guiding,
and rectifying of mine understanding."

Contents

Acknowledgments

As I offer thanks to the many people who have helped me towards this book, I know how little my acknowledgment repays their kindness, and I do not pretend, like a Harold Skimpole, that I have given them something of value by providing them an opportunity to be generous. But they were happy to give to me gratis. And I have taken eagerly, with warm feelings of gratitude. If thankfulness is a passion, it seems to me a wonderful rarity: a passion without a darker side, one to be indulged in naively. I am unashamedly delighted to owe so much to mentors and friends.

I cannot now name everyone to whom I am indebted for help in this project. But I can begin by thanking my teachers at Stanford, who tried to show me how to recover and understand the past: Professors Virgil Whitaker, George Sensabaugh, Lawrence Ryan, David Riggs, and Murray Roston, and especially Professors Ronald Rebholz and Martin Evans. William Allan, of the Stanford Libraries, and many another librarian in places remote and near have made much of my work possible, and all of it easier. My senior colleagues at Harvard have offered encouragement and have tried to fill my ever-deepening need for instruction. I am grateful to Professors Herschel Baker, Walter Kaiser, and Morton Bloomfield for assistance of various kinds, and to Professor Gwynne Evans, whose patient and learned attention to this study at different stages of its existence has rescued it from many an insanity and whose benefactions to me have been legion. Professor Maynard Mack has given me timely advice from another quarter. In yet another, Professors David Bergeron, George Reinecke, Malcolm Magaw, and Leslie Whitbread know what they have done to prepare my way. My colleagues Andrew Delbanco and Heather Mc-Clave, and my superior at present, Richard Marius, have shown more generosity than a friend has a right to expect. Many of my strongest obligations are of the longest standing: to Anne Klause, Donald Gelpi, Albert Gelpi, E. J. Romagosa, John Edwards, Garth Hallett, and that "best philosopher," Youree Watson.

I wish to thank the Harvard English Department for assuming some of the costs of preparing the manuscript, the Hyder E. Rollins Fund for a grant to support this study's publication, and Mr. James Thorpe III, of Archon Books, for his understanding editorship.

To Tricia Hill I owe thanks for help with this book and for many things of far greater worth.

J. K.

1

Introduction

One touch of nature makes the whole world kin.

Troilus and Cressida

An "epicureanism of the imagination" is as easy to despise as to admire. When a man enjoys the spectacle of contrary "truths," delighting as much in the defeat of reason as in its triumph, when he feels unconstrained by the necessity to choose from competing versions a single truth that may direct a life, he may be more blamed for his dilettantism than praised for his acuteness and honesty.[1] A readiness for any truth may seem wise:

> *In utrumque paratus!* To be ready for everything, there perhaps is wisdom. To abandon oneself at the appropriate time to confidence, skepticism, optimism, irony, is to be sure that at least for some moments one has participated in the truth.[2]

But the readiness is not all. Abstention from error is neither the most noble nor the most useful moral action; intelligence is not courage; and a self-conscious distaste for the "crudity" of partisanship may spring from the coyest effeteness.

The intellectual and moral coyness of Andrew Marvell, however, is rarely held against him. Marvell has over the last few decades become esteemed as one of the major poets of the seventeenth century, even though he spoke with an apparent detachment that has rendered him almost anonymous.[3] A public figure who emerged reluctantly from his privacy after the great revolutions of the 1640s, who finally took sides on matters of state and religion in an age that pressured men into the starkest loyalties, he yet did his best to keep his true predilections secret and has left us reason to wonder about the depth and sincerity of his commitments. Even where Marvell's motives seem unambiguous, they were not closely

1

bound up with ideologies, the reassuring clarity and absoluteness of which he did not need. He preoccupied himself, as this study will propose, with large questions of justice—that is, with the constraints of an absolute moral norm upon human action, indeed, upon the action of God himself. Providence had left itself open to challenge, and must be defended in a "theodicy" if the most basic verities were to be secure. But Marvell's writings have often been read as demonstrating that very few truths could hold him in thrall.

This has mattered little to those readers of his poetry who have been interested in the play of his mind rather than in the ideas that engaged it or in the effects of these ideas upon action. Rosalie Colie, for instance, assumed that "Marvell's chief reason for writing lyric poetry was an overriding interest in the problem of lyric poetry," that he was not "committed to any particular theme or obsessed by it," that he played "games" with both "mental sets" and "philosophies."[4] J. B. Leishman was undisturbed by the contradictory attitudes expressed in Marvell's poems—by the eternity-loving "drop of dew" and the eternity-dreading courter of the "coy mistress," by the misogynous haunter of gardens and the amorous admirer of "fair singers" and "tender shepherdesses," by the eulogist of Cromwell the revolutionary and the detractor of the "Chronicler to Spartacus." Leishman suggested that Marvell's "detachment and uncommittedness" produced poetry which was "a kind of highly sophisticated game," poetry written out of "the sheer desire to exercise an exceptional gift for making something with words." Whereas Donne and Shakespeare wrote of "love experienced," Marvell "[wrote] of (or rather, perhaps, on) love as a topic," used religious issues as mere "subject matter" on which to exercise his poetic "technique." Marvell looked upon the drama played out by Cromwell and Charles I with the "connoisseurship" of a theatergoer, contemplating the rise of the Lord Protector "as disinterestedly—one might almost say, as artistically—as if he were contemplating some classic hero in the pages of Plutarch."[5]

Not everyone has found Marvell so Olympian. But his old image as England's "watchful sentinel"—the indignant satirist, the inflexible and incorruptible Protestant and patriot—has for for the most part yielded to that of the detached, ironic connoisseur.[6] This Argus-eyed Marvell, it is now believed, was seriously concerned about some few important moral issues, aware of their complexity but never overmastered by it, and almost never a singleminded proponent or follower of causes. And he was the wariest of artists. Gerard Manley Hopkins's estimate of Marvell as "a most rich and nervous poet" is generally accepted,[7] but now defined in characteristically modern ways, ways charted by T. S. Eliot in an essay of

1921.[8] The *rich* poet displays "wit," a quality which "involves . . . a recognition, implicit in the expression of every experience, of other kinds of experience which are possible."[9] Marvell is a master ironist and a devotee of paradox.[10] The *nervous* poet manifests only the cool intensity of a superior gamesman. His verse is play.[11] And the "equipoise," the "balance and proportion" which Eliot found in the poetry, "the alliance of levity and seriousness (by which the seriousness is intensified)," have become attributes of the poet's character, in spite of Eliot's insistence that the qualities he described were "literary rather than personal."[12] Marvell shows himself in command of the games of art and life through rhetorical and philosophical "strategies."[13] His mind is "equable and stable," even "serene," for he has "an assured sense of values" and "has made his peace with things of great account."[14]

And how has he concluded his peace? With detachment. Through his "ability to accept paradox and to recognize the validity, *in loco,* of more than one philosophy."[15] Through his appreciation of an Hegelian dialectic which makes him comfortable with intellectual syntheses.[16] Through stoic resolution before fierce necessity—"*scaeva necessitas*"—and "negative capability" in the face of doubt.[17] Through "loyalism" in politics, a dextrous casuistry that allows one to change allegiances without betraying principles.[18] Whatever the answers, they all imply that Marvell is in complete control, truly the "easie Philosopher" of *Appleton House* who, sometimes without the consolation of "final solutions,"[19] makes his crucial personal and political decisions with the sang-froid that comes from godlike strength and vision.[20] At most, the early poems, the greatest poems, give evidence of internal "conflict," says Christopher Hill.[21] But the poet who stuggles is a champion, a master of the "dialectic," and "by the time of 'The First Anniversary' and 'On Blake's Victory over the Spaniards' [i.e., by the mid-1650s], all Marvell's problems are solved."[22]

To suggest that this received version of Marvell's character suffers from idealization, distortion, and omission is not, one hopes, to react to the "British Aristides" (an epithet earned by Marvell, according to an early biographer) as a mean-spirited citizen did to Plutarch's noble Greek in voting to ostracize him from Athens. Asked "if Aristides had ever done him any injury," the citizen replied, "None at all, neither know I the man; but I am tired of hearing him everywhere called the Just."[23] Surely a portrait of Marvell as a poised, equable sage would be in some respects a true one. There are, however, grounds on which the authenticity of certain features might be questioned. We should suspect on general principle the preternatural ease with which Marvell is said to maneuver through metaphysical and ethical problems. If he did find it easy to lead in the world a morally upright life that was true to his deepest perceptions, we might wonder whether he had not cheated, or failed to take life's struggles seriously. They do him no justice who would have him too wise to be good or too good to be believable.

There is, in fact, evidence enough that Marvell did not enjoy an overwhelming sense of "security." His brief conversion by the Jesuits, for instance, and his premature departure from Cambridge may be signs of mere youthful volatility.[24] They also foreshadow more serious spiritual irresolution, more pronounced dissatisfaction with traditional intellectual structures, and more painful restlessness. Aubrey's picture of a laconic solitary who "would drinke liberally by himselfe" and "was wont to say that, he would not play the good fellow in any man's company in whose hands he would not trust his life" should not be too quickly shrugged off.[25] We can tell from Marvell's writings that he was "facetious" like his father, not an utterly dour melancholic.[26] If he feared for his life, he lived in dangerous times and took positions that gained him enemies. Yet it was not a secure, superior man who once clapped a pistol to the head of a stubborn wagoner to make him pull his load, or who exchanged blows with a fellow member in the House of Commons, or who advised a friend in Persia:

> Stand upon your Guard; for in this World a good Cause signifys little, unless it be as well defended. A Man may starve at the Feast of good Conscience. My Fencing-master in *Spain*, after he had instructed me all he could, told me, I remember, there was yet one Secret, against which there was no Defence, and that was, to give the first Blow.[27]

There is also a hint of the obsessive in Marvell's secretiveness. His constant pleas for preserving the confidentiality of his official communications are understandable.[28] But his words in a letter to the Hull Corporation say more than his correspondents can know: "The best of it is that none of us I belieue either do say or write any thing but what we care not though it be publick although we do not desire it."[29] A note of more than ordinary triumph can be heard in these lines (indeed, the triumph obliterates concern for syntax), especially when the sentiments are considered in the context of other statements by the author. "I am sorry [my letter] by the *Armenian* miscarryed," Marvell writes the friend in Persia. "Tho there was nothing material in it, the Thoughts of Friends are too valuable to fall into the Hands of a Stranger."[30] Thoughts such as "A Man may starve at the Feast of good Conscience," perhaps. Thoughts that come too close to revealing and committing his soul. For "the soul is too precious to be let out at interest upon any humane security, that does or may fail; . . . it is only safe when under God's custody, in its own cabinet."[31] Lancelot-Joseph de Maniban, a harmless graphologist, obviously scratched a sensitive nerve in the poet who wrote forty-six Latin lines ridiculing attempts of the soothsayer *("Aruspex")* to peer into the depths of the soul *("animi recessus")*.[32]

Marvell's secretiveness is more than a temperamental quirk in one "naturally . . . inclined to keep [his] thoughts private."[33] More than the extreme caution of a public man who fears that his position, if known, would prove unpopular. It is the nervousness of a skeptic at the mercy of his doubts, who wants to be free to change his stance without inconvenience, either because he has been forced to take it without conviction or because the conviction from which it resulted was only provisional. That he refused to publish most of his lyrics is not surprising; they were *too* personal and private to be let out of his cabinet.[34]

Marvell's doubts, his obstacles to conviction, and his responses to uncertainty will be central concerns of this study. And it should be stated at the outset that some of the charges his enemies leveled against him, although not ultimately damaging, seem not entirely groundless; that his motto should have been *Quo me vertam nescio* ("I know not where to turn"),[35] or that he was "a notable English Italo-Machavillian."[36] His skepticism tempered the strength of his commitments, making them flexible in ways that he would have been embarrassed to acknowledge at a time when partisanship was considered an imperative of virtue.

His criticism of Samuel Parker in *The Rehearsal Transpros'd* sounds very much like an *apologia pro vita sua*:

> Though a man may be allowed once in his life to change his party, and the whole Scene of his Affairs, either for his Safety or Preferment; nay, though every man be obliged to change an hundred times backward and forward, if his Judgement be so weak and variable; yet there are some drudgeries that no man of Honour would put himself upon, and but few submit to if they were imposed.[37]

Marvell does not seem to have been always and everywhere sure where a man of "variable" judgment should make his stand on a point of "Honour." The lines of the principled poet in "Tom May's Death" ring with the confidence of firm conviction:

> When the sword glitters ore the Judges head,
> And fear has Coward Churchmen silenced,

Then is the Poets time, 'tis then he drawes,
And single fights forsaken Vertues cause.
He, when the wheel of Empire, whirleth back,
And though the World's disjointed Axel crack,
Sings still of ancient Rights and better Times,
Seeks wretched good, arraigns successful Crimes.[38]

[63-70]

Perhaps the Civil War, through much of which Marvell was making his grand tour of the Continent, was not yet the "Poets time." But only a few months before "Tom May" the same poet had declared in "An Horatian Ode upon Cromwell's Return from Ireland" that "wretched good" was not good enough, that "the antient Rights . . . do hold or break / As men are strong or weak."[39] We could hear again in the background, "A Man may starve at the Feast of good Conscience." The passage about the poet's singlehanded fight in "forsaken Vertues cause" is, as John Carey has said, "wonderfully public." It does not at all sound detached. Yet we find "no trace of publication until thirty years after it was written, nor the least evidence that it was made public in manuscript. Marvell, so far as we know, was haranguing an empty room."[40] We need to look at more evidence before calling this an instance of *Quo me vertam nescio*, but the case is not implausible. On the other hand, some of Marvell's *certitudes* also lead him into inconsistencies. In the "Horatian Ode" he scorns the "party-colour'd Mind" of the Scots, but there is little more "party-colour'd" than his commendation of the ruffians Thomas Blood and James Mitchell. His satires do not spare in the least the most hapless sinners among his opposition. Yet Monmouth and Buckingham, who support the right causes, win his approval; even Buckingham—atheist, libertine, humiliator of Marvell's former pupil at Appleton House, Maria Fairfax.[41]

In view of what the epithet implied in his day, Marvell would justly have resented hearing himself called a Machiavellian.[42] He could speak powerfully in defense of moral scrupulousness:

St. Paul hath said, "God forbid we should do evil that good may come of it." . . . No man ought to cheat another, though to the true belief. Not by interlining the Scripture. Not by false quotation of Scripture, or a Father. Not by forging a Heathen prophecy, or altering an Author. Not by a false syllogisme. Not by telling a lye for God.[43]

Then, too, the courage he showed in his parliamentary years cannot fail to impress. The letter to his friend in Persia is a little disturbing, however, and we know that if Marvell would not "lye for God," he would bend the truth in other causes. His praise for Charles II throughout *The Rehearsal Transpros'd* he bestows not always in admiration, certainly, but often out of a sense that adulation is expedient—as when he claims that "Princes, as they derive the Right of Succession from their Ancestors, so they inherit from that ancient and illustrious extraction, a Generosity that runs in the Blood above the allay of the rest of mankind."[44] Through his flattery of Louis XIV in "Inscribenda Luparae" Marvell hopes to win prize money in a competition,[45] not to advance what he sees to be the cause of truth and justice:

> Sunt geminae Jani portae, sunt tecta tonantis;
> Nec deerit numen dum Ludovicus adest.[46]

In *The Rehearsal Transpros'd,* again, he protests against an insinuation of Parker which comes too near the truth:

> As to myself, I never had any, not the remotest relation to publick matters, nor correspondence with the persons then predominant, until the year 1657, when indeed I enter'd into an imployment, for which I was not altogether improper, and which I consider'd to be the most innocent and inoffensive toward his Majesties affairs of any in that usurped and irregular Government, to which all men were then exposed.[47]

Considering that this defense is offered by one who spent most of the seven years just prior to 1657 as tutor to Lord Fairfax's daughter and to Cromwell's ward, who corresponded with Cromwell in 1653, whose application for a post in the Commonwealth was advanced by Milton in the same year, and whose eulogies of the Lord Protector, whatever their hesitancies, reveal the poet's increasing admiration for the "Wars and Fortunes Son," we might judge the biographers' reactions overly generous when they say that in this passage Marvell "exaggerates his detachment" or that he speaks "not without mental reservation."[48]

To admit Marvell's *"flexibilité,"*[49] then, does not require us to see him "living with irreconcilable contradictions easily [and] finely."[50] We may disagree both with those who find in him a "security of unquestioned and untroubled belief" and with those who claim that like a master alchemist he turns his doubts into the gold of "creative skepticism" in the furnace of his wit.[51] It will be seen that his nervousness is not merely the exhilaration of an artist fully aware of his powers, but also a disquiet born of conflicts, even contradictions, in his inherited schemes of value. His mind, however agile, cannot resolve these conflicts, the defeat of reason becoming for him one of the dominant facts of his moral life.[52] Nor can paradox as an intellectual category render the contradictions acceptable to him, for in his view, paradox as a metaphysical condition is part of the problem of evil, not a feature of redemption. If over the course of his life he seems evasive and occasionally less than ingenuous, it is partly because like most mortals he is not consummately virtuous and partly because he cannot always see where or why he should invest utterly his moral energy.

The following inquiry into the mind of Andrew Marvell, then, is a search for premises that lead to intellectual impasse. A serious and reflective soul, desiring the world to make sense, Marvell asks elementary questions about the nature of things: not merely about proper modes of living or appropriate ethical choices—"Should I lead a contemplative or an active life? Should I embrace these politics and politicians or those?"— but about the principles that determine "good" or "evil" and establish them in the world—"What is justice? Are Nature and its Architect just? What are the sources of value and of moral obligation, *my* obligation? How do I accommodate myself to the 'mystery of iniquity'?" These are religious questions, posed by a Christian whose unaffective piety never melts, trembles, or breathes even the smallest sigh, who in his thoughts sometimes risks irreligion, yet believes that Transcendence can be this world's only ultimate source of explanation and rescue. When Marvell searches his mind for answers he finds very few, because the axioms from which he proceeds virtually preclude rational solutions. He would ground his actions on considerations of divine and human justice, but the former he finds incomprehensible and the latter only dimly perceptible in the institutions that must embody it. Impasse turns into game. But this game, unlike that of art, is crucial and dangerous. Marvell does not always play it with grace, nor does he always win, but unlike a dilettante he feels compelled to guide it to a conclusion. By the end of his life he believes, chooses to believe, versions of religious and political truth which he has long tested; and he acts with a brave prudence to promote them, even if his belief is not much helped by understanding.

The axioms that direct Marvell into this condition are simple in themselves, complex in their corollaries. They reside in what William James would have called "the hot place" in Marvell's consciousness, a "group of ideas to which he devotes himself, and from which he works," concerns at "the habitual centre of his personal energy."[53] Although these ideas are not always clearly developed in his mind, they are never far from being fully conceptualized.[54] They are embodied with such consistency in certain themes and images that we can conceive of a strongly charac- terized "moral imagination" which informs his work, dictating subject and manner of treatment. It is in his quarrel with God that this imaginative faculty most faithfully reveals itself. So high an argument, therefore, should serve as the starting point and a constant point of reference for this study of Marvell's mind.

Before the discussion proceeds, however, two of its assumptions ought to be made explicit. The first, of course, is that such an undertaking is legitimate. Some critics have suggested that the evidence will not permit a study of Marvell's thought, there being no "essential unity of idea" in the poems and no "straight equivalences" between them and the "general set of [the poet's] mind."[55] One may respectfully disagree. Contradictions there are in Marvell's writings, but these do not disprove "equivalences" between his poems and his mind any more than anomalies in a person's biography prove that he did not live them.[56] The poet may speak through a multitude of masks; but as Yeats has said, "There is always a living face behind the mask," and there is some point to the apothegm of Oscar Wilde: "Man is least himself when he talks in his own person. Give him a mask and he will tell you the truth."[57]

Unlike Bunyan or Wordsworth or Newman, Marvell produced no formal spiritual testament, and few of his lyrics can be dated with certainty. Some dates, however, are certain, others probable;[58] and a sufficient number of the author's preoccupations are evident in his writings to warrant a treatment of his moral imagination and its self-contentiousness. This study will not attempt to give a yearly chronology of all of Marvell's spiritual conflicts, but will instead describe large patterns of thought and feeling that tend in retrospect to arrange themselves in a history. (The imperfect evidence about dates allows *only* a speculative retrospect of a changing awareness, hence the somewhat eccentric position of the chronologically organized discussion in the final chapter of this study.) Since the search for Marvell must rely to some extent on conjecture, sober critics have cause to be wary. Nevertheless, the character that he reveals to most readers is in some ways so attractive, in others so disquieting, and in either case so compelling, that there is surely reason enough to try to make what evidence we have tell all it can about him.

The second assumption is that a knowledge of a mind requires an understanding of what it did not think as well as of what it did. Predilections and choices are better appreciated when related to the large range of options from which choices are taken—even when some of the options are only dimly perceived by the mind in question, or not perceived at all. The best way, therefore, to consider Marvell's quarrel with God is to place it in the context of the classic and perennial debates about the divine justice. Marvell will be seen to belong to a side, to share with some thinkers a temperament and a set of ultimate values that can raise in a believing Christian the most anxious perplexity—as they do, for all his suavity of manner, in the poet himself.

It may be objected that the attempt to locate a shadowy figure within an intellectual tradition can turn the critic into a Malvolio, who, when frustrated by an inconvenient anagram, will yet not abandon his beloved hypothesis: "To crush this a little, it would bow to me." But no critical approach is of itself proof against Malvolioism. The threat and even the inevitability of subjective analysis should daunt the student of a poet's mind no more than they do other kinds of commentators. No critic or historian of any persuasion can deny having had an experience like James Thurber's. After fumbling for a while with his microscope at a botany lesson, Thurber finally found a setting that seemed to show him the cell he was supposed to see. He drew a "constellation of flecks, specks and dots." But his instructor was not impressed. "'That's your eye!' he shouted. 'You've fixed the lens so that it reflects! You've drawn your eye.'"[59] Some philosophers, consumed with the problems of epistemology, claim that one can draw little else. Those of us who set out in search of an author, indeed, of his "mind's eye," may appreciate this view, acknowledging how difficult it is to know another. But we would not take the first step if we did not believe, like true Metaphysical wits, that the "pictures in our eyes" are not our own.

2

Rightly Dividing

If thou didst offer rightly, but didst not
rightly divide . . ., hast thou not sinned?
Be silent.

Translation of Genesis 4:7,
from the Septuagint

O if we but knew what we do,
   When we delve or hew—
Hack and rack the growing green!
. . . .
   Where we, even where we mean
      To mend her we end her,
   When we hew or delve:
After-comers cannot guess the beauty been.

G. M. Hopkins, "Binsey Poplars"

   Nothing can be sole or whole
That has not been rent.

Yeats, "Crazy Jane Talks
with the Bishop"

We may never know exactly what Hopkins meant in calling Marvell "nervous" (and he confessed to having read only "excerpts" from the writings),[1] but in fact the two poets show themselves nervous about some of the same things. There is consanguinity evident in Marvell's "Picture of little T. C." and Hopkins's "Spring and Fall," in the Protestant's "Resolved Soul and Created Pleasure" and the Jesuit's "Habit of Perfection," in the former's attitude toward the "Architects" in "A Dialogue between the Soul and Body" and the latter's toward the ravagers of "Binsey Poplars."[2] Not so evident, yet very real, is the kinship between Marvell

11

and the author of "The Wreck of the Deutschland," of "Thou art indeed just, Lord, if I contend / With Thee," and of the troubled sermon rhetoric that follows:

> Not a sparrow, Our Lord says, falls to the ground without your Father, that is / without his noticing and allowing and meaning it. But we men, he added, are worth many, that is / any number of, sparrows. So then God heeds all things and cares and provides for all things but for us men he cares most and provides best. . . .
>
> But yet this providence is imperfect, plainly imperfect. The sun shines too long and withers the harvest, the rain is too heavy and rots it or in floods spreading washes it away, the air and water carry in their currents the poison of disease; there are poison plants, venomous snakes and scorpions; the beasts our subjects rebel; . . . we contend with cold, want, weakness, hunger, disease, death, and often we fight a losing battle, never a triumphant one; everything is full of fault, flaw, imperfection, shortcoming. . . . But yet there is good in it. . . .[3]

Hopkins in his poetry and prose wrestles strenuously with the God of Power, Justice, and Love, and utters his submission, when he does submit, almost out of breath. But where does Marvell so much as show his sweat? Indeed, in a letter of condolence to Sir John Trott, a Hampshire baronet who has just lost his second and only surviving son, an admonitory, perhaps even attitudinizing Marvell speaks in a voice of firm, self-satisfied faith:

> Upon a private loss, and sweetened with so many circumstances as yours, to be impatient, to be uncomfortable, would be to dispute with God and beg the question. Though in respect of an only gourd an only Son be inestimable, yet in comparison to God man bears a thousand times less proportion: so that it is like *Jonah's* sin to be angry at God for the withering of his Shadow. *Zipporah,* though the delay had almost cost her husband his life, yet when he did but circumcise her Son, in a womanish pevishness reproacht *Moses* as a bloody husband. But if God take the Son himself, but spare the Father, shall we say that he is a bloody God. He that gave his own Son, may he not take ours? 'Tis pride that makes a Rebel.[4]

In the eulogy "On Mr. Milton's Paradise lost," the poet expresses reservations, which are eventually overcome, about Milton's ambitious attempt to justify the ways of God to men, on the grounds that the project might set off a retreat from certainty:

> I lik'd his Project, the success did fear;
> Through that wide Field how he his way should find
> O're which lame Faith leads Understanding blind;
> Lest he perplext the things he would explain,
> And what was easie he should render vain.
>
> [12–16]

And in his own brief, informal theodicy, *Remarks upon a Late Disingenuous Discourse, Writ by one T. D. under the Pretense De Causa Dei . . .*, Marvell lashes out impatiently at those "controversial, female appetites" which hunger after the "very knowledge of good and evil" and drive men to "the disquisition of the causes from whence, and in what manner they are derived." Good is from God, evil from man: *scriptura locuta est* (to paraphrase St. Augustine), *causa finita est* (scripture has spoken, the case is closed).[5] This seems like prompt, cool, unexhausting obeisance.

It should be noted, however, that all these statements come from Marvell in his later years; all of them are public, and therefore not necessarily representative of this very private man's complete thought;[6] and all betray a touchiness about the problem that could well be the result of a troubled decision to cut off debate on an unresolved issue and live in fideistic certitude. Marvell does not deny that God has wreaked a "dreadful . . . vengeance" upon the posterity of Adam.[7] He devotes many of his lyrics to describing the effects of that vengeance. Never protesting in outrage or proclaiming defiance (except, perhaps, in his elegy "Upon the Death of Lord Hastings"),[8] he lets his personae murmur their perplexities, almost afraid to admit that their chagrin is his own, that his, in fact, goes deeper. He wonders whether his God might not be, after all, "bloody."

This last claim is a sweeping and an eccentric one, attributing to Marvell thoughts and moods which few, if any, observers have found fully grown in him.[9] Marvell himself would perhaps have recoiled from the suggestion that his engagement with "the problem of evil" was intense and solemn; for he had reason to feel, as will be seen, that earnest, perennial, uncombated questionings of the divine power and goodness, doubts which one could not dominate and dismiss with a fillip of the will, were, more than temptations, accomplished sins. Yet I believe that the struggles which issued in the unexceptionable platitudes of his later years were genuine, and fiercely, intelligently waged. To understand how this private "war of truth" may have been conducted, we must consider in some detail (over the rest of this chapter) and define with precision the philosophical and theological problems at issue. The project will require a journey into abstraction, in the course of which Marvell will disappear from view, but at the end the man and poet should be able to emerge more visible than before. And the causes of a particular religious anxiety will also provide a starting point for studying other concerns which appear in his writings because they were important enough to affect the course of his life.

Theodicy requires a debate of some of the ultimate questions in Christian theology, as Marvell was quick to acknowledge: "All the most important doctrines of Christianity serve on the one side, and all the fiercest questions of Religion on the other, depending for truth and falshood upon the success of this engagement."[10] In justifying the ways of Providence, one must consider the nature of God and of man, provide a theory of human freedom, argue points of right, responsibility, and sanction, articulate and apply the "law of love." The apologist often assumes, however, that in accomplishing the elementary task of defining good and evil he can be somewhat elliptical, counting on a universal assent to his presuppositions about the issue. Yet what is left unspoken and unexamined can provide matter for disagreements so basic that no amount of argument can resolve them; in the debate the disputants move to a point where the major premises of their syllogisms are no longer logically demonstrable—to the point, that is, where each must make a final appeal to his "intuitive reason."[11] One such disagreement results from what can be called, for the moment, the opposition between "aesthetic" and "ethical" perceptions of value. The adjectives are timeworn; and since they have had a long, complicated history and have often been given meanings that are unrelated to previous usages,[12] I will offer my own descriptive definitions, with the help of statements by authors ancient and modern from whose writings the concepts can be clearly delineated.

In the history of philosophy, the concept of the aesthetic (or beautiful) has been applied to the moral good in different, potentially confusing, ways: sometimes the aesthetic is seen as indicative, even constitutive in some way, of moral quality; sometimes moral goodness is defined in opposition to the aesthetic, which is then a disinterested quality—distinct from, either higher or lower in value than, the moral.

The former application can be found in one of the dialogues of Plutarch's *Moralia*. In the "Gryllus," Odysseus tries to persuade a character of that name, a Greek who has been changed by Circe into a swine, to resume his humanity. Resisting the hero's exhortation, Gryllus establishes with Odysseus the proposition that fertile soil which yields crops spontaneously is better than the dusty acreage of Ithaca, which surrenders little even to the most industrious laborer. He then poses an analogous question: Is "the *spiritual* soil . . . better which produces a harvest of virtue as a spontaneous crop without toil?"[13] Although Odysseus' concession on this point may make arguing for a strenuous human life difficult, he agrees that such a soil is better, adhering, in effect, to the Aristotelian doctrine that temperance, or freedom from excessive or evil desires, is superior to continence, or restraint of immoderate impulses which assail a man.[14] This attitude (which, one will recall, is shared by Signor Ottaviano in Castiglione's *Courtier*)[15] might be termed "aesthetic" for a number of reasons. Classical philosophers tended to speak of the moral good as "beautiful" not only because virtue was thought to reflect the aesthetic qualities of order, measure, and symmetry,[16] not only because it was in itself attractive, but because it embodied a "fittingness" which was to be found in conduct as well as in art.[17] Neither the epicurean Gryllus nor the heroic Odysseus would dissent from this view, both of them implying that temperance possesses a higher degree of fittingness than continence. The aesthetic moralist believes that nothing is more fitting or proper than the possession of an end, that an end realized is better than an involvement with means toward it. Thus Aristotle considered that the contemplation of truth is superior to the search for it, and Plutarch assumed that the possession of a good is more important than the choosing of it.[18] If moral ends are preeminently conditions, such as a state of justice or a habit of generosity, rather than processes toward a condition, such as struggle, even heroic struggle, to be just or generous, then the quick and easy agreement of Gryllus and Odysseus about the nature of virtue is quite understandable.

But why does the aesthetic philosopher insist on the primacy of final states? One can only say it is because of his predilection for certain aesthetic values, of which the most notable is "wholeness." In proposing that the "first condition of beauty" is "wholeness or completeness" *(integritas sive perfectio)*,[19] Thomas Aquinas was writing in the tradition of the Greeks. Plato, in a Socratic exploration of the continuities between the good and the beautiful, found that the complete *(to teleon)* and the sufficient *(to hikanon)* were common to both.[20] Aristotle maintained that every kind of excellence *(arete)*, including moral and aesthetic excellence, was "a kind of completeness" *(teleiosis tis)*.[21]

This attitude can actually blossom into disparate, even antithetical philosophies, as we shall see. Our present concern, however, is with the type of mind (here it is Artistotle's) that judges temperance superior to continence for the reason that the latter is "not a virtue" in the full and proper sense, but a "mixture" *(tis mikte)*—aesthetic wholeness in this case requiring a uniform purity, and amalgamation implying incompleteness.[22] The continent man's moral state is impure because he combines in himself the ordered with the disordered, the completely achieved—his self-rule—with the incipient or provisional—his need to struggle continually toward self-conquest. Aristotle can, in a moment of contemplative transport, with his philosophical eye on the divine perfection, go so far as to dismiss the "circumstances of action," the broken ephemeral processes of human moral striving (which are never in practice "unmixed"), as silly trifles indeed:

> We assume the gods to be above all other beings blessed and happy; but what sort of actions must we ascribe to them? Acts of justice? Will not the gods seem absurd if they make contracts and return deposits, and so on? Acts of a brave man, then, confronting dangers and running risks because it is noble to do so? Or liberal acts? To whom will they give? . . . And what would their temperate acts be? Is it not tasteless to praise them for having no bad desires? If we were to run through them all, the circumstances of action would be found trivial and unworthy of gods.[23]

Plato has Socrates declare with characteristic crispness a similar bias against unaesthetic mixtures:

> Fixed and pure and true and what we call unalloyed knowledge has to do with the things which are eternally the same without change or mixture, or with that which is not akin to them; . . . all others are to be regarded as secondary and inferior.[24]

One might demur at finding Plato, a lover of absolutes and a spokesman for otherworldly perfection, placed in cozy agreement on this point with Aristotle, a pragmatic regarder and accommodator of the relative and the mundane. Aristotelian ethical theory most certainly recognizes that man is a composite creature and that human virtue must therefore be mixed:

> Being connected with the passions, [the moral virtues] are related to our composite nature; now the virtues of our composite nature are purely human; so therefore also is the life that manifests these virtues and the happiness that belongs to it.[25]

But while he respects this properly human virtue which leads to a properly human happiness, Aristotle does not consider the metaphysical "compromise" which constitutes humanity to be ideal. The life of a hybrid moral virtue "is happy only in a secondary degree."[26] What is primary is the pure *(he kathareiotes)*, the permanent *(to bebaion)*, the self-sufficient *(he autarkeia)*,[27] these qualities being found not in mixed virtues[28] such as continence or martial valor, but in the activity of reason, contemplation, which makes man godlike. And Aristotle does not know why men should not strive to transcend the limitations of their amalgamated state by replacing as much as possible of the baser alloy with the more precious:

> By as much as [the divine thing within a man] is superior to his composite nature, by so much is its activity superior to the exercise of the other forms of virtue. . . . And we ought not to obey those who enjoin that a man should have man's thoughts and a mortal the thoughts of mortality, but we ought so far as possible to achieve immortality, and do all that man may to live in accordance with the highest thing in him.[29]

In this aesthetic dissatisfaction with the impure and incomplete, then, Aristotle does not differ markedly from the mentor with whom he clashed decisively on many other issues. When in Plato's *Phaedrus* Socrates prays that his soul may be "made beautiful,"[30] he too realizes that he cannnot ignore and must accept as a melancholy necessity the antinomic, "mixed" character of his best self:

> We will liken the soul to the composite nature of a pair of winged horses and a charioteer. Now the horses and charioteers of the gods are all good and of good descent, but those of other races are mixed; and . . . the charioteer of the human soul drives a pair; and . . . one of the horses is noble and of noble breed, but the other quite the opposite in breed and character. Therefore in our case the driving is necessarily difficult and troublesome.[31]

Plato finds men and gods alike as helpless before the perpetual opposition of good and evil as they seem to be before the mystical inevitability of pleasure and pain, which deity once tried to reconcile without success, and so "fastened their heads together," so that "when one comes the other follows."[32] And it is not man's chief glory that he can triumph over the difficulty, the trouble, the evil (although Plato certainly admires the courage and strength which self-conquest implies); rather that he can, to some extent at least, escape from them into a realm of pure perfection where one is *too* virtuous to experience tribulation.

> Evils . . . can never pass away; for there must always remain
> something which is antagonistic to good. Having no place
> among the gods in heaven, of necessity they hover around the
> mortal nature, and this earthly sphere. Wherefore we ought to
> fly away from earth to heaven as quickly as we can; and to fly
> away is to become like God, as far as this is possible; and to
> become like him, is to become holy, just, and wise.[33]

His mind hostile to mixtures, then, the aesthetic philosopher will not
admit that light is enhanced by darkness or that a condition of peace is
richer for having been established through a process of war. His quest for
wholeness leads him to depreciate choices in which one good must be
denied for the sake of another, because the sacrifice, the moral "violence"
involved, does not give rise to a good greater than possession of both
objects of choice. He rejoices in conjunctions rather than disjunctions,
lamenting any cleavage between or subordination among the right and the
good, the good and the beautiful. Aristotle and Epicurus can agree on this
point at least:

> That which is good without qualification is also without
> qualification pleasant. . . . Happiness is the best, noblest, and
> most pleasant thing in the world.[34]

> It is impossible to live pleasantly without living prudently, well,
> and justly, and to live prudently, well, and justly without living
> pleasantly.[35]

Aristotle does not aver, of course, as Epicurus does elsewhere, that the
pleasant *is* the good; nor does he make the preposterous assertion that in
the world as we know it all good is in reality pleasant; but he does imply
that ideally, metaphysically speaking, the moral good should be pleasant
for the "good man,"[36] there being no higher moral value that can result
from the discontinuity of goods, none either that can be realized by a
division of man into elements—intellect, will, emotions—with *rival*
claims.

Whatever the aesthetic philosopher's vision of the ideal, however, he
finds himself and the good divided; and his experience tells him that
choices must be made, that virtue is often difficult, limiting, maiming,
"ugly." He looks sadly upon the loss of some values to the exigencies of
moral choice. At the destruction of others, his sadness swells into a
perplexed grief and an indignant, helpless fear as he contemplates the
unrelievedly "tragic." Reading the *Antigone* with an Hegelian sense of the

clash of opposites, he would find no Hegelian consolation in a "synthesis" beyond tragedy; he would be more likely to reflect that where "a value cannot be realized without the destruction of another value, equally positive—there . . . is the tragic."[37] The aesthetic philosopher cannot find consolation for loss in the human "grandeur" which tragedy may occasion, for such nobility would be achieved through moral paradoxes which he does not embrace.[38] One does not gain his life by losing it, redeem his suffering by accepting it, vindicate justice by bearing the oppressor's wrong or the proud man's contumely. Once born, evil is everlasting and intractable. As it is with suffering, so with other evils: *souffrir passe; avoir souffert ne passe jamais.* Wisdom may come through suffering, as tragedians in the tradition of Aeschylus have sought to demonstrate, but it need not—the gods are wise yet do not suffer.[39] And if the ways to wisdom are arbitrary, it is doubly tragic that mankind must often travel those that are tearful and bloody.

Why do the gods create or allow such a state of affairs? Are they jealous or malicious? Hesiod suspected as much, and his primitive complaint resounded through much of classical literature: "The gods keep hidden from men the means of life. . . . Zeus in the anger of his heart hid it because Prometheus the crafty deceived him: therefore he planned sorrow and mischief against men."[40] But to complain is not necessarily to blaspheme. Evil remains a fact rather than a problem, as suffering might remain a phenomenon in the nervous system, without moral valence, unless the apparent injustice of it suggests scandal and inspires at least the thought of rebellion or the project of theodicy. Aristotle's relentlessly scientific mind, which could indeed be "shocked" by the spectacle of a just man's undeserved misfortune,[41] did not, it seems, feel pressure to understand, much less to challenge or defend, a divine providence. (He has left us no discussion of the subject, probably because his God was utterly self-centered and related to the universe only as First Mover.)[42] Epicurus and his followers were certain that the "defects" of the universe disproved any divine responsibility for the *rerum natura;* yet instead of protesting against the gods' indifference toward man and his universe, the Epicureans admired and envied it.[43]

When the aesthetic philosopher does feel that the question of divine complicity in the evils of the world demands urgent and devout attention, his theodicy has but few avenues to take. He cannot claim that the gods have allowed evils in order to try man's virtue, for the most truly virtuous man is beyond trial, which is itself only incidental to moral perfection. The "virtues" sacrificed in a world of aesthetically perfect goodness, says Plutarch, might be well lost indeed:

Whenever the universe shall have been turned to fire [in the Stoics' eschatological cataclysm], no evil whatever will remain, but the whole will be at that time prudent and sage. So, then, there will be prudence though evil does not exist; and it is not necessary that there be evil for prudence to be possible. Even supposing, however, that prudence must be the knowledge of things good and evil, what's to dread if because of the abolition of evils prudence would not exist and we should have instead of it another virtue, which is knowledge, not of things good and evil but of things good alone?[44]

Nor can it be argued from this point of view that evil is the price man must pay for his freedom. Many physical evils are not at all attributable to an abuse of the power of moral choice. Besides, if he sees no special value in the conflict between discrete faculties in the soul, the aesthetic philosopher would not be grateful for the "gift" of that "freedom" which involved the ability to choose against reason. Plato, of course, knew no strict disconnection of will from intellect, believing that one who had full knowledge of the good could not choose evil; and Aristotle, though strongly critical of this view, was in fact not far from it himself.[45]

To a skeptic like Cicero's Cotta, then, who demands to know why the gods have denied man that full knowledge which would preclude vice, or why they have not bestowed the gift of a more limited reason on those men only who they know will not misuse it,[46] the defender of an aesthetic faith cannot reply by appealing to the divine concern for a higher moral good. If the apologist should suggest that evil is a punishment for sin,[47] the skeptic would first counter with the universal human experience that the wicked often prosper while the just come to grief,[48] and would then return to Cotta's original questions, the implications of which are spelled out by the modern philosopher Josiah Royce:

One justifies the surgery but not the disease; the toil, but not the existence of the need for toil; the penalty, but not the situation which has made the penalty necessary. . . . Talk of medicinal and disciplinary evil, perfectly fair when applied to our poor fate-bound human surgeons, judges, sailors, or teachers, becomes cruelly, even cynically trivial when applied to explain the ways of a God who must choose, not only the physical means to an end, but the very *Physis* itself in which path and goal are to exist together.[49]

In order to "save" the divine goodness, the aesthetic philosopher must forego any thoughts of the usefulness of evil and either allow the gods indifference (which many inquirers will doubt belongs to goodness) or limit their power, his axioms leaving him no other consistent way out of the dilemma of Epicurus:

> God either wishes to take away evils, and is unable; or He is able and unwilling; or He is neither willing nor able; or He is both willing and able. If He is willing and is unable, He is feeble, which is not in accordance with the character of God; if He is able and unwilling, He is envious, and envy is equally foreign to God; if He is neither willing nor able, He is both envious and feeble, and therefore not God; if He is both willing and able, as is alone suitable to God, from what sources then are evils? Or why does He not remove them?[50]

God does not because he cannot; if not feeble, he is clearly not omnipotent.[51] The theoretical solution to the problem of evil must be a cosmic dualism: as in Plato's vision, spiritual perfection must share the universe with the imperfection and evil necessitated by matter; or as in Plutarch's, rival cosmic "Artificers" must share the work:

> It is impossible for anything bad whatsoever to be engendered where God is the Author of all, or anything good where God is the Author of nothing.... Inasmuch as Nature brings, in this life of ours, many experiences in which both evil and good are commingled ... we may assert that it is not one keeper of two great vases who like a barmaid deals out to us our failures and successes in mixture; we must admit, rather, two opposed principles and two antagonistic forces ... two gods, as it were, the one the Artificer of good and the other of evil.[52]

Thus is the world to be "rightly divided."

It is inevitable that this theoretical explanation should suggest certain practical responses. Since God cannot "remove evils," since neither he nor their victims can redeem them, evils must be endured without compensation and, whenever possible, fled: "Evils can never pass away.... Wherefore we ought to fly away from earth to heaven as quickly as we can."[53] The term of one's flight may indeed be "heaven," but those with less mystical yearnings may settle for Aristotle's ideal of an earthly life of contemplation or dream dreams of pastoral escape or, in the pleasant Horatian tradition of "the happy man," attempt to make those dreams come true.[54]

A pastoral impulse arises most naturally in the aesthetic philosopher, a lover of "both/and" (i.e., of wholeness) who only grudgingly accepts the necessity of "either/or," for the pastoral way of life may aim to keep as much as possible out of the greedy hands of necessity. There is, of course, more than one kind of pastoral vision.[55] But a certain kind of pastoral devot would not know how to appreciate Cardinal Newman's motto, Holiness *rather than* peace. Renato Poggioli has observed that "the psychological root of the pastoral is a double longing after innocence and happiness."[56] If the psychological origins are in fact more complex than this "double" yet stark desire, such a desire always contributes to the complexity. The longing is after innocence *and* happiness (or pleasure) especially, but, as the more sophisticated pastorals indicate, after every other kind of "incompatible" as well. The pastoral life may in practice disappoint Touchstone's aesthetic and, under the circumstances, unrealistic desires:

> In respect of itself, it is a good life; but in respect that it is a shepherd's life, it is naught. In respect that it is solitary, I like it very well; but in respect that it is private, it is a very vild life. Now in respect it is in the fields, it pleaseth me well; but in respect it is not in the court, it is tedious.[57]

But it is the project of the aristocratic exiles in Arden to mitigate "the penalty of Adam" by combining as far as possible the advantages of "the court" with those of "the fields."[58] That their project fails—tongues in trees, books in the running brooks, and sermons in stones do not in fact make the pastoral life so attractive that the courtiers persevere in their resolution "not [to] change it"[59]—is not surprising in a flawed or fallen world.

If what Touchstone and other aesthetic philosophers object to is finitude, or "metaphysical evil," as some authors have called it,[60] which is by definition incomplete and exclusionary, then they are, we might say, preternaturally critical. Would it be better that only the infinite exist? To pose the question in this way, however, would unfairly make the objections to privation appear absurd. An aesthetic apologist admits the value of the limited without surrendering the right to deplore its incommodities, its "limitations." The aesthetically-principled skeptic insists that few physical and no moral evils are strictly logical consequences of finitude and that each finite nature is capable of its own proper, finite completeness, which a different world order need not risk or deny. The principle of contradiction may render some values of the court and of the field incompatible, but many more are incompatible than need be because nature as we know it is riven in the wrong places. Whether apologist or skeptic is right, whether or not evil can be helped, whether or not the project of Arden is entirely feasible, wholeness is health and may be sought with all one's heart.

The "ethical" philosopher, defining the good to some extent in opposition to the beautiful, approaches the problem of evil with radically different presuppositions, as can be seen in Seneca's attitude towards the men of the Golden Age. These innocents, he says, though "noble" and "guileless," and thus of "an exalted spirit," were not in the strict sense "virtuous," for they were not tempted and "did not know how to sin. . . . Virtue does not belong to the soul until the end of a period of training, until that soul is brought to perfection by trial." Although the men of gold came "fresh from the gods," they are not to be envied.[61]

In this view, means become as important as ends—often more important, as when heroism eclipses the moral cause that may occasion it. Aesthetic means thus become, in a way, ethical ends. The ethical good is defined by process, acts of choice,[62] and in that process it is separable from and sometimes pitted against the beautiful. The ethical man's "either/or" philosophy inclines him to welcome the opportunity to choose between conflicting values, because the highest good, the moral good—the *only* good, assert some Stoics[63]—can be achieved by no other means. Without choice made difficult by disjunctions in the wholeness of being, there is no "trial,"[64] and without trial, no "virtue."[65] In the ethical mind's dissatis-faction with the integral, the unified, and the composed, it makes room in the concept of goodness for the truncated, the divided, and the disturbed. Violence and ugliness become sources of value:

> True worth is eager for danger and thinks rather of its goal than what it may have to suffer, since even what it will have to suffer is part of its glory. Warriors glory in their wounds and rejoice to display the blood spilled with luckier fortune. Those who return from the battle unhurt may have fought as well, but the man who returns with a wound wins the greater regard.[66]

The image of "wounds" underscores the fact that the ethical philosopher arrives at his good through a process of excision, making authentic goodness, or virtue, stand apart in glorious isolation from such "indif-ferent things" as "life, health, pleasure, beauty, strength, wealth, reputa-tion."[67] The thought that there is not really very much to rescue from a rampant, predatory evil whose only authentic hypostasis is vice renders the ethical apologist confident of the success of his theodicy: "The task is not difficult," Seneca boasts. "I shall be pleading the cause of the gods."[68]

And he has good reason to feel his argument secure. If nothing is evil but moral evil,[69] or, to speak less extremely, if a narrowly conceived moral good is the *summum bonum* and worth any sacrifice to attain—indeed, if only sacrifice will attain it—one can hardly blame God for making the world an *"occasio virtutis"*[70] or, in Keats's famous phrase, a "vale of soul-making." Instead of absolving God from complete responsibility for nature by advancing theories of a dualistic universe, we should proudly proclaim that he is the one ultimate cause of things as they are.[71] Questions about the appropriateness or justice of the rewards and punishments he allots are senseless, for virtue is its own reward and vice its own punishment.[72] His failure to prevent mankind's lapse from a state of pristine innocence and bliss can only be fortunate, for had we not fallen from a golden age into one of iron, we would have been forever deprived of our greatest glory, our apotheosis: "Endure with fortitude," urges Seneca. "In this you may outstrip God; he is exempt from enduring evil, while you are superior to it."[73]

In the flush of this enthusiasm, the ethical philosopher will not retreat from evils. Although he may attach some value to a life of contemplation, he believes that "the whole glory of virtue is in activity,"[74] which may be solely self-regarding, undertaken to enhance his own moral superiority,[75] or directed toward the moral good of society.[76] In either case, it is the activity of warfare that he seeks, eager to wield, like the God of Cleanthes, a "sword two-edged,"[77] knowing that the greater loss will bring the greater victory: "Virtue rejoices when it pays dear for its existence."[78] Evils are not to be fled, but "divided" and conquered.

Up to this point, while speaking of aesthetic and ethical men or frames of mind, I have simply been epitomizing ideologies, and most intellectual programs are too inflexible to keep their proponents from inconsistencies of thought or action. Plato, for instance, did not "fly away from earth to heaven" as quickly as he could, but exerted himself to establish his ideal Republic on earth. Aristotle, despite his aestheticism, felt compelled to admit that "the good is better when it is harder," and manifested some uncertainty about the equation of the good and the beautiful.[79] The Stoics in their quest for *apatheia,* which is in essence a retreat from experience, seemed hardly consistent in professing eagerness for moral conquest or commitment to political activity.[80] The fact is that within each of the philosophies we have been considering, there is an inquietude which pushes first principles in the direction of greater comprehensiveness, and sometimes into contradiction.

The aesthetic "principle of plenitude," advanced by Plato in the *Timaeus* and later elaborated by Plotinus and others,[81] was meant as a contribution to the Platonic theodicy, which rests on the assumption that

God and evil have nothing to do with each other (we have already noted the cosmic dualism proposed in the *Timaeus*) and that God is not only good in his own being, but responsible for whatever goodness exists apart from himself. This principle attributes the creation of the world to an overflow of a divine benevolence which could not out of envy begrudge existence to a world distinct from the godhead. The product of God's creative activity is the most beautiful of all possible worlds—possessing the beauty of completeness, a fullness of forms, all gradations of being from the most perfect to the least, and embodying the aesthetic ideal of order-in-variety.[82] According to this doctrine, the universe is better for realizing all the possibilities of being—and therefore all grades of privation, which is the only source of distinction among grades of being—than it would be if it contained only the highest. Thus the aesthetic theory of the beautiful earlier enunciated is temporized: dualism shades into monism; the "glory of the imperfect"[83] joins or supersedes the splendor of the pure and self-sufficient in Ideal Goodness; a complete escape from evil is no longer warranted (although, of course, evil is still to be resisted), because things are best as they are. Perhaps the equivocation is due to a qualm about ceding too much to evil in a dualistic cosmos. But whatever their psychological or strategical origins, the contradictions in Platonic thought are genuine, and beyond reconciliation.

The ethical philosopher manages to avoid such literal inconsistencies by being careful of his definitions as he attempts to accommodate his moral theory and the theodicy consequent upon it to a more complex sense of the problem of evil than his cut-and-dried formulas seem to allow. Unwilling to concede the realm of the beautiful to his opponents, he declares that his own "wounded" good possesses a more profound beauty than does any unmarked perfection. It has its harmonies, but harmonies which incorporate dissonance.[84] It has its completeness: "The reason why the Stoics characterize the perfect good as beautiful is that it has in full all the factors required by nature or has perfect proportion."[85] For the Stoics, however, this integrity is achieved, as we have seen, by ruthless circumscription of those "factors required by nature." We must look to thinkers generally considered Romantic for candid proclamations, in accordance with certain corollaries of the principle of plenitude, that incompleteness is the necessary condition of true completeness; that evolutionary process, operating through strife, contradiction, and mutilation—what Hegel called the "slaughter bench" of history—is the only means to the fullness of peace; or even that "fullness" itself is something of an idea abhorrent, confining and stifling in comparison with the dream of perpetual striving.[86] "Beauty" will have a competitor in "The Sublime."

It must now be admitted that these ambiguities hovering around the concept of the beautiful point up the inadequacy, for purposes of analysis, of both "aesthetic" and "ethical" classes, which have proved useful but not sufficiently inclusive. A more fundamental opposition seems to be that between the "categorical" and the "dialectical" or "paradoxical."[87] It is the categorist whose sturdy, stubborn sense of insurmountable oppositions leads him to find wholeness only in purity, to love conjunctions (but only of "pure" perfections) and mourn divisions as tragic, to seek the highest good in the serenity of finality, to describe the world as dualities in perpetual conflict, and to despair of any redemption of evil. His moral good is beautiful or aesthetic, but the beauty is categorically defined. It is the paradoxist whose urge to be "transcending" disposes him to think of the integral as mixed, to accept divisions as opportunities, to honor above all else the good won through loss in violent, sacrificial process, to reconcile opposites in a cosmic monism, and to discover in evil a redeeming usefulness. His moral good is also beautiful, but the beauty is dialectically defined.[88]

The paradoxist would accuse the categorist of being blind to the complexities of a world in which tinctures and hybrids have real, independent, and valuable existence. The categorist's narrow principles, it might be said, dismiss too much in the universe as useless detritus and, in violation of a genuinely aesthetic code, severely restrict the possibilities of legitimate variety. Indeed, what true artist would not exalt the dappled over the monochromous, or, more to the point, would not consider *chiaroscuro* an advance over the flat, uniform radiance of a *trecento* fresco? The categorical ideal of achieved, indefectible perfection only serves to enshrine the torpid and the static. "If there were only unity," says the philosopher Schelling, "and if everything were at peace, then truly nothing would want to stir, and everything would sink into listlessness."[89] In depreciating heroism, the categorist perversely suppresses the universal human instinct to admire it. He reveals a lack of imagination, both in his inability to see that the good of a whole can be served by injury done to its parts, and in his insensitivity to what Schiller called the "Spieltrieb," the play-impulse, which impels man to participate in the grave yet exciting cosmic game of reconciling opposites.[90]

The categorist, of course, would have his own case to make in rebuttal. He would charge his opponent with trying to lend his vision greater depth by the use of epistemological tricks. After all, light in a painting is not *in itself* enhanced by the darkness into which it recedes; there is only an appearance of greater mystery or splendor. (One might even contend that the darkness and light on an artist's canvas are not really opposites, since darkness is perceived simply as another color. Black is not genuinely privative in the way that evil is.)[91] Neither, then, is good in itself enhanced by evil, which can have utility only as a foil. Is the slaughter bench of history to be justified in the name of appearances? The words of Yeats's Crazy Jane, "Fair and foul are near of kin, / And fair needs foul . . . ," are but paradoxical cant, as are those of Goethe's Faust:

> I vow myself to excitement, intoxication,
> the bitterest pleasures, amorous hatred,
> and stirring remorse. My heart, now free
> of the longing for learning, shall close itself
> to no future pain. I mean to enjoy
> in my innermost being all that is offered to mankind,
> to seize the highest and the lowest,
> to mix all kinds of good and evil,
> and thus expand my Self till it includes
> the spirit of all men. . . .

In his counsel to the Romantic hero that light and dark must be kept separate, even when one experiences both—

> You can believe me that this world was made
> to suit a god who dwells in eternal light.
> He has cast us into darkness;
> for you it's enough to have only night and day—

it is, ironically, Mephistopheles who unwittingly suggests a categorical reading of the Gospel text, "if . . . thine eye be single, thy whole body shall be full of light."[92]

To the complaints that his ideal world is monotonous and stagnant, the categorist would also have his replies. There is variety enough in positive perfections, he would say, so that we need not counterfeit new ones by making pseudocompounds out of negations. Furthermore, not all variety is admirable, only that which is controlled by a proper principle of selection. Since an infinite variety or a fullness of forms (*plenum formarum*) is impossible in the real order,[93] that is, since our finite universe must do without much, why should it not do without the worst? As for process, one can contemplate several kinds: the simple, inevitable, purposeful dilation of one's being through time;[94] random or purposeless or futile motion; the alteration of being for the worse; an evolutionary change which may combine all of these. If "Mutabilitie" is a necessity, if indeed it is tempting to believe that through change more positive values may be realized in the universe than in a world of eternal, undeveloping, fully realized good (so that we might, for instance, enjoy the perfection of the child as well as of the adult), then we should prefer the first kind of process and regret the existence of the rest. The paradoxist who extols the glories of an evolution that thrives on destruction and waste, declaring that this sacrifice of parts to whole promotes the highest, most comprehensive good of all, labors under serious misconceptions. Finality does not necessarily imply stasis: one can conceive, even for a finite being, of the most intense activity in an everlasting prime, at an extended peak of perfection.[95] Moreover, destructive evolution subordinates concrete, individual, and (in the case of man) personal goods to the "good" of a "whole" which is only an impersonal principle—and a bogus aesthetic one at that. An evolutionary vale of soul-making does make heroic virtue possible; heroism does merit praise, for it involves an admirable outpouring of moral energy. But in reality heroism is something of a *vertu manquée*. The (internal) difficulty which a hero must overcome is a relative quality, a kind of negative quality made possible by weakness—that is, by a relative deficiency in him of that same moral energy which is a source of our admiration for the virtuous. The strongest love makes the most "difficult" actions undertaken for the beloved *easy* to perform, and to that extent "unheroic."

Finally, the paradoxist may exult in the rigors and excitement of his cosmic game, but only by remaining heedless of or indifferent to the sacredness of the values that are toyed with, put at hazard, and lost.[96] No matter how much Romantic "profundity" the paradoxical thinker aims at, his optimism is as hollow as the rhythms and wisdom of Kipling's verse are facile:

> In all time of our distress,
> And in our triumph too,
> The game is more than the player of the game,
> And the ship is more than the crew.[97]

While recognizing antinomies, the categorist claims to be too honest to dissolve them out of a temperamental need for the *frisson* afforded by paradoxical mysteries, or under pressure from a desire for redemption.

To such an impasse, then, come aesthetical and ethical, categorical and paradoxical quests for solutions to the problem of evil. At this point, where contradictory assumptions make arguments futile, leaving disputants no choice but to point to premises and plead for the careful attention to them that may win recognition and acknowledgment, the religious man (for the rest of this discussion, the Christian) must examine the evidence and appropriate what truth he can discover.

The Christian's God, whose universal sovereignty no dualistic Manichaean heresy may impugn, loves his creation and therefore cannot be
indifferent or malicious. For those whom he loves he desires the best,
which in his omnipotence he can bring about and does. The nature of the
"best," however, is difficult to define. It is not simply the categorical
good—not from Yahweh, "the Lord of Hosts," or from Jesus, who came
"not to send peace on earth, but a sword" and left the legacy of a supernal
"peace" to be won through warfare. "The kingdom of heaven suffereth
violence, and the violent take it by force."[98] The paradoxical ideal would
seem more compatible with the religion of the Cross, did not the self-
sufficiency of Stoic virtue eliminate man's need for and dependence on the
divine.[99] Indeed, despite this major incompatibility, biblical and post-
biblical theodicies have continually relied on paradoxical arguments,
raising in the process as many questions as they have professed to settle.[100]

Although the account in Genesis of the disobedience of Adam and
Eve has not always been offered as an answer to the problem of evil,[101]
Christian apologists, beginning with St. Paul, have discovered in it the
issues crucial to their defense of God. At the very beginning of the Bible
the Lord God stands open to accusation and requires a defense, for he is a
God who prohibits, who divides possibilities arbirarily, allowing his
creatures neither knowledge nor, once they have known, immortality.
His disposition is at least subject to unkind interpretation. The Yahwist
author himself seems to have considered "the knowledge of good and
evil" to be scientific rather than moral, God's command to Adam and Eve
to abstain from the fruit of the Tree of Knowledge motivated by a desire
to keep them in a state of child-like, albeit blissful, ignorance.[102] And the
enemies of Yahweh could easily put the worst color on his close guarding
of the Tree of Life, as did, for example, the emperor Julian:

> [The Galileans'] God must be called envious. For when he saw
> that man had attained to a share of wisdom, that he might not,
> God said, taste of the tree of life, he cast him out of the garden,
> saying in so many words, "Behold, Adam has become one of us;
> . . . and now let him not put forth his hand and take also of the
> tree of life and eat and thus live forever."[103]

To counter such suggestions, the divine prohibitions must be made to
serve a benevolent purpose—in the opinion of many Christian theologians, a paradoxical moral purpose. The forbidden fruit, writes
Augustine, contained in itself no power for good or evil:

> It was well to show man, whose submission to such a Master [as
> God] was so very useful to him, how much good belonged

> simply to the obedience. . . .[Adam and Eve] were in fact
> forbidden the use of a tree, which, if it had not been for the
> prohibition, they might have used without suffering any evil
> result whatever.

God thus called the tree "the tree of the knowledge of good and evil" in order "to signify [to Adam and Eve] by this name the consequence of their discovering both what good they would experience if they kept the prohibition, and what evil if they transgressed."[104] Since Adam and Eve disobeyed God's commandment, they were kept from the immortality-giving tree of life not out of jealousy but in condign punishment for their crime. According to the Pauline theology, "by one man sin entered into the world, and death by sin,"[105] and all other evils that the world knows. As Augustine states in his *Commentary on Genesis*, "*omne quod dicitur malum, aut peccatum [est] aut [poena] peccati.*"[106] Many theological perplexities inevitably arise from the imputation of the "original sin" of the first parents to their children, or from the rehabilitation of the once rejected biblical proverb, "The fathers have eaten sour grapes and the children's teeth are set on edge."[107] Nevertheless, it is clear that the tacit assumptions of a theodicy read out of Genesis become the paradoxical ones that the *occasio virtutis* is worth the risk of all other values and that virtue is attainable only through a trial in which some of those values must be freely and with difficulty sacrificed.

One might ask, however, whether these assumptions are perfectly congruent with the rest of Christian doctrine.[108] It is not really evident, for example, that Christianity unequivocally prizes virtue, or virtue paradoxically defined, as the highest good. The Christian's God does not overcome obstacles and achieve virtue through trial, yet no man, however heroic, can "outstrip" him.[109] Nor can one say that virtue is simply the highest good for a finite creature, since in orthodox Christian dispensations man is not by himself capable of virtue in the strict ethical sense. If one cannot do what virtue requires without the help of grace, he can call no victory, and hence no worth, his own.[110] It may be claimed that this less than heroic condition is a punishment for sin, the transgression of Adam and Eve having deprived their posterity of a chance for the highest good. But this is not a Christian view. All men somehow sinned in Adam, it is true, but they are redeemable, and their redemption does not leave them deprived of, incapable of the highest good. A Christian does not consider the saints in their "everlasting rest" to be in any way diminished because they have been given a reward without fully earning it (if earning it at all), or because, immune to temptation, they cannot deviate from the good.[111]

Augustine maintained, in fact, that the state of the saints in heaven, who cannot sin (*non possunt peccare*), is more exalted than that of Adam and Eve in Eden, who were capable of sinning (*poterant non peccare*) and for a time did not. This position is stated in more general terms by Thomas Aquinas: "The higher degree of goodness is that a thing be good and unable to fail from goodness, and the lower degree is of that which can fail."[112]

For the Christian theologian, as for Aristotle, virtue must have the nature not of an end but of a means. "All moral deeds," says Aquinas, "can be directed to something else [as an end]," the ultimate end being the possession through knowledge and love of the Supreme Good.[113] Now if creatures who infallibly choose this end possess a "higher degree of goodness" than those whose virtue is liable to fail, God's creation of fallible creatures and consequent permission of evil cannot be justified as a *necessary means* to a "higher" moral good. In the opinion of Calvin, God in his omnipotence could have forestalled evil by creating man "altogether incapable either of choosing or of committing any sin." God refrained from doing so not on any rational grounds that it is better to allow evil to be chosen—the infallible nature "would have been more excellent"—but simply "because it was at his choice to bestow as little as He pleased."[114] Augustine and Aquinas provide a reason why God makes room in his creation both for those who can and who cannot sin. But the rationale is not ultimately based on moral considerations.

This may seem an odd point to try to establish, for one of the major trends in the history of Christian theodicy has been the development of the "free-will defense" of Providence.[115] And of course moral good may be described as the good created by the will through its free choices. But freedom has been difficult to define, and the moral dimension of freedom, however it is defined, has not in fact been paramount in attempts to justify the ways of God.

The free-will defense may be outlined as follows. All evil, physical and moral, is in one way or another (as sin, the effect of sin, or punishment for sin)[116] attributable to the free choices of rational creatures. Freedom makes these rational agents, and not their Creator, responsible for their actions and the consequences of the actions. Even so, it is better that God created angels and men free than that he should have made them unable to choose between good and evil. And he could not without contradiction have made them both free and unable to sin. Hence the fact of evil, a consequence of the gift of freedom, counts neither against God's goodness nor (since omnipotence does not imply an ability to work contradictions) against his power.

There are two main points to be made here about this argument.

First, it can be valid only if freedom is defined as involving the ability to choose evil as well as good—as though the free will were poised in balance between opposing choices[117]—and only if this freedom is better than its converse or opposite. But God's will is not so poised: he cannot choose evil. Either, then, the divine will is not free (to choose good or evil), or freedom must be described on a model other than that of the balance.

This alternate model is predicated on the theory that the moral choice of a rational agent will never be totally indeterminate, "free" in that sense, for it will always be directed at least by one reason or another. (Wholly irrational choices have no moral dimension.) Free will would consist in the ability to have the choice determined by one's knowledge of the goodness or badness of the object chosen *rather than* by any other constraint (such as "passion" or external force). Freedom would then be a continuum rather than a balance: the more the will is free, the more its choices will be determined by the mind's knowledge of good and evil. And since the will never desires evil *as* evil, but always under "the appearance of good" *(sub ratione boni),*[118] greater knowledge (precluding action upon mere appearances) will mean less ability to choose evil. The greatest freedom, therefore, would entail, as Augustine and Aquinas affirm, the impossibility of choosing evil. God is incapable of sin, yet acts freely; and even man in his definitive state of holiness in heaven will have a "freedom much greater [than his first, in Eden]—in not being able to sin."[119]

Now either of these conceptions of freedom poses difficulties for the free-will defense of Providence. According to the balance-model, God and the saints confirmed in goodness are not free to choose between good and evil. It would then seem that the ability to choose only the good is more valuable than freedom, and God's permission of evil for the sake of freedom is questionable as a "favor" to his creatures. According to the continuum-model, God and the saints are most free, and freedom is a gift of the highest value, but evil would have been excluded from the universe if God had given his creatures more freedom than he did. In either case, the goodness of the Creator falls short of vindication.[120]

Second, the creation of agents who can according to the balance-model freely choose good or evil does not *necessarily* increase the moral perfection of the universe, for it is at least logically possible that these agents will always choose evil. As we shall see, some theologians have recognized that the existence of beings *qui possunt peccare* is ultimately an aesthetic fact, contributing to the variety, hence to the beauty, of the universe, rather than in a necessary way to its moral goodness. Indeed, if—as Christian theologians have taught—God has punished sin by weakening the human will (when other punishments were possible), he may not be said to have made the fostering of virtue his highest priority.

A moral theory, then, a paradoxical moral theory—exalting disjunction, trial, risk, and loss—cannot by itself explain for the Christian why God has allowed evil to exist in the world.

Nor, on a less abstract and philosophical level, can such a theory turn the biblical story of the fall into a theodicy. Even if the trial of Adam and Eve was pure, one in which they had to rely on their own resources, those resources came from God. He may have given Adam and Eve godlike strength and wisdom, as affirmed by the "maximal" theologies,[121] which represent the first couple (Adam especially) as mature and pefect specimens in whom reason controlled appetite without struggle and whose intellectual powers were profound.[122] Under such circumstances it is difficult to understand how creatures so blessed, or the angels before them, could have fallen at all. One can only bow, insists Augustine, before the great mystery of the freedom of the will, for to seek the causes of defection from good is "to try to see darkness, or hear silence"; there is "no cause of willing . . . which is prior to willing."[123] In accepting the mystery of the fall, however, we must ignore the fact of experience that circumstances may render certain choices implausible, sometimes practically, even when not logically, impossible. And there is little less plausible than the gratuitous choice of evil by a creature of perfect rationality, whose reason controls his appetite and who is naturally disposed to love and delight in the good.[124]

On the other hand, God may have, as postulated in the "minimal" theologies,[125] created man a "child" who "had need to grow so as to come to his full perfection."[126] Adam and Eve's limited vision and strength, then, render temptation plausible and the fall understandable,[127] but their weakness also raises objections about the purpose of their trial and the justice of their punishment. Throwing an inexperienced swimmer into the water may insure that there will be a struggle, but what does that struggle prove? What does the seduction of a child prove, and what does the fallen child deserve? These problems become more acute still when we add to the analogies the consideration that God gives his children whatever resources they possess in the first place and decides where those resources are to end. Even on the assumption that Adam and Eve were not children but relatively mature adults somewhere between childhood and godhead, the whole affair might yet seem a game, in which the gamemaster so constitutes the players as to guarantee a trial and creates odds that the contestants might lose and thereby assure the defeat of all their descendants—who as a result of original sin are incapable of winning such a contest and must be rescued from above. To what end are odds set? If, as has been suggested, the cause of human virtue is problematic, and if it is unthinkable that God should desire the violence and the risk for their own sakes, a more satisfactory rationale must be found for the divine plan.

The paradox of the *felix culpa*, although perhaps originally a hyperbolical expression of faith not meant to bear rigorous theological scrutiny, has often been offered in strict literalness as just such a rationale. *O certe necessarium Adae peccatum, quod Christi morte deletum est! O felix culpa, quae talem ac tantum meruit habere redemptorem!*[128] The fall was fortunate not because the trial that led to it or the condition that resulted from it might occasion greater virtue in man but because it warranted the Incarnation and Redemption,[129] the state of redemption being, in the words of St. François de Sales, "a hundred times greater than the state of innocence."[130] The superiority of the Redemption need not, either, be taken solely on faith, but can be established on conceptual principles—as in the reasoning of the seventeenth-century apologist Richard Sibbes:

> The infinite love and mercy of God . . . is greater in the works of Redemption, then in the Creation of the world, for the distance betweene nothing and something was lesse then the distance between sin and happinesse. For nothing adds no opposition, but to be in a sinfull state there is opposition, therefore it was greater love and mercy for God when wee were sinfull, (and so obnoxious to eternall destruction) to make us of sinners not onely men, but to make us happie, to make us heires of heaven out of a sinfull and cursed state, then to make us of nothing something, to make us men in *Adam,* for there God prevailed over nothing, but here his mercy triumphed over that which is opposite to God, over sinfullnesse and cursednesse.[131]

What Sibbes seems to imply is that man's sin is felicitous because it presents *God* an opportunity for triumph, for paradoxical "virtue." Du Bartas had seen the issue in simple terms: "But for sinne, *Justice* and *Mercie* were / But idle names . . . ";[132] and something like the same thought probably lay behind many of the countless formulations of the theme *Deus humanae substantiae dignitatem mirabiliter condidit et mirabilius reformavit,*[133] as, indeed, it may have prompted the utterance of St. Paul: "God hath concluded them all in unbelief, that he might have mercy upon all."[134]

Such arguments may console those, like Shakespeare's Edgar, who can rejoice that "the clearest Gods . . . make them honours of men's impossibilities"—or liabilities. Other temperaments, however, would more likely ask with some bitterness, "Is it the mark of majesty of

Power / To make offenses that it may forgive?"[135] If it is objected that God only allows, does not "make" offenses, one might reply with an observation of Calvin: "It offends the ears of some, when it is said God *willed* [the] fall; but what else, I pray, is the permission of Him, who has the power of preventing, and in whose hand the whole matter is placed, but His will?"[136] Even if Calvin's contention is not utterly persuasive in its denial of a distinction between God's permissive will and his "will of good pleasure," and God is seen merely to allow sin in the cause of a higher good, one can ask if the end can really justify the means.[137] One might also wonder in what sense Adam's sin was *certe necessarium*. What would have happened had Adam *not* sinned and not made possible a greater outpouring of the divine goodness? Would God's glory have suffered?[138]

Redemption may be superior to unfallen innocence in another respect, if it brings, in the words of Milton's Adam, not only "To God more glory" but also "more good will to Men / From God."[139] This part of the paradox, however, like the first, disturbingly requires end to justify means.[140] Furthermore, it introduces into God's decisions an arbitrariness which many (Calvinists definitely excepted) would find difficult to accept; for redeemed man can do no more to earn the more excellent rewards made possible by the fall than Adam and Eve could have done to earn the lesser rewards belonging to unsullied innocence. The God-man Christ could merit infinitely more, but there was no *reason* for Christ to win greater gifts for sinners. Theologians of a minimalist bent would be likely anyway to look with suspicion on the paradox, because of their belief that man was destined to progress beyond his primal state even had he not sinned. Milton, for example, felt that Adam and Eve's obedience would have insured for them a physical and spiritual evolution,[141] a reward of the highest value, to judge from God's own declaration that Adam would have been "Happier, had it suffic'd him to have known / Good by itself, and Evil not at all."[142] Perhaps that is why Milton's Adam stands "full of doubt" as he utters his *felix culpa,* in what may in fact be an excess of grateful enthusiasm.[143]

But then, the evocation of gratitude and love could be precisely the desired result of God's permission of evil, as Irenaeus suggests in a variation on the *felix culpa* theme:

> This . . . was the [object of the] long-suffering of God, that man,
> passing through all things, and acquiring the knowledge of
> moral discipline, then attaining the resurrection from the dead,
> and learning by experience what is the source of his deliv-
> erance, may always live in a state of gratitude to the Lord,

having obtained from Him the gift of incorruptibility, that he might love Him the more; for "he to whom more is forgiven, loveth more" (Luke vii. 43).[144]

Such a paradox, however, is clearly liable to the same criticisms as the others. In addition, it portrays God as he is seen in the engraving prefatory to the first editions of Sir Thomas Browne's *Religio Medici,* as a hand ready to rescue a man plunging from a precipice, but adds the detail that the same hand had placed the man on the edge (or at least refused to prevent him from climbing the rock) and had allowed him to fall in order to make him grateful for the rescue. A questionable tactic, this, for a father to use to inspire love in his children.

Paradoxical theodicies that rely on a fortunate fall are further embarrassed by the Christian God's concern for each individual soul, on the one hand—He "will have all men to be saved, and to come unto the knowledge of the truth"[145]—and on the other, the obvious fact that some men through no fault of their own do not *become* mature moral personalities capable of "profiting" from adversity. At least as far back as the days of Origen apologists have been troubled by the knowledge that

> many people have been brought up in such circumstances that they have not been allowed to receive even a suggestion of better things; but even from their earliest years they have always been either in the position of favourite to licentious men or masters, or in some unfortunate condition which prevents their soul from looking to higher things.

So it must be confessed that "probably the causes of these inequalities lie entirely in the sphere of providence, and it is not easy for men to come upon their explanation."[146] Then there is the problem of the children,[147] who suffer and die as victims only and cannot actively contribute to the collective heroism of the race. If their God does indeed love or tolerate paradoxical violence, they may seem simply part of the inevitable debris from the cutting and planing and troweling of Origen's carpenter-God.

> Evils which are few in comparison with the orderly arrangement of the universe have been the consequence of the works which were [God's] primary intention, just as spiral shavings and sawdust are a consequence of the primary works of a carpenter, and as builders may seem to cause the mess that lies beside buildings, such as the dirt that falls off the stones and the plaster.[148]

Since God deeply desires the moral perfection of all, surely "the little ones"—even if their cause may not be pleaded on other grounds—cannot be so expendable. A Christian vale of soul-making should be so ordered that every soul have the opportunity to be "made."

It appears, then, that the solely moral grounds of Christian theodicy, those relating it to the perfection of the divine or human will, are extremely tenuous, and it is not surprising that theologians have tried to transcend them. Over the centuries the most influential attempt has been that of Augustine, whose ultimate argument in defense of God actually rests on the subordination, through a paradoxical aesthetic, of the moral good to the beautiful.[149] In the tradition of Plato and Plotinus, Augustine seeks in the variety made possible by privation a good higher than moral, sufficiently grand to justify the creation of a world more deficient in moral goodness than it need otherwise be.[150] According to the Augustinian principle of plenitude, while sin itself is not essential to the "perfection of the universe, . . . souls as such are necessary which have power to sin if they so will."[151] The argument is made explicit by Aquinas: "As . . . the perfection of the universe requires that there should be not only beings incorruptible, but also corruptible beings, so the perfection of the universe requires that there should be some which can fail in goodness, and thence it follows that sometimes they do fail."[152] It is not to be regretted that souls who are able to sin people the world, even though they are inferior to souls confirmed in goodness, for the aesthetic "perfection of the universe" requires such imperfection. Nor do the actual lapses of fallible creatures mar the cosmic beauty, for, as Augustine declares, the sins of individuals contribute to a special loveliness in the whole: "As the beauty of a picture is increased by well-managed shadows, so, to the eye that has skill to discern it, the universe is beautified even by sinners, though, considered by themselves, their deformity is a sad blemish." As long as God punishes sin, the order essential to the beauty of the universe is maintained: "There is no interval of time between failure to do what ought to be done and suffering what ought to be suffered, lest for a moment the beauty of the universe should be defiled by having the uncomeliness of sin without the comeliness [*decus*] of penalty."[153] "Comeliness." In the most remarkable of paradoxes, the Lord "glorious in holiness," who has "loved righteousness and hated iniquity," whose loving-kindness extends to each of his children, places the perfection of the Divine Artistry above the holiness, righteousness, and happiness of "the work of His hands."[154]

The adequacy for the Christian of this solution to the problem of evil is certainly open to question. Even if one ignores the conceptual difficulties involved in the principle of plenitude itself,[155] and, as well, the problems which theologians have encountered in trying to suit the deterministic philosophy of Plotinus to the philosophical requirements of a religion whose God is free,[156] one is still faced with propositions which are no more evident than the doctrines they are intended to support: the propositions, for instance, that the beauty of variety warrants the permission of all kinds of evil; that sin contributes to the beauty of the universe; that, indeed, "if evil were taken away from certain parts of the universe, the perfection of the universe would be much diminished."[157] One must believe that the God revealed in the Bible as a loving father should, like an artist or, in the terms of the seventeenth-century theologian Henry More, like the author of a "Tragick Comedy,"[158] make an impersonal aesthetic principle his governing motive in dealing with his creation; that God is above moral categories—for the principle of double effect can no more justify the paradoxical aesthetic end than it can the moral ends previously discussed.[159]

Religious souls whose capacity for faith is large may cut the Gordian knot by affirming that God is just under any circumstances, as Job, after his encounter with the God of the whirlwind, and Calvin were inclined to do. Theodicy thus becomes an impertinence. Most Christian thinkers, however, have preferred to live with inconsistencies, allowing the aesthetic and moral elements in the divine motives to remain uncombined, as though separately suspended in the same solution, or trusting that paradox will fuse them in ways too mysterious for finite intelligence fully to understand.

Thus God brandishes a "sharp two edged sword,"[160] providing for paradoxical violence in any number of ways. He hides himself and makes it difficult for men to find him, perhaps because he considers the love which direct knowledge engenders not as valuable as the love which the will must in some way force. Hence the tradition of *credo quia impossibile* ("I believe because it is impossible"), appearing throughout Christian history in various and often diluted forms. By hiding, God insures that he will be in a contest with his creation for the loyalty and love of individual men, a competition in which men must even choose between God and themselves: "Two cities have been formed by two loves: the earthly by the love of self, even to the contempt of God; the heavenly by the love of God, even to the contempt of self."[161] This God possesses the paradoxical conviction that much in creation is expendable. He chooses, for his own good reasons, a single people out of many as the repository of his revelation and the beneficiary of his choicest favors,[162] gives grace to whom he will, and can accept the "loss" of the nonelect as long as the moral balance of the universe is maintained. He loves process, as is evident from his operation through history, even though in the process which he has chosen (as in any evolutionary action) some participants are more deprived than others, and the sins of the fathers are visited upon the children in ways that mock equity, if not justice. In God's sight, the beauty of *integritas*—of life, of health, of the unimpeded development of faculties and fulfillment of potential—is not an ultimate end but a means, liable to the violence which establishes the kingdom of heaven. Job's family may be ravaged for no other reason than to create a trial for the patriarch, and even the God-man himself may be sacrificed on "the altar of the cross" to redress moral grievances. The divine law is a paradox whose validity can be accepted only on faith: a grain of wheat must, and should, die before it can have more abundant life.[163]

Yet this law has a limited application. Ultimate Goodness himself, say the theologians, is one, complete, immutable, serene, and his love or generosity cannot be intensified by difficulty.[164] Although he did not, he could have created a world as peaceful as his own inner life and as morally superior to the one we know as the saint in blessedness is to the meanest reprobate on earth. Since the sway of divine grace over the virtues necessary for salvation is essential—*amare Deum, Dei donum est*[165]—a man's sacrificial offering is not his own (or not entirely his own) to make, and necessary for him as an individual only because God wills it so. The grain of wheat does not die on its own behalf, after all, but for the beauty of a richly variegated meadow in which nothing is wasted, not even "waste" itself.

This uneasy alliance of opposites at the ground of the Christian's faith, perceived as such, may well tempt the believer towards agnosticism, especially if contradictions are seen not to arise out of metaphysical necessities but as within the competence of a divine "edict" to resolve:

> Just are the ways of God,
> And justifiable to Men,
> Unless there be who think not God at all.
> . . . .
> Yet more there be who doubt his ways not just,
> As to his own edicts, found contradicting,
> Then give the reins to wand'ring thought,
> Regardless of his glory's diminution;
> Till by thir own perplexities involv'd
> They ravel more, still less resolved,
> But never find self-satisfying solution.[166]

Even if the religious man's faith is secure, the antinomies may make it difficult for him to interpret his Master's injunction, "Be ye . . . perfect, even as your Father which is in heaven is perfect."[167] Does perfection require involvement in the world of process or escape from it? Is virtue restless and sweaty or halcyon and cold? Beauty a *skandalon,* a stumbling block in perfection's way, or perfection's goal? And when answers do not come easily or do not prove entirely satisfactory, what is one to do?

These problems can appear particularly tenacious to a Christian mind unreceptive to or unappreciative of paradox—as was that of Pierre Bayle, for instance, whose doubts and challenges in the seventeenth and early eighteenth centuries prompted the systematic theodicies of Leibniz and Bishop King. In the overcrowded, often vagabond pages of his remarkable *Dictionnaire historique et critique,*[168] Bayle showed himself a true congener of the categorists among the ancient philosophers, and at the same time demonstrated how a strain could be placed by their assumptions on the rational ramparts of faith.

To Bayle's reason it was evident that if we depend "only upon one cause, Almighty, infinitely good, and infinitely free, and which disposes universally of all beings, according to the good pleasure of his own will, we ought not to feel any evil, all our good ought to be pure, and we ought never to have the least disgust."[169] The paradoxical, mixed goods of Stoic sages and Christian theologians, of Zeno and Chrysippus, of Lactantius and St. Basil, have no authentic standing in themselves or as warrants for evil.[170] And indeed, no rational justification of an omnipotent God's ways to men is at all possible. Reason must reel lame and impotent from the truths of revealed religion:

> It is evident that evil ought to be prevented, if it be possible, and that it is a sinful thing to permit it when it can be prevented. Nevertheless, our theology shows us that this is false: it teaches us that God does nothing but what becomes his perfections when he permits all the disorders that are in the world, and which he might easily have prevented. . . . It is evident that a creature which does not exist cannot be an accomplice of an ill action. . . . And that it is unjust to punish that creature as an accomplice of that action. Nevertheless, our doctrine concerning original sin shows us the falsity of those evidences. . . . It is evident that what is honest ought to be preferred before what is profitable, and that the more holy a Being is, the less freedom he has to prefer what is profitable to what is honest. Nevertheless, our Divines tell us, that it being in God's choice to make a world

perfectly well regulated, and adorned with all virtures, and a world like ours, wherein sin and disorder prevail, he preferred the latter to the former, as being more consistent with the interest of his glory.[171]

Bayle found arguments *a fortiori* especially destructive of rational theodicy, as he asked continually, "If a human parent would (or would not) . . . how much more (or less) should our Heavenly Father? . . . " To the suggestion that Adam's sin was a *felix culpa,* he responds:

> If you say that God permitted sin to manifest his wisdom, which shines the more brightly by the disorders which the wickedness of men produces every day, than it would have done in a state of innocence; it may be answered that this is to compare the Deity to a father who should suffer his children to break their legs on purpose to show to all the city his great art in setting their broken bones; or to a king who should suffer seditions and factions to increase through all his kingdom, that he might purchase the glory of quelling them.[172]

To those who try to exculpate God from responsibility for the fall by proposing that God could not foresee the sins of a free creature, because free actions cannot be *deduced* from determinate causes, Bayle answers:

> At least [God] knew very certainly, that the first man ran the hazard of losing his innocence, and introducing into the world all the evils of punishment and guilt, which followed his apostacy. Neither his goodness, nor his holiness, nor his wisdom could permit that he should run the hazard of these events; for our reason convinces us very evidently, that a mother who should suffer her daughters to go to a ball, when she knew most certainly that they would run a great hazard with respect to their honour, would show thereby that she neither loved her daughters, nor chastity: and if it be supposed that she has an infallible preservative against all temptations, and that she gives it not to her daughters when she sends them to a ball, it is most evident that she is guilty, and that she takes but little care that her daughters should preserve their virginity. Let us carry on the comparison a little further; if that mother should go to this ball, and through a window should see and hear that one of her daughters defends herself but weakly in the corner of a closet against the sollicitations of a young gallant; if even when she sees that her daughter is but one step from yielding to the desires

of the tempter, she should not go then to assist her and deliver her from the snare, would not every one have reason to say, that she acts like a cruel stepmother, and that she would not scruple to sell the honour of her own daughter?[173]

For a number of reasons Bayle shows little respect for the "free-will defense" of Providence. Since he has difficulty comprehending how a being who depends on its creator at every moment for its existence and for the operation of its faculties is capable of any completely independent action, he wonders how much freedom man can rightly claim.[174] And, categorist that he is, he severely limits the amount of indeterminacy to which man might legitimately aspire. In disdain of *"le funeste privilège de pouvoir pécher,"*[175] he calls *"la liberté d'indifférence"* an imperfection[176]—as he is taught to do by the examples of infallibility provided by the blessed angels and saints and by God himself.[177] Of limited value in itself, vagrant, capricious human freedom is by no means worth all the immolations made for its sake. Concern for means is appropriate until punctilious respect for them subverts entirely the end they were supposed to attain:

> If a son should see his father ready to throw himself out at the window . . . he would do well to chain him, if he could not restrain him otherwise. If a queen should fall into the water, any footman that should get her out of it, either by embracing her, or taking her by the hair, tho he should pluck off above one half of it, would do a very good action; she would certainly not complain of his want of respect for her. . . . To have a regard to the free-will of man, and carefully to abstain from laying any restraint upon his inclination, when he is going to lose his innocence for ever, and to be eternally damned, do you call that a lawful observation of the privileges of liberty?[178]

But, of course, there need be no question at all of unseemly violence done to a human prerogative, for "all Divines own that God can infallibly produce a good act of the will in a human soul without depriving it of the use of liberty."[179]

Why, then, does God not avail himself of this power, save all of his children, and prevent the moral defilement of the universe? Reason has no unimpeachable answers; and of the solutions to the problem of evil which rational inquiry can produce, those most convincing to Bayle are the heretical ones of the Manichaeans, who attribute good to God and evil to those principles in the world which Divine Goodness is powerless to overcome.[180] No philosophical monism, apprehended through eyes keen for paradoxes which turn the world into a divine "sport,"[181] can obviate for the Christian the necessity of fideism: "You must necessarily make an option betwixt Philosophy and the Gospel. . . . If the conveniences of a round table do not satisfy you, make a square one, and do not pretend that the same table should furnish you with the conveniences both of a round and of a square table."[182]

Bayle first published his *Dictionary* two decades after Andrew Marvell's death, and it is proper that each man be placed in his own era, lest, as Dogberry would say, comparisons become "odorous." Yet neither writer was an absolute period-figure. As was inevitable in a time of transition, Bayle was attached to some pre-Enlightenment pieties; Marvell, to some post-Renaissance canons of thought. In a number of biographical details there are tantalizing parallelisms: Marvell and Bayle were both sons of Protestant ministers; both flirted with Roman Catholicism in their youth and were shortly reconverted—to a Protestant faith which stopped short of a rigid, doctrinaire Calvinism. By temperament each man was solitary (neither married),[183] nervous, humorous, skeptical, ironical, tolerant (at least each wrote energetically in the cause of religious toleration), and religiously devout with the kind of dry fervor that bespeaks earnestness but no ardent, mystical engagement with a personal God. Marvell and Bayle have remained in many ways inscrutable. But each has revealed something of his deepest convictions in attempting to come to terms with the problems of theodicy. And those views are sufficiently similar to have made a consideration of Bayle's thought on this subject an appropriate prolegomenon to a study of Marvell's.[184]

In all probability, Marvell did not travel down all the corridors of the metaphysical labyrinth we have just traced, but it is certain that he explored some of them. Categorical and paradoxical principles warred within his breast "for regiment," not just as unconscious urges but often as examined concepts that contributed to a rationale for action or acquiescence. Categorical and paradoxical issues underlay to a great extent his Platonic and pastoral reveries, his apprehensions about love, his confusions about the means and ends of political arrangements, his metaphysical perplexities and doubts, the chief of which led to his quite un-Miltonic attempts to justify the ways of God to men. That is what his writings suggest, if we are willing to look in them not so much for consistent viewpoints as for lingering preoccupations.

3

The Temptations of Elysium

But, Lord, thise grisly feendly rokkes blake,
That semen rather a foul confusion
Of werk than any fair creacion
Of swich a parfit wys God and a stable,
Why han ye wroght this werk unresonable?
. . . . .
I woot wel clerkes wol seyn as hem leste,
By argumentz, that al is for the beste,
Though I ne kan the causes nat yknowe.

Chaucer, The Franklin's Tale

Miranda.
Had I been any god of power, I would
Have sunk the sea within the earth or ere
It should the good ship so have swallow'd, and
The fraughting souls within her.
Prospero.
Be collected.
No more amazement. Tell your piteous heart
There's no harm done.

The Tempest

Que Dieu serait cruel, s'il n'était pas si grand!
Lamartine, Premières Méditations,
"Les Oiseaux"

Marvell's translation of lines from a chorus in Seneca's *Thyestes* may seem an unlikely witness to the secrets of the seventeenth-century poet's heart. The sentiments expressed are smug, moralistic, entirely conventional:

44

Climb at *Court* for me that will
Tottering favors Pinnacle;
All I seek is to lye still.
Settled in some secret Nest
In calm Leisure let me rest;
And far of the publick Stage
Pass away my silent Age.
Thus when without noise, unknown,
I have liv'd out all my span,
I shall dye, without a groan,
An old honest Country man.
Who expos'd to others Ey's,
Into his own Heart ne'r pry's,
Death to him's a Strange surprise.[1]

Yet Marvell chose to give this passage his time (though, we must say, not his best effort), and its tenor is reminiscent of the codes of other characters in his lyrics who praise a withdrawn life of quiet contemplation. Marvell in fact adds his personal mark to the piece by taking it slightly beyond the original author's emphasis. Whereas Seneca's speakers admit some motion into the happy life (*aetas per tacitum fluat* ["let my life flow in silence"]), Marvell's seek to "lye still," to pass away the time "in some secret Nest." It is not clear whether the position Marvell allows his chorus is supposed to stem from disgust with the corruption at court, impatience at the flickleness of fortune, an attraction toward the contemplative delights of "delicious solitude," laziness, or cowardice. Whatever the motives behind the philosophy, it might appear rather bloodless beside Sir Thomas Wyatt's response to the same text:

Stond who so list upon the Slipper toppe
Of courtes estates, and lett me heare reioyce;
And use me quyet without lett or stoppe,
Unknowen in courte, that hath suche brackish joyes.
In hidden place, so lett my dayes forthe passe,
That when my yeares be done, withouten noyse,
I may dye aged after the common trace.
For hym death greep'the right hard by the croppe
That is moche knowen of other, and of him self alas,
Doth dye unknowen, dazed with dreadfull face.[2]

Even allowing for the change in poetic taste over the century and more that separates the two translations, we have to judge the temperament that desires to "use . . . quyet without lett or stoppe" and conceives of death as a violent wrenching to be fundamentally different from, more assertive and perhaps more combative than, one that seeks to lie still in the security of a nest and fancies death a pale ghost of a thief in the night.

This is not to accuse Marvell of a fecklessness which his biography will easily disprove. It is to suggest, however, what other evidence tends to confirm, that Marvell, like the categorist described in the previous chapter, was neither by temperament nor by any intense intellectual conviction disposed to find value in struggle—not even in the "spiritual combat" so dear to his Puritan confreres. He could prove at times a violent man himself and call for violent action against others, but then he did not live in the world of his dreams. And his dreams were quite unlike those of paradoxists like Donne and Milton, whose visions of the ideal he knew.

Most certainly Donne tended to conceive of the good in paradoxical ways, alive as he was to the powerful appeal of mixed beauty. "[There is] scarce any purchase that is not cloggd with secret encumbrances," he mused,

> scarce any *happines,* that hath not in it so much of the *nature* of false and base money, as that the *Allay* is more than the *Mettall.* Nay is it not so . . . even in the exercise of *Vertues?* I must be poore, and want, before I can exercise the vertue of *Gratitude;* miserable, and in torment, before I can exercise the vertue *patience.* . . .[3]

He believed that a glory, or at least a wisdom, might be distilled from corruption:

> Our soule, whose country'is heaven, and God her father,
>   Into this world, corruptions sinke, is sent,
> Yet, so much in her travaile she doth gather,
>   That she returnes home, wiser then she went.[4]

In contrast, the soul in Marvell's "On a Drop of Dew" categorically refuses to seek any opportunities in the world of its exile, and will touch it only where compelled to:

> So the Soul, that Drop, that Ray
> Of the clear Fountain of Eternal Day,
> Could it within the humane flow'r be seen,
>   Remembring still its former height,
>   Shuns the sweat leaves and blossoms green;
>   And, recollecting its own Light,

Does, in its pure and circling thoughts, express
The greater Heaven in an Heaven less.
    In how coy a Figure wound,
    Every way it turns away:
    So the World excluding round,
    Yet receiving in the Day.
    Dark beneath, but bright above:
    Here disdaining, there in Love.
How loose and easie hence to go:
How girt and ready to ascend.
Moving but on a point below,
It all about does upwards bend.

                                              [19-36]

Donne was not of a mind to reject the beauties or benefits of schism.
Reflecting on the relative values of "unity" and "interruption" in general
and of religious unity and divergence in particular, he could note with
satisfaction that "God himselfe, who only is one, seems to have been
eternally delighted, with a disunion of persons."[5] And although Donne
sometimes asks to enjoy an "evennesse [of] Pietie," and to be delivered
"from needing danger, to be good,"[6] he seems to have found something
salutary in violence, the consequence of division. Many of the *Songs and
Sonets* dramatize contests of wits and emotions between lovers, or between lovers and unsympathetic third parties, in ways that suggest love is
better off for having to overcome opposition. Not only is the lover
gratified when he triumphs over unruly suns, expostulators like the one in
"The Canonization," and mistresses who provide resistance, as in "The
Flea," "The Dampe," "The Dreame"; he is also ennobled when he
accepts love's violent paradoxes: "Wee can dye by it, if not live by love
. . . And . . . all shall approve / Us *Canoniz'd* for Love" ("The Canonization," 28, 35-36). The imperfections of love, the difficulties which make
"true love" almost unattainable in this world, establish opportunities
which will dissolve in the all too perfect world to come:

    And then wee shall be throughly blest,
      But wee no more, then all the rest:
    Here upon earth, we'are Kings. . . .

                          ["The Anniversarie," 21-23]

Donne does not entirely regret, either, the resistance that divine love
encounters as it pulses through creation. "From the gods who sit in
grandeur, grace comes somehow violent," observed Aeschylus (*Agamem-
non*, 182-83). And that violence seems for Donne almost exhilarating:

Batter my heart, three person'd God. . . .
. . . .
That I may rise, and stand, o'erthrow mee,'and bend
Your force, to breake, blowe, burn and make me new.
["Holy Sonnet XIV," 1, 3–4]

Those are my best dayes, when I shake with feare.
["Holy Sonnet XIX," 14]

No Crosse is so extreme, as to have none.
["The Crosse," 14]

O thinke mee worth thine anger, punish mee,
Burne off my rusts, and my deformity.
["Goodfriday, 1613," 39–40]

The case of Job does not indict the divine goodness, for

> Gods first intention even when he destroyes is to preserve . . . ;
> even Gods demolitions are super-edifications, his Anatomies,
> his dissections are so many re-compactings, so many resurrec-
> tions; God windes us off the Skein, that he may weave us up into
> the whole peece, and he cuts us out of the whole peece into
> peeces, that he may make us up into a whole garment.

Indeed, one ought to worry about experiencing *too much* peace:

> Peace is a blessed state, but it must be the peece of God. . . . Wo
> be to that man that is so at peace, as that the spirit fights not
> against the flesh in him; and wo to them too, who would make
> them friends, or reconcile them, between whom, God hath
> perpetuated an everlasting war. . . .

And one should be grateful even for wars that bring defeat:

> Many times we are better for [Satan's] tentations. . . . Nay, I am
> sometimes the safer, and the readier for a victory, by having
> been overcome by him. The sense, and the remorse of sin, after I
> have fallen into it, puts me into a better state, and establishes
> better conditions between God and me then were before, when
> I felt no tentations to sin.[7]

Even if we were to judge that Donne found more satisfaction in the
violence done by paradox to the intellect than in the therapeutic lacera-
tion of flesh or spirit themselves (perhaps he felt that paradox was the only
conceptual category that could foster in man a sense of the miraculous

nature of human love or divine majesty),[8] we would still have to admit that the Lord who "throws down" in order that "he may raise" and the meditative Donne who is the object of his wrath and redemption are, officially, of a single mind.[9]

Milton's bent was not so paradoxical as Donne's, as may be judged from the former's apparent hesitancy about the *felix culpa*.[10] "It was from out the rinde of one apple tasted," says Milton, "that the knowledge of good and evill as two twins cleaving together leapt forth into the World. And perhaps this is that doom which *Adam* fell into of knowing good and evill, that is to say, of knowing good by evill."[11] The "doom" cannot be considered utterly tragic, since, "as . . . the state of man now is . . . , where does virtue shine, where is it usually exercized, if not in evil?"[12] As the state of man now is. But we have God's own word that Adam had been "Happier, had it suffic'd him to have known / Good by itself, and Evil not at all" (*Paradise Lost,* 11. 88–89)—happier not, certainly, for being *less* virtuous.[13] Milton knew the limitations of heroism, condemning alike the "heroic Virtue" (*Paradise Lost,* 11. 690)[14] of classical paganism (which the Satan of *Paradise Lost* possesses to an eminent degree) and the magnanimity of the man who sins and risks his soul in "glorious trial of exceeding love" (*Paradise Lost,* 9. 960–76).

Yet, though he participated in the lament of the prophet "Wo is me my mother, that thou hast borne me a man of strife, and contention,"[15] Milton intensely admired the heroic energy which in "the state of man [as it] now is" meets and overcomes opposition. Indeed, in this vale of soul-making, he could not "praise a fugitive and cloistered virtue . . . that never sallies out and sees her adversary . . . ," nor deny that the exertions, the trials of his protagonists are "happy" (*Comus,* 592), even if their falls may not be entirely fortunate. The poet's condemnation of the pagan heroic ideal in *Paradise Lost* does not prevent the Son of God from leading his loyal angel warriors to glorious victory on chariot wheels more terrifying than any Greek's or Persian's (for all their reminiscences of Ezekiel)[16] and with thunderbolts mightier than Jove's. In the "Nativity Ode," Christ lies in his cradle like an infant Hercules, routing the pagan gods and overturning their altars. A relentless, ascetic Christ regains Paradise for mankind—in somewhat heterodox fashion—by actively and conspicuously defeating Satan in face-to-face combat, the more passive (or outwardly so, at least) crucified Redeemer having been relegated to an uninspired and unfinished poem on "The Passion." It is a privilege as well as a necessity for mere mortals to follow Christ's model, and God does men the highest of favors by establishing within and without them an order that pits force against force in the coil of spiritual warfare:

Many there be that complain of divin Providence for suffering *Adam* to transgresse, foolish tongues! when God gave him reason, he gave him freedom to choose, for reason is but choosing; he had bin else a meer artificiall *Adam, such an Adam* as he is in the motions. . . . God therefore left him free, set before him a provoking object, ever almost in his eyes; herein consisted his merit, herein the right of his reward, the praise of his abstinence. Wherefore did he creat passions within us, pleasures round about us, but that these rightly temper'd are the very ingredients of virtu? . . . This justifies the high providence of God, who though he command us temperance, justice, continence, yet powrs out before us ev'n to a profusenes all desirable things, and gives us minds that can wander beyond all limit and satiety.[17]

In reflecting these values, Milton's Garden of Eden departs radically from the versions, traditional by his day, that described Paradise in the terms of (what Arthur Lovejoy and George Boas have called) "soft primitivism."[18] The men of the classical "golden age," according to Hesiod, lived

like gods without sorrow of heart, remote and free from toil and grief: miserable age rested not on them; but with arms and legs never failing they made merry with feasting beyond the reach of all evils. . . . They had all good things; for the fruitful earth unforced bore them fruit abundantly and without stint. They dwelt with ease and peace upon their lands.[19]

Although this golden age could be and was by many Christian thinkers transported into Eden, Milton would not be satisfied with a garden that required little or no strenuous effort to maintain.[20] His Eden involves "the threat of [an] encroaching wilderness";[21] its plants are "wanton," sometimes "overgrown," and "lie bestrowne unsightly and unsmooth," awaiting the labor of attendants, who find their toil "plesant" but not for that reason unexacting.[22] In the garden of innocence as in the soul of unfallen man there must be lopping and pruning, for there is an energy which only the prospect of sacrifice can elicit and turn toward the highest value.

Now if, as Robert Ellrodt maintains, "nothing is more characteristic of the temperament of a poet than the image of Paradise which he proposes to himself and to us,"[23] we may learn much by comparing Milton's Eden with the "Elizium" described in Marvell's writings. The inference to be drawn from an observation in the *Defence of John Howe* is that an arduous paradise—even the biblical Eden, which required dressing and keeping—is decidedly inferior to a state in which all inconvenient and peripheral activity, all concern for temporary expedients, can be abandoned for what is momentous, ultimate, fulfilling: engagement with God himself.

> It hath seemed to me as if they who have chosen, and are set apart for that work [of the Ministry] did, by the continual opportunity of conversing with their Maker, enjoy a state like that of Paradise, and in this superiour, that they are not also, as Adam, put in "to dress and keep a garden. . . ."[24]

Marvell's remark is offered by the way, but much of his poetry indicates that the attitude suggested here is not adventitious.

In "A Dialogue between Thyrsis and Dorinda,"[25] Marvell has a shepherd describe for his love how the two of them will "in Elizium . . . / Pass Eternity away":

> *Thyrsis.* Oh, ther's, neither hope nor fear
> Ther's no Wolf, no Fox, nor Bear.
> No need of Dog to fetch our stray,
> Our Lightfoot we may give away;
> . . . .
> There, sheep are full
> Of sweetest grass, and softest wooll;
> There, birds sing Consorts, garlands grow,
> Cool winds do whisper, springs do flow.
> There, always is, a rising Sun,
> And day is ever, but begun.
> Shepheards there, bear equal sway,
> And every Nimph's a Queen of *May*.
>
> [19, 21-24, 31-38]

This is not the sweaty paradise in which Milton would feel comfortable—not even fragrant *"Alexanders sweat'*[26] would be welcome in such a retreat. There is no recalcitrance to overcome. The hierarchical arrangements which create the dynamic tension requisite for "virtue" in *Paradise Lost* are absent where egalitarianism forestalls competition. No threats loom from within or from without. Yes, but surely Thyrsis envisions a heaven, not an Eden; the final, restful goal of one's striving, not a primeval testing ground. He knows, or seems to know, that "'Tis a sure but *rugged* way / That leads to Everlasting day" (11-12; emphasis mine). Knowledge, however, if it be such in this instance, does not beget action, for Thyrsis joins Dorinda in abandoning the strenuous ideal for the nearest and smoothest way:

> Then let us give *Carillo* charge o'th Sheep,
> And thou and I'le pick poppies and them steep
> In wine, and drink on't even till we weep,
> So shall we smoothly pass away in sleep.

[45–48]

Of course, Marvell may feel that Thyrsis simply succumbs to the temptation to give all, too much, for love—as did Milton's Adam[27]—and that Dorinda's impatience with painful processes and yearning for effortless perfection are puerile and cowardly. Her monosyllabic, iterative, and wholly pathetic exclamations bespeak anything but hardiness or maturity: "Oh sweet! oh sweet!" "Ah me, ah me!" "I'm sick, I'm sick" (27, 39, 40). But as we shall see in considering the poet's Mower and dying Nymph, Marvell is fond of using the foolish of the world to confound wisdom, the weak to confound strength. And Dorinda's naive enthusiasms are like the preposterous yet disconcerting questions of a child, to which a parent knows all the right answers, but can offer them only with the secretly embarrassing suspicion that adult truth may be liable to subversion by infantile logic or insight. At the least, since "Thyrsis and Dorinda" is an objectively dramatic scene, and the young girl's single- and literal-minded pursuit of the Platonic ideal of immediate escape from this world to the next[28] is not explicitly disparaged, anyone who condemns her must be predisposed to do so. There is much in Marvell's poetry to discourage such a predisposition and to encourage the catgegorical view that Eden and Elysium are ideally equivalent, that the road to Elysium need not be any more "rugged" than the fields of the blest.

"Thyrsis and Dorinda" may seem less than wholly serious, a playful daydream captured in words before stern realities can reclaim and dominate the poet's attention. Like most of Marvell's poetry, the dialogue is based on a literary convention, a fact which may seem to place it at a good remove from spontaneous or ingenuous personal conviction. But we may legitimately wonder about the predilections that dictate a poet's choice and use of standard topics, tropes, and poses. As Marvell's modern readers are almost unanimous in affirming, his use of conventions is idiosyncratic and intriguing. And his thoughts about Elysium, if imaginative vagaries, are recurrent enough to suggest at least his fascination with the vision and his susceptibility to its attractiveness. He seems to share in some degree Dorinda's impatience, for he tends to find inspiration for his Elysian visions in an idealized but earthly present rather than in a distant heavenly future. He gives Paradise localities and names: the "sweet Canary Isles," for example,

> One of which doubtless is by Nature blest
> Above both Worlds, since 'tis above the rest.
> For least some Gloominess might stain her sky,
> Trees there the duty of the Clouds supply;
> O noble Trust which Heaven on this Isle poures,
> Fertile to be, yet never need her showres.
> A happy People, which at once do gain
> The benefits without the ills of rain.
> Both health and profit, Fate cannot deny;
> Where still the Earth is moist, the Air still dry;
> The jarring Elements no discord know,
> Fewel and Rain together kindly grow;
> And coolness there, with heat doth never fight,
> This only rules by day, and that by Night.
> [*On the Victory obtained by Blake*, 25–38]

Or the Bermudas, where castaways may anticipate "a grassy Stage . . . / Safe from . . . Storms," where God, they may be sure, gives

> eternal Spring
> Which here enamells every thing
> And sends the Fowl's to us in care,
> On daily Visits through the Air.
> He hangs in shades the Orange bright,
> Like golden Lamps in a green Night.
> And does in the Pomgranates close,
> Jewels more rich than *Ormus* show's.
> He makes the Figs our mouths to meet;
> And throws the Melons at our feet.
> ["Bermudas," 11–22]

Or, he may picture a second Eden come to an English garden, in which a recluse experiences without complication or hindrance the goods of body and spirit:

> What wond'rous Life in this I lead!
> Ripe Apples drop about my head;
> The Luscious Clusters of the Vine
> Upon my Mouth do crush their Wine;
> The Nectaren, and curious Peach,

Into my hands themselves do reach;
Stumbling on Melons, as I pass,
Insnar'd with Flow'rs, I fall on Grass.

Mean while the Mind, from pleasure less,
Withdraws into its happiness. . . .

["The Garden," 33-42]

In his poem "On a Drop of Dew" Marvell reveals his sympathy with the soul who, like Dorinda, thirsts for "the clear Fountain of Eternal Day" (20), and who desires to pass "smoothly" into it ("Thyrsis and Dorinda," 48), to be *dissolved* into the "Glories of the Almighty Sun" ("On a Drop of Dew," 39-40) without a struggle along a rugged way.

If these enthusiasms are the products of moods (which, it is true, have antitheses elsewhere in Marvell's writings), they are not mere whimsies. The pictures described in "Bermudas" and "The Garden," as will be seen later, are for Marvell problematical, and he cannot dote on them un-critically. But just as Milton's garden reflects a state of mind, a complex of values, a "philosophy," so do Marvell's gardens and happy isles—a philosophy, to be sure, that must be debated, but in the debate, stood up for, given its due. In the midst of the categorically perfect places of Marvell's imagination we can begin to hear Gryllus's pointed questions: is "the spiritual soil . . . better which produces a harvest of virtue as a spontaneous crop without toil?"[29] We can catch glimpses of a both/and philosophy that tries to find room for "Fewel and Rain together," that cherishes "Both health and profit," pleasure and virtue. We can sense a distaste for the "fight" and for "jarring . . . discord"—perhaps even for *concordia discors*. We may be reminded of the garden of Epicurus.

Indeed, Marvell and the Epicurean poet Lucretius share a number of important sentiments.[30] "Nothing is more delightful," Lucretius muses, "than to possess well fortified sanctuaries serene, built up by the teachings of the wise." Sanctuaries such as these are not only pleasant but necessary, for men find themselves everywhere exposed to senseless violence that threatens to destroy their peace of mind: violence in personal relation-ships—especially in love—violence in political relationships, and in nature; violence so endemic in the physics and metaphysics of things as to preclude any possibility that the *natura rerum* was "made for us by divine power"—so "great are the faults wherewith it stands endowed."[31]

Marvell too appreciates the security of sanctuaries. Part of the attractiveness of "Elizium" lies in the safety to be found there ("Thyrsis and Dorinda," 21-22). Safe is the Senecan "secret Nest" ("Senec. Traged.," 4), the religious utopia ("Bermudas," 12), and the sylvan, contemplative retreat:

> How safe, methinks, and strong, behind
> These Trees have I incamp'd my Mind;
> Where Beauty, aiming at the Heart,
> Bends in some Tree its useless Dart;
> And where the World no certain Shot
> Can make, or me it toucheth not.
> But I on it securely play. . . .

[*Upon Appleton House,* 601-7]

The soul is "only safe when under God's custody, in its own cabinet,"[32] and, of course, should be kept there. In imagination, at least, Marvell seeks this security in shunning the same kinds of broils that Lucretius sought to rise above, as becomes evident when the Lucretian schema just presented is applied to Marvell's case.

The seventeenth-century poet doubts that love is either enriched by the more ardent passions or ennobled by a struggle against odds. He can write approvingly of "young love," the cool, uncombative, and unconsuming affection of which a child is capable:

> Come little Infant, Love me now.
>   While thine unsuspected years
> Clear thine aged Fathers brow
>   From cold Jealousie and Fears.
>
> Pretty surely 'twere to see
>   By young Love old Time beguil'd:
> While our Sportings are as free
>   As the Nurses with the Child.
>
> Common Beauties stay fifteen;
>   Such as yours should swifter move;
> Whose fair Blossoms are too green
>   Yet for Lust, but not for Love.[33]

["Young Love," 1-12]

When young love threatens to mature, however, the poet begins to withdraw his approbation, feeling that the most intense "Glories" of a "conquering" mistress are best experienced at a safe distance:

> This is She whose chaster Laws
> The wanton Love shall one day fear,

And, under her command severe,
See his Bow broke and Ensigns torn.
    Happy, who can
Appease this virtuous Enemy of Man!

O then let me in time compound,
And parly with those conquering Eyes;
Ere they have try'd their force to wound,
Ere, with their glancing wheels, they drive
In Triumph over Hearts that strive,
And them that yield but more despise.
    Let me be laid,
Where I may see thy Glories from some shade.
                    ["The Picture of little T. C.," 11-24]

It is true that Marvell does not utterly condemn the passion which the sexually riper nymphs in his poems possess and inspire. But he feels comfortable only with passion that does not threaten, that meets and offers no resistance. Thus, of the pictures of Clora which adorn the "gallery" of the poet's mind, the one that pleases him best is that of

A tender Shepherdess, whose Hair
Hangs loosely playing in the Air,
Transplanting Flow'rs from the green Hill,
To crown her Head, and Bosome fill.
                    ["The Gallery," 53-56]

The portraits of the "Inhumane Murtheress" and the "Enchantress" "torment" him with their suggestions of "cruel Arts," "Engines" of torture, and haruspical "Entrails." And even though the goddesses Aurora and Venus do not displease him, they seem somehow much too formidable in comparison with the simple and tender girl of the fields who wins his preference. In the interchange between Ametas and Thestylis, then, it is more than likely that Marvell sympathizes with the lover who feels no need to have his love founded on or fortified by opposition:

Ametas
Think'st Thou that this Love can stand,
Whilst Thou still dost say me nay?
Love unpaid does soon disband:
Love binds Love as Hay binds Hay.
Thestylis
Think'st Thou that this Rope would twine
If we both should turn one way?

Where both parties so combine,
Neither Love will twist nor Hay.
                    Ametas
Thus you vain Excuses find,
Which your selve and us delay:
And Love tyes a Womans Mind
Looser then with Ropes of Hay.
                    Thestylis
What you cannot constant hope
Must be taken as you may.
                    Ametas
Then let's both lay by our Rope,
And go kiss within the Hay.

["Ametas and Thestylis making Hay-Ropes"]

Marvell shows himself *out* of sympathy with lovers who court
violence or who fall martyrs to it—he is at least critical of the violence
and the martyrdom themselves. Daphnis, for example, manages to make
something of a fool of himself in his laborious pursuit of Chloe.

He, well read in all the wayes
By which men their Siege maintain,
Knew not that the Fort to gain
Better 'twas the Siege to raise.

["Daphnis and Chloe," 17-20]

When the siege fails, precisely for being a siege, and he realizes that his
exertions have gone for naught, he lapses into the somewhat laughable
pseudo-death throes of a courtly lover. Then, oddly enough, after a
relenting Chloe proposes to grant him his heart's desire, he refuses to
accept it, preferring instead to roll his eyes, tear his locks, and curse his
fate in self-pity, while insisting on punctilios that create just as large a
barrier to his own happiness and Chloe's as she did in the first place by her
coy resistance. He mouths a categorical philosophy that deprecates
violence:

Gentler times for Love are ment.
Who for parting pleasure strain
Gather Roses in the rain,
Wet themselves and spoil their Sent.

[85–88]

But he cannot himself abide by its implications. Continuing to look upon

Chloe as a "Foe" (58), he slinks off to pine in what he calls "manly stubborness" (70), not without a bit of melodramatic posturing:

> Fate I come, as dark, as sad,
> As thy Malice could desire. . . .
>
> [93–94]

The poet, tongue in cheek, then offers a warning:

> But hence Virgins all beware.
> Last night he with *Phlogis*[34] slept;
> This night for *Dorinda* kept;
> And but rid to take the Air.
>
> [101–4]

And his final observations are made with a knowing irony:

> Yet he does himself excuse;
> Nor indeed without a Cause.
> For, according to the Lawes,
> Why did *Chloe* once refuse?
>
> [105–8]

Indeed; and why did Daphnis?

In "The unfortunate Lover," love's martyr deserves more pity than Daphnis, largely because the former seems more a victim. The "poor Lover" is (metaphorically) born and orphaned in a *Cesarian Section* amid the clash of elements, alternately fed and devoured by cormorants of despair, and lashed to bleeding by "angry Heaven." Yet the poem's narrator[35] is sufficiently detached and analytical to condemn the sin, so to speak, while pitying the sinner. The narrator's paradise is graced by "Fountains cool, and Shadows green" (4), and when a young lover abandons this pleasance with its temperate joys for a violent life, his actions become liable to criticism that is not entirely invalidated by his heroic suffering. The unfortunate lover's woes are hyperbolical to the point of grotesqueness[36]—surely the speaker's voice is disparagingly casual, his meters and rhymes disrespectfully comical in such lines as

> Till at the last the master-Wave
> Upon the Rock his Mother drave;
> And there she split against the Stone,
> In a *Cesarian Section*.
>
> [13–16]

And the narrator is careful to indicate that the absurdity lies in the hero's situation rather than in the description of it. Not only does the speaker compare the lover to Ajax,[37] whose behavior in the *Iliad* is often reprehensible and whose defiance of higher powers, if true to character, is more ridiculous than admirable;[38] he emphasizes the fictitious quality of his hero[39] (the storm is a "masque" [26], the unfortunate lover himself a figure on an escutcheon, "In a Field *Sable* a Lover *Gules*" [64])[40] and then proceeds to denigrate the fiction by claiming that the lover "in Story only rules"—that is, "only in Story."[41] This attitude Marvell could find in Lucretius, whose work he recalls more than once in composing this poem;[42] and perhaps it is the *De rerum natura* itself which suggested both the project of dispelling the mystique surrounding heroic passion and the specific image of the helpless, pitiable, but foolish and hardly august lover devoured by cormorants. "There is no Tityos lying in Acheron rummaged by vultures," Lucretius protested like a euhemerist against mythologizers. "But our Tityos is here, grovelling in love, and the winged things that tear him (anxious care eating him up) or rend him with some other lust, are his passions."[43]

An unfortunate lover also "rules," outside of "Story" but not for that reason in truth, in the kind of philosophical system proposed by Giordano Bruno in *De gli eroici furori*, a work which "The unfortunate Lover" is meant to parody.[44] Bruno had attempted to eternize and push to "heaven" the fires of love. At the beginning of Marvell's poem, however, cool flames belong to unheroic couples who "lose their light" like ephemeral "Meteors," failing to reach "that Region" where they might "make impression upon Time."[45] But even the brave passion of Marvell's afflicted lover, although hotter and brighter a fire than that of the unheroic, is in the final analysis earth-bound and in itself (rather than in its "fame") mortal. The Italian philosopher had preached a pure strain of paradoxical doctrine: "Nothing results from an absolutely uncontested principle," he claimed, "but everything results from contrary principles through the triumph and conquest of one of the contraries."[46] His *infortunato amante*[47] was a man "amphibious, divided, afflicted," and for that very reason a candidate for heroic sainthood in the service of "absolute goodness and beauty."[48] Marvell's "*Amphibium* of Life and Death" (40), "Torn into Flames, and ragg'd with Wounds" (54), even as he cuffs "the Thunder with one hand" and grapples Prometheus-like with his rock (50-52), is diminished to a pitiful figure—a plaything of an "angry Heaven" (43, 41) that delights in violence for no reason discernible. This unfortunate lover, unlike his pacific counterparts with whom the "Infant Love" plays only harmless games (2), does indeed make impression upon Time, for his "Flames" become notorious. Such immortality, however, is neither awe-inspiring nor consoling. The words of pain and defiance that Marvell's unfortunate utters may be what "a Lover drest / In his own Blood does relish best" (55–56), but a detached observer wonders whether there is not something perverse in *relishing* those words, in self-consciously regarding such dress a garb of honor, in fancying that "Storms and Wars" produce "Perfume... / And Musick" (60–62). It is true that Josiah, one of Judah's most revered kings, had also left to his posterity a reputation as sweet as "perfume and music";[49] but the monarch was memorable more for his character and his public accomplishments than for the spectacle of his death, of which the Bible gives very little description.[50] The perfume left by the battered lover is rather the odor of blood, rising (as the epic poets say) in the smoke that issues from wounds. The music is the noise of slaughter. To a paradoxist—as to Browning's Abt Vogler—the ugliness may appear lovely:

> The high that proved too high, the heroic for earth too hard,
> The passion that left the ground to lose itself in the sky,
> Are music sent up to God by the lover and the bard.
>
> [77–79]

To Marvell's narrator, the beauty of a lover's tribulation seems to reside in story only, and the "masque" seems mostly grotesque. However deep his sympathy for the agonies of his poor lover (11) (is there not condescension as well as pity in that epithet?), however warm his admiration for the sufferer's patience and fortitude, he insists in an indirect, burlesquing way that courage cannot rescue from criticism every outrage committed in its name. There is no reason to believe that Marvell would disagree with him. Not even the Marvell who wrote of tearing pleasure with rough strife through iron gates.

In the light of "Daphnis and Chloe" and "The unfortunate Lover," it is tempting to read "To His Coy Mistress" as a dramatic monologue in which the speaker, after making wittily ironic and telling points against a lady's willful stubbornness, becomes himself a victim of dramatic irony. This lover too seems to get carried away at the end of his argument—not so much, as Daphnis does, through personal vanity, as through an obsession with tragedy:

> And now, like am'rous birds of prey,
> Rather at once our Time devour,
> Than languish in his slow-chapt pow'r.
> Let us roll all our Strength, and all
> Our sweetness, up into one Ball:

And tear our Pleasures with rough strife,
Thorough the Iron gates of Life.
Thus, though we cannot make our Sun
Stand still, yet we will make him run.

[38-46]

These are the words of an importuner who has forgotten his original purpose, for he cannot hope to win over his coy mistress by proposing that, like "birds of prey," they "devour" and "tear" their way through pleasure. His voice trembles towards a crescendo of outraged defiance as he loses sight of his first intention—"let us sport us" (37)—in his preoccupation with the fierce challenge of "Time." He is certainly a categorist in his hatred of process, suggesting that anticipation and preparation can do no more to beatify love's moment than mere duration ("Eternity") can do to make the "Desarts" bloom; and he feels the inseparability of pleasure and "rough strife" to be tragic. His final boast, however, sounds paradoxical, heroic:

Though we cannot make our Sun
Stand still, yet we will make him run.

Does Marvell want him admired for taking a heroic stance? Perhaps it is stretching interpretation a bit to criticize the lover for losing his equilibrium, and with it his suit. Perhaps in a singular mood Marvell contemplates the possibility that rough strife is love's only proper resort in a situation which categorical principles render otherwise unendurable. But even if the lover is not open to ironic criticism, he does not win praise, nor does he ask it, for his unflinching acceptance of violence, his ability to receive wounds with courage. His partial triumph over time (by his own admission, "we cannot make our Sun / Stand still") consists rather in his ability to get as much "Strength" and "sweetness" through the gates as possible. The pain cannot be helped; neither can it be redeemed by martyrdom.

There is likewise little help for the suffering lovers in "The Definition of Love." The love which binds them,

But Fate so enviously debarrs,
Is the conjunction of the Mind
And Opposition of the Stars.

[30-32]

Though some critics have considered the "Opposition" fortunate,[51] there is no warrant in the poem for such a sanguine judgment. Love begotten by

Despair upon Impossibility is cynically called "divine" only because the impossible (in a different sense, that is: the miraculous) is a divine prerogative. Despair is ironically called "Magnanimous" because it mockingly offers the lovers a perfection that is less than perfect; Despair is not genuinely magnanimous in spite of itself. The speaker sees no value in an opposition which he has tried to *surmount* (9-12), only to be defeated by forces brutal (11-12) and jealous (13-16). He does not see any logical reason why love cannot be perfect while at the same time fulfilled, and attributes the disjunction to a "Tyrannick pow'r" whom he does not in any way pretend to defeat.[52]

The "perfect" couple of "The Match" do not fare much better. As the poem's title suggests, their matching perfections, equal in intensity but not for that reason necessarily compatible, are just as truly parallel as the lovers' lines in "The Definition of Love," and perhaps just as doomed to separation. In spite of cosmic conspiracies to deny perfection to mortals, Celia contains within herself Nature's "choicest store" of beauty, and her lover burns with love's hottest fires. The lover claims that as a result they are both "happy" (37); yet each is self-contained, having broken through the walls of "several Cells" (13-14, 21), but apparently not through the walls that divide them from one another. If Celia is all beauty without intensity of feeling, and her lover is on fire with "all that burns the Mind" (24) but a solitary flame, their future holds little promise. Their self-containment can yield no more happiness than will the self-sufficiency of the lady in "Mourning":

> And, while vain Pomp does her restrain
> Within her solitary Bowr,
> She courts her self in am'rous Rain;
> Her self both *Danae* and the Showr.
>
> [17-20]

Marvell may want to imply that the same attraction, "magnetically strong," which united the parts will eventually unite the wholes also—in which case the poem would be uncharacteristically optimistic. We must suspect, however, that the poet does not really approve of a love "that burns the Mind." He is aware that his lover contradicts himself by describing the raging fire in his heart (33-36) while claiming to be at "rest" (37). This lover is just as much a victim of his passion as Damon the Mower, whose mind is also on fire ("Damon the Mower," 17-24), but who is not too sophisticated to admit his victimization.

Damon knows only the "hurts" of love, which make all other

injuries seem negligible ("Damon the Mower," 81-82). His plaints are those of a man-child devastated in growing up:

> My Mind was once the true survey
> Of all these Medows fresh and gay;
> And in the greenness of the Grass
> Did see its Hopes as in a Glass;
> When *Juliana* came, and She
> What I do to the Grass, does to my Thoughts and Me.
>
> ["The Mower's Song," 1-6]

> Since *Juliana* here is come,
> . . . She my Mind hath so displac'd
> That I shall never find my home.
>
> ["The Mower to the Glo-Worms," 14-16]

> How happy might I still have mow'd,
> Had not Love here his Thistles sow'd!
> But now I all the day complain,
> Joyning my Labour to my Pain;
> And with my Sythe cut down the Grass,
> Yet still my Grief is where it was:
>
> . . . .
> . . . for him no Cure is found,
> Whom *Julianas* Eyes do wound.
> 'Tis death alone that this must do:
> For Death thou art a Mower too.
>
> ["Damon the Mower," 65-70, 85-88]

Perhaps Damon should be blamed for his naiveté and lack of resiliency, or for not stoically suppressing his grief. But which of Marvell's more "mature" lovers can, speaking from a position of superiority, exonerate love at Damon's expense, when love has in some way "displac'd" the minds of all who have exchanged cool caves and gelid fountains for sunburnt meadows?[53]

The private or personal values embodied in Marvell's poems about love have their correspondences in his political writings, though, as I have suggested, Marvell is not perfectly consistent in his political principles, the world of fact tending to be even crueler to public ideals, about which most men can do little, than to private ones.[54] Thus while Marvell displays a categorist's distaste for politically inspired violence, "all the horrid destruction, devastation, ravage and slaughter of war,"[55] he does not hesitate to advocate it himself—in a "proper" cause. He fulminates against ecclesiastics of "precipitate, brutish, and sanguinary Counsels," who move the "Ecclesiastical *Militia*" to "*scourge* [*men*] *into order*" and incite princes to "fill the world with Blood, Execution, and Massacre."[56] But he praises Cromwell for having "first put Armes into *Religions* hand, / And tim'rous *Conscience* unto *Courage* man'd" (*A Poem upon the Death of O. C.,* 179–80). At one time, he believes "Publick Tranquility" to be among the highest of goods;[57] at other times, he cheers the fanatic James Mitchell for having shot a bishop,[58] the hot-headed Thomas Blood for having stabbed his way—but not fiercely enough—to the crown jewels.[59] It should not be forgotten that, as Legouis has had to remind critics who think the poet too "sane" to have exhorted to violence, "Marvell favoured foreign war, to the end of his life, whenever an occasion arose."[60]

We may allow, however, for the irrationality that usually attends and sometimes forms political convictions. Then, too, Marvell is no more inconsistent than anyone else who has sponsored a "just war" to end war, and we need not doubt the sincerity of his statements on the subject:

> Though it may happen that both the Parties may be guilty of War, as both of Schisme, yet there are many cases in which War is just, and few however where there is not more Justice on one side then the other. To repell an Invasion from abroad,[61] or extinguish an Usurpation at home would not require a long consultation with Conscience. The *Jews* themselves learnt at last that 'twas lawful to fight a battel on the Sabbath day, rather then submit their throats to the Enemy. . . .[62]

The following lines from "Blake's Victory" are not to be discounted for being part of a somewhat obsequious tribute addressed to Cromwell:

> Ah would those Treasures which both Indies have,
> Were buryed in as large, and deep a grave,[63]
> Wars chief support with them would buried be,
> And the Land owe her peace unto the Sea.
> Ages to come, your conquering Arms will bless,
> There they destroy, what had destroy'd their Peace.
> And in one War the present age may boast,
> The certain seeds of many Wars are lost.
>
> [153–60]

The same sentiments may be found in the (again, often excessive) *First Anniversary of the Government under O. C.* and are evidently genuine—a fact which helps to explain the poet's commitment and attachment to the Lord

Protector, one of whose mottoes was *Pax quaeritur bello* ("peace is sought through warfare"). Marvell proposes violence with mixed feelings, and with a confusion intensified by the temperament of a categorist, as *The First Anniversary* can bear witness.

In this poem as elsewhere, Marvell looks upon time, categorically, as an implacable enemy.[64] The temporal is a punishment for sin:

> The great Justice that did first suspend
> The World by Sin, does by the same extend.
>
> [153-154]

Otherwise time is "useless" (41, 139). The great world of process is in itself vain, wearisome, suffocating:

> Like the vain Curlings of the Watry maze
> Which in smooth streams a sinking Weight does raise;
> So Man, declining always, disappears
> In the weak Circles of increasing Years;
> And his short Tumults of themselves Compose,
> While flowing Time above his Head does close.
>
> [1-6]

Cromwell's appeal lies precisely in his ability to triumph over time by destroying it, or at least by hastening its destruction:

> 'Tis he the force of scatter'd Time contracts,
> And in one Year the work of Ages acts.
>
> [13-14]

This tribute is exceedingly hyperbolical, as is so much else in a poem that was certainly not intended to be a sober and cautious evaluation of the Protector's virtues. But the hyperbole should not be allowed to obscure the fact that Marvell places real millennial hopes in Cromwell, hopes so cherished that the poet hedges them about, as he does nowhere else in the poem, with a welter of provisos to insure that they are neither too fantastic nor fanatical:

> Hence oft I think, if in some happy Hour
> High Grace should meet in one with highest Pow'r,
> And then a seasonable People still
> Should bend to his, and he to Heavens will,
> What we might hope, what wonderful Effect
> From such a wish'd Conjuncture might reflect.
> Sure, the mysterious Work, where none withstand,

Would forthwith finish under such a Hand:
Fore-shortned Time its useless Course would stay,
And soon precipitate the latest Day.
But a thick Cloud about that Morning lyes,
And intercepts the Beams of Mortal eyes,
That 'tis the most which we determine can,
If these the Times, then this must be the Man.
And well he therefore does, and well has guest,
Who in his Age has always forward prest:
And knowing not where Heavens choice may light,
Girds yet his Sword, and ready stands to fight;
But Men, alas, as if they nothing car'd,
Look on, all unconcern'd, or unprepar'd;
And Stars still fall, and still the Dragons Tail
Swinges the Volumes of its horrid Flail.
For the great Justice that did first suspend
The World by Sin, does by the same extend.
Hence that blest Day still counterpoysed wastes,
The Ill delaying, what the'Elected hastes;
Hence landing Nature to new Seas is tost,
And good Designes still with their Authors lost.

[131-58]

"The latest Day . . . , that blest Day," that is what Marvell so deeply
desires: the end of all that is imperfect and tragic. So, of course, does
everyone. Yet Marvell yearns with a special impatience (difficult, perhaps, for us to understand, who live in an age increasingly unfamiliar with
the notion that an apocalyptical event can be a fulfillment), straining like
his Drop of Dew for the end that lies beyond the irrelevance of history.
Although a man as obsessively cautious as he would not have had as much
assurance about the immediate prospects for the millennium as many of
his contemporaries did, although (as critics have been at pains to show) he
was scrupulous to "distinguish prophecy from fancy,"[65] he could, when
events seemed suggestively to conspire towards a welcome crisis, allow
himself to indulge his hopes. And Cromwell, if he is "the Man," with his
lightning-swift force that reveals Hope a sluggard, promises to dispense
with aeons upon aeons of messy and pointless means to the end. Like an
angel (126), he does not have to labor under the ponderous weight of
matter; like an angelic artist, he can shape the world to his and Marvell's
aesthetic desires without having to struggle with his medium:

> Indefatigable *Cromwell* hyes,
> And cuts his way still nearer to the Skyes,
> Learning a Musique in the Region clear,
> To tune this lower to that higher Sphere.
>   So when *Amphion* did the Lute command,
> Which the God gave him, with his gentle hand,
> The rougher Stones, unto his Measures hew'd,
> Dans'd up in order from the Quarreys rude;
> This took a Lower, that an Higher place,
> As he the Treble alter'd, or the Base:
> No Note he struck, but a new Story lay'd,
> And the great Work ascended while he play'd.
> . . . .
> Thus, ere he ceas'd, his sacred Lute creates
> Th'harmonious City of the seven Gates.
>   Such was that wondrous Order and Consent,
> When *Cromwell* tun'd the ruling Instrument.

                                                    [45-56, 65-68]

Again, hyperbole, licensed if not excused by the canons of epideictic poetry and oratory.[66] But Marvell's genuine enthusiasms are still evident. He wants the preliminaries done with as quickly and as gracefully as possible. He wants the cosmic dance to begin its dress performance with no more fumbling towards a tentative choreography.

And what of the divinely sanctioned "Force" (239) that will bring the end to pass? Since, as the state of man now is, society cannot like Thyrsis and Dorinda "smoothly pass away" into Elysium, the poet sanctions the use of violent instruments—Cromwell's terrible swift sword, the sacred "Arks of War" in the British fleet (357)—that will establish harmony in a "Kingdom blest of Peace and Love" (66, 218) on earth.

It would be too much to claim that these prescriptions for hastening the millennium are utterly pure and high-minded; *The First Anniversary*, for all its restraint and qualification, is full of crass flattery, and its bellicose spirit is as jingoistic as it is eschatological.[67] Marvell gropes for rationalizations in the poem, teasing facts and tormenting his own deep-seated beliefs. His purpose, however, is not merely to eulogize Cromwell, or (if we can accept a disputed reading of the poem) to go further and persuade the Protector that he should become a "Davidic King,"[68] but to resolve broad philosophical issues that are of private and practical concern to him.

He has Cromwell "walk still middle betwixt War and Peace" (244), in violation of the classical wisdom that "*inter bellum et pacem medium nihil* [*est*]."[69] The poet who wrote the lyrics would try desperately to find this middle ground if the high ground of peace seemed unattainable—especially if an escape from violence seemed likely to call for more of a struggle than would accommodation. He tries to remove from the necessary violence its ugliest features by having Cromwell's sword cut cleanly, quickly, effortlessly, artfully. This is in part (and we must return to this subject later) an attempt to save categorical principles from complete irrelevancy to the world as it is. That the attempt does not quite succeed Marvell was forced in some measure to admit when the sword and the power to wield it fell into different hands.

The Restoration forces Marvell to confess that in the Civil War

> the Cause was too good to have been fought for. Men ought to have trusted God; they ought and might have trusted the King with that whole matter. The *Arms of the Church are Prayers and Tears,* the Arms of the Subjects are Patience and Petitions. The King himself being of so accurate and piercing a judgment, would soon have felt where it stuck. For men may spare their pains where Nature is at work, and the world will not go the faster for our driving.[70]

This admission was in great part tactical, made in a work which Charles II was meant to read and approve of.[71] Marvell's whole political career under the restored monarchy points up the disingenuousness of his statement that "even as his present Majesties happy Restauration did it self, so all things else happen in their best and proper time, without any need of our officiousness."[72] Yet in some ways Marvell really did believe that a cause could be too good to fight for, ways that would probably not occur to his opponents, who twitted him about his "Cause Too Good."[73] Parker found the idea a sign of "Cowardize" rather than "Loyalty," "for it seems," he said in reproving Marvell, "you think all Causes too dear when they are bought with danger or blood."[74] But a categorist feels that he can pay no greater compliment to a good than to say that it is too clearly and compellingly attractive for anyone to dispute its value or fight over it. Value is not gauged by the amount of violence provoked in its service, nor is violence of itself a source of value. In his love poems Marvell presents this ideology in a more or less unadulterated form; in his political writings he compromises it somewhat but does not completely abandon it. He speaks with contempt of those who think that violence contributes to nobility:

> The People, which what most they fear esteem,
> Death when more horrid so more noble deem;
> And blame the last *Act,* like *Spectators* vain,
> Unless the *Prince* whom they applaud be slain.
>
> [*A Poem upon the Death of O. C.,* 7–10]

Whereas Milton's Samson was a heroic figure, splendid in defeat, divinely blessed in wreaking catastrophe, Marvell's assessment of the great destroyer is not at all positive:

> *Sampson* groap'd the Temples Posts in spight . . .
> The World o'rewhelming to revenge his Sight.
>
> ["On Mr. Milton's Paradise lost," 9–10]

Marvell considers the *Book of Martyrs* "Fanatical" and "will not with some call the Bible so."[75] Though he cannot get around the fact of Christ's martyrdom, he bristles when Jesus is called a "zealot," preferring to believe with Grotius, and against Milton, that the Son of God rid the Temple of moneychangers "*by the Majesty of his Divine Power, not of any external violence.*"[76]

Marvell deems it one of the functions of governments both civil and ecclesiastical to forestall and eliminate causes that have to be fought for. Thus he is angered by clerics who are bent on "making true piety difficult" and "innovating laws to revenge themselves upon it," who multiply "Creeds" and turn them into "Test[s]."[77] He urges Princes not "to command things unnecessary, and where the profit cannot countervail the hazard," for "even Law is force, and the execution of that Law a greater Violence; and therefore with rational creatures not to be used but upon the utmost extremity."[78] The game is too vicious and too absurd in which magistrates invent means by which to run "their Subjects into Disobedience, and then invent and apply the Tortures for their Disobeying."[79] And such a game can hardly be in the prince's self-interest:

> Whoever shall cast his eye thorow the History of all Ages, will find that nothing has always succeeded better with Princes then the Clemency of Government. . . . The wealth of a Shepheard depends upon the multitude of his flock, the goodness of their Pasture, and the Quietness of their feeding: and Princes, whose dominion over mankind resembles in some measure that of man over other creatures, cannot expect any considerable increase to themselves, if by continual terrour they amaze, shatter, and hare their People, driving them into Woods, & running them upon Precipices.[80]

While in this mood, Marvell, like his God, "will have mercy and not sacrifice."[81]

Marvell was aware, however, all too anxiously aware, that his God *would* have sacrifice. God did run his sheep upon precipices at the risk of diminishing his flock; he did instigate trials in which the "profit" might not "countervail the hazard." Marvell saw with a special vividness the violence required by the *rerum natura,* which was the work of God, and it was not easy for him to forgive God for actions similar (by a somewhat perilous but not altogether implausible analogy) to those which he found reprehensible in God's deputies. When in his final days Marvell determined to write a theodicy, he used the *argumentum a fortiori* to defend God: "If a well natur'd man would not do so, it is much more disagreeable to God's nature."[82] As Pierre Bayle was to make distressingly evident, however, this very proposition could lead as well to skepticism as to faith.[83] Marvell knew that this was so. We might, then, be alert to listen in his public, theological voice for the tremolo of rejected doubt qualifying the full, clear notes of confidence.

It is significant that Marvell very often describes violence in images of dividing or splitting. And since he has a tendency to think of integrity in categorical terms, celebrating the unmixed and inviolable purity of his Drop of Dew, suggesting by his Mower's hostility to botanical mixtures the poet-moralist's instinct that alloyed goods in general are adulterations,[84] it seems inevitable he should conclude that the world as we know it cannot be *rightly* divided. Fate drives "iron wedges" into the very nature of love and keeps perfect lovers perpetually apart.[85] Brought into the world through "*Cesarian Section,*" his mother "split against the Stone," the Unfortunate Lover grows up to be "Torn with Flames and ragg'd with Wounds" (14-16, 54); the Coy Mistress's lover, less passive, proposes to "tear" pleasures "Thorough the Iron gates of Life." The Mower's scythe[86] slices not only through grass but, in accordance with the biblical equation, through the flesh of man and beast as well—and what Damon does to the grass, Juliana does to his thoughts and him ("Damon the Mower," 73-80; *Upon Appleton House,* 393-400; "The Mower's Song," 6ff.). There i. a terrible irony in the fact that the procreative act of love, ominously described by Marvell in one place as the thrusting of a sickle at a virgin harvest (*Falcem virginiae . . . immit[t]ere messi),*[87] is symptomatic of a fatal condition, "The Mower mown" ("Damon," 80), to which state there is an analogue in the psychology of man the mircrocosm: "The Cramp of Hope does tear" the Body, which the Soul so "impales" that it becomes its own "Precipice," a perpetual cutting-edge unto itself ("A Dialogue between the Soul and Body," 33, 13-14). In nature Cromwell's lightning, a spark of the divine, divides its way to its destination, rending palaces and temples ("An Horatian Ode," 16, 22). Architects "square and hew";[88] the hewel's beak hacks, mines, and fells (*Upon Appleton House*, 545–52). Indeed, "Necessity" has with its hammer split the whole of Nature down the middle: "There is . . . a necessity . . . that was pre-eternal to all things, and exercised dominion not only over all humane things, but over *Jupiter* himself and the rest of the Deities and drove the great Iron nail thorough the Axle-tree of Nature."[89] The ultimate cosmic catastrophe, even *in potentia*, is conceived of by the poet as an unnatural separation in which (we might infer) the divided parts no longer cleave to the stake:

> Nature so her self does use
> To lay by her wonted State,
> Lest the world should separate.
>
> ["Daphnis and Chloe," 13–15]

And the ultimate personal tragedy is for the soul to be haplessly "divided from the Sphear" which is its true home ("On a Drop of Dew," 14). These images arise naturally in the imagination of one who loves wholeness to such an extent that he complains, not in loud defiance but with controlled acrimony, against the supernatural forces responsible for tragic division, antagonism, and incompleteness.[90]

Marvell is both pained and bewildered by the kind of dilemma later defined by the Princess in Johnson's *Rasselas*:

> Every hour . . . confirms my prejudice in favor of the position so often uttered by the mouth of Imlac, "that nature sets her gifts on the right hand and on the left." Those conditions, which flatter hope and desire, are so constituted, that, as we approach one, we recede from another.[91]

In "The Definition of Love," Marvell makes "Fate" responsible for this condition; in "The Match," he blames "Nature," "Love," and ultimately the force that rules them; in the elegy for "Lord Hastings," he indicts "Heaven" or "the *Democratick* Stars" (19–26). It is, of course, important to consider what the names refer to. The poet may think of Fate or Nature or Stars as a *logical* necessity, by which even God is bound. Not even the deity can make parallel lines meet or "immure / The *Circle* in the *Quadrature*."[92] If this is the necessity which "exercised dominion . . . over *Jupiter* himself and the rest of the Deities and drove the great Iron nail," there would be little point in reproaching God for failing to close the rift.

Marvell does not, however, direct most of his complaints against impersonal forces that are beyond all appeal. In "The Definition of

Love," there is no logical necessity for love to be defined by "the Conjunction of the Mind, / And Opposition of the Stars." Whereas a contradiction is in itself not conceivable, Fate does "see / Two perfect Loves" (13–14) and "enviously" (30, 13) proceeds to separate them. Parallels cannot logically cross, but lovers do not logically have to constitute parallels. Fate with its wedges capriciously drives the lovers apart by arbitrarily defining love in terms of separation and opposition. A kind of supernatural jealousy, or chariness, also makes itself felt in "The Match," causing divisions that are not at all necessary.

> Nature had long a Treasure made
>   Of all her choisest store;
> Fearing, when She should be decay'd,
>   To beg in vain for more.
>
> Her *Orientest* Colours there,
>   And Essences most pure,
> With sweetest Perfumes hoarded were,
>   All as she thought secure.
>
> [1–8]

Nature (as does Love later on) hoards, packs away, locks up her treasures in "separate" compartments (14) out of fear rather than necessity, with the result that the world is deprived of the *integritas* it might so easily possess.

> She seldom them unlock'd or us'd,
>   But with the nicest care;
> For, with one grain of them diffus'd,
>   She could the World repair.
>
> [9–12]

It is difficult to avoid placing the blame for this situation on the Lord of Nature. For if Nature is right in fearing that poverty will force her to "beg" from him (4), her Lord may be judged less than fully generous in supporting her; if Nature's apprehensions spring rather from her own selfishness, insecurity, and jealousy, her Lord may be judged less than fully competent in creating her—or one would at least want to ask him why he should wish to inflict this flawed stepmother on the world.[93] He does not, it is true, prevent Nature's stores from leaving their compartments in some measure; but their escape is only a limited blessing, for it does not "repair" the world, which remains "poor" (38) in the midst of whatever wealth Celia and her lover may themselves, separately, enjoy.[94]

When Marvell speaks of Nature's mistakes, he cannot be referring to necessities, since a mistake by its very nature need not be made. The poet envisions, then, that Nature's law of either/or may be otherwise as he exhorts the "Darling of the Gods," little T. C., to "Reform the errours of the Spring" ("The Picture of little T. C.," 27). Perfection need not be bought at the cost of perfection:

Make that the Tulips may have share
Of sweetness, seeing they are fair;
And Roses of their thorns disarm:
   But most procure
That Violets may a longer Age endure.[95]

[28-32]

Man's attempts to rectify the errors of the spring on his own do not always meet with success and are sometimes blameworthy, as the Mower makes clear in his tirade against gardens, but Marvell must in some way sympathize with those attempts at "reform," however hopeless, that are motivated by a yearning for a completeness that nature cannot or will not provide. Fields left to themselves, after all, do not produce the gardens of Elysium.[96] And the gods, who dwell with the Mowers in the wild ("The Mower against Gardens," 40), may also be liable to criticism for tolerating Nature's errancy. A complaint against Nature need not always result in a quarrel with God, but it may—as the devout often realized in spite of theologians' insistence that Nature has "fallen" along with man and might be expected to appear at least as halt and incompetent as he. Donne claimed that "it is a *halfe Atheisme* to murmure against *Nature,* who is *Gods immediate Commissioner.* . . ."[97] Ralph Cudworth and Henry More, two of the more systematic seventeenth-century defenders of the *causa Dei,* both began their theodicies by combating Lucretius's remarks about the faultiness of Nature.[98] Since the declarations of poets do not have to be as precise as those of theologians, we should not judge from Marvell's criticisms of Nature by themselves that he was a "half-atheist" (the term "atheist" was often applied in the Renaissance to men who were mere skeptics). When those statements, however, are read in the context of other related grievances which Marvell had with Providence, they help to define and measure his less than holy discontent.

There is no logical necessity that man lack wholeness within himself; the theologians say he actually possessed it in Eden. Yet his body and soul, despite their interdependence, have competing interests that cannot now be reconciled, and their hostility, in a baleful paradox, sunders what must remain a unity. Hence the "Dialogue between the Soul and Body":

Soul

O who shall, from this Dungeon, raise
A Soul inslav'd so many wayes?
With bolts of Bones, that fetter'd stands
In Feet; and manacled in Hands.
Here blinded with an Eye; and there
Deaf with the drumming of an Ear.
A Soul hung up, as 'twere, in Chains
Of Nerves, and Arteries, and Veins.
Tortur'd, besides each other part,
In a Vain Head, and double Heart.

Body

O who shall me deliver whole,
From bonds of this Tyrannic Soul?
Which, stretcht upright, impales me so,
That mine own Precipice I go;
And warms and moves this needless Frame:
(A Fever could but do the same.)
And, wanting where its spight to try
Has made me live to let me dye.
A Body that could never rest,
Since this ill Spirit it possesst.

Soul

What Magick could me thus confine
Within anothers Grief to pine?
Where whatsoever it complain,
I feel, that cannot feel, the pain.
And all my Care its self employes,
That to preserve, which me destroyes:
Constrain'd not only to indure
Diseases, but, whats worse, the Cure:
And ready oft the Port to gain,
Am Shipwrackt into Health again.

Body

But Physick yet could never reach
The Maladies Thou me dost teach;
Whom first the Cramp of Hope does Tear;
And then the Palsie Shakes of Fear.
The Pestilence of Love does heat:
Or Hatred's hidden Ulcer eat.
Joy's chearful Madness does perplex:

Or Sorrow's other Madness vex.
Which Knowledge forces me to know;
And Memory will not forgoe.
What but a Soul could have the wit
To build me up for Sin so fit?
So Architects do square and hew,
Green Trees that in the Forest grew.

Why must the good of one principle preclude the good of the other? The orthdox answer is that this "wearisome Condition of Humanity," as Fulke Greville calls "selfe-division,"[99] is a punishment warranted by the fall, hence a juridical, not a logical, requirement. Even so, a man of skeptical temper may lament the punishment and, flirting with heterodoxy, question the grounds on which it was levied. More sanguine and more militant spirits, believing in a *felix poena*, or fortunate punishment, may glorify the strife between soul and body—as does Samuel Parker, Marvell's adversary in *The Rehearsal Transpros'd:*

> Mankind is compounded of contrary Principles, endued with
> contrary desires and inclinations, to the end that there might be
> an order of Beings in the world . . . capable of all those Heroick
> Vertues, which consist in the Empire of Reason over the brutish
> and sensual Faculties.[100]

But Marvell in his dialogue of soul and body is far from such consolation. He refuses to derive comfort from a paradoxical view of the human composite or "compound," allowing no synthesis (we might think of Yeats's "Self" in "A Dialogue of Self and Soul") to overcome the dreadful antitheses that produce destructive ironies rather than healing paradoxes. Contrary to the dictates of traditional theology, he does not provide the soul with arguments to put the body permanently in its place. By arranging the dialogue so that none of the assertions of either disputant is refuted, he makes victory and the joy of victory impossible. (The body is given a few extra words, as well as the last word, not to establish its superiority in the debate but to underscore the cogency of its claims, which are usually considered weak.)[101] Soul and body have equally limited vision, for neither realizes that a triumph in an argument which determines who suffers the most must be Pyrrhic indeed. Marvell pities more than he condemns them, however, as he looks beyond their almost childish bickering to a predicament for which they cannot be held totally responsible.

When the body asks, "What but a Soul could have the wit / To build

me up for Sin so fit?" it directs all of its resentment against its immediate
adversary, neglecting to consider that it is the Divine Architect who
preeminently possesses the wit, the power, and the ultimate responsibility. The poet's awareness cannot be so circumscribed. He is used to
thinking about the complicity of supernatural forces in setting the world
at cross purposes with itself, and therefore he is likely to recognize that
the body's rhetorical question can have an answer. He knows how to trace
effects to their ultimate causes. (He states, for example, in *The Rehearsal
Transpros'd*, that "the Body is in the power of the mind; . . . the Mind is in
the hand of God. . . .")[102] Now if God's is the "Magick" (21) that has
devised the plight of body and soul, if it is his wit that has fashioned a
composite "fit" for sin and thus for punishment that leads to more sin, so
that (to paraphrase St. Paul) where retribution doth abound, sin doth
more abound, a defense of the divine aims and actions would seem in
order. How can the Lord's hatred of iniquity have allowed him to select,
from all the penalties for an original fall available to him, the one that
would make the proliferation of moral evil a virtual certainty? Although
Marvell provides a defense of God elsewhere, he is not willing to do so in
the "Dialogue," whose speakers ask questions that are not answered and
suggest additional questions, also unanswered, that are more dangerous
than they realize. It is clear from this cautious, indirect protest that the
poet does not breathe here the heady atmosphere of rebellion, but we can
hear between the lines a murmuring not quieted by appeal to traditional
wisdom. It is perhaps this very kind of repining that James Howell looked
upon with some alarm in *The Vision: or a Dialog between the Soul and the Bodie*
(1651).[103] In Howell's dialogue, the body charges the "Intellectual soul"
with subjecting man to ills that make him *"Heautontimorumenos,* a self-
tormentor and crucifier of himself," while serving "to puzzle the brain
with sturdie doubts and odd surmises, touching the mysteries of saving
Faith, whereas indeed, as *sense* should vail to *reason,* so *reason* should strike
sail to *faith;* moreover the soul is forward oftentimes to question the very
works of Creation, and quarrel with Nature the hand-maid of the
Almighty in the method of her Productions. . . ."[104]

In a more explicit protest against the ways of "Heaven," the elegy
"Upon the Death of Lord Hastings," Marvell speaks again of a necessity,
which constrains the young nobleman to accept its terms. As in the case of
little T. C., the violet cannot a longer age endure:

> Alas, his Vertues did his *Death* presage:
> Needs must he die, that doth out-run his Age.

[9–10]

Again, heaven does not obey this necessity but decrees it—and out of the basest motives, which Marvell makes no attempt to disguise. Had Hastings

> on *the Tree of Life* once made a Feast,
> As that of *Knowledge;* what Loves had he given
> To Earth, and then what Jealousies to Heaven!
> But 'tis a *Maxime* of that State, That none,
> Lest He become like Them, taste more than one.
> Therefore the *Democratick* Stars did rise,
> And all that Worth from hence did *Ostracize.*
>
> [20–26]

This sour reminiscence and pejorative interpretation of the fall echoes the charges which opponents of biblical religion have perennially leveled against the God of Genesis,[105] and it reveals how intensely Marvell can doubt the premises of Christian theodicy when he thinks too hard about a jealous God whose policy is forever to allow no "more than one" (24), never both. In such a mood of doubt and resentment, Marvell is willing to entertain the worst thoughts about the divine goodness. He aligns himself with Aesculapius (47ff.) against the destructive gods, who, in the paradigmatic case of Lord Hastings, arbitrarily and irresistibly enforce their envious will. What could the "good man," the kind physician, do in opposition, "although he bruis'd / All herbs, and them a thousand ways infus'd"?[106] Tragically, nothing.

> All he had try'd, but all in vain, he saw,
> And wept, as we, without Redress or Law.
>
> [55–58]

The poet must also have reflected that once, when the herbs of Aesculapius did bring a dead man back to life, Zeus struck down the great healer with a lightning bolt.[107]

Nowhere else in his writings does Marvell let his anger and frustration over the problem of evil run unchecked.[108] Indeed, I have already referred to some of the statements he makes in support of the *causa Dei* which prove that he could see and take God's side of the argument. But the categorist's temperament presents significant obstacles to an easy faith in the goodness of a Creator whose idea of perfection is quite different from his own; and Marvell frequently expresses attitudes, some categorical, others not inherently so, that are likely to have caused him trouble with specific tenets of the theology which was supposed to uphold or complement faith. Some of these attitudes have already been discussed: Marvell's love of the beauty and integrity of Elysium as goods of the highest order in themselves; his hatred of incompleteness—and of the paradoxes meant to glorify it; his less than profound esteem of the heroic ideal, which defines good by appeal to violent, sacrificial process; his suspicion that "heroic" struggles are games which do not prove all that they are supposed to— especially if the players are ultimately but "the *Heavens* sport" ("Upon the Death of Lord Hastings," 59). It is probable that a man of such dispositions would find it difficult to bless what happened, what was allowed to happen, in Eden in the name of the "higher" goods which, theologians declared, could not have been otherwise achieved.

Some paradoxical arguments in defense of God, it may be recalled, postulated that the fall and the conditions which led to it contributed to the moral stature of man and enhanced the moral perfection of God. If I have interpreted the evidence correctly, Marvell had his doubts about the overriding value of the moral benefits men were to reap at the cost of categorical perfection. He certainly felt that there were goods greater than virtue (paradoxically defined) which God could bestow upon his creatures, or so, as the Transproser, Marvell said to Parker, who in speaking of perfection had tried to attribute more dignity to means than to end:

> To prove that the fruits of the Spirit are no more than Morality, [Mr. Bayes (Parker)] quotes Saint *Paul*, Gal. 5.22. Where the Apostle enumerates them: *Love, Joy, Peace, Patience, Gentleness, Goodness, Faith, Meekness* and *Temperance:* but our Author translates Joy to *Chearfulness*, Peace to *Peaceableness*, and Faith to *Faithfulness:* What Ignorance, or rather what Forgery is this of Scripture and Religion?[109]

What is more, Marvell would not even hear talk of God's "moral accomplishments." He became furious at Parker for presuming to use such an expression:

> Gods Morall accomplishments! If it were an Oath I should not think it binds me: but in the mean time methinks it has something in it bordering upon Blasphemy. . . . 'Twere proper enough to speak of the *Moral Accomplishments* of some young Gentleman at the Inns of Court that were upon his Preferment; but I do not remember to have heard it used at any time upon this Occasion. I hope you see by this time that a man might at your rate of talking have made God as well only a notional and Moral existence.[110]

Virtue, it seems, is not a good sufficiently exalted to be predicated of God.[111] And, all things considered, it was not sufficiently esteemed by Marvell to console him for the horrors of what he called the "humane condition."[112]

Marvell did not accept the paradox of the *felix culpa* and in effect says so (in an apostrophe to England, "that dear and happy Isle" which should be a picture of *"Paradise"* but is not):

What *luckless* Apple did we tast,
To make us Mortal, and The Wast?

[*Upon Appleton House,* 327–28;
emphasis mine]

The poet who complained of the errors of the spring did not in all probability believe in anything like the principle of plenitude, which turned privation into a source of value. Nor did the lay theologian who defended John Howe against Thomas Danson conceive of God as being in any way beyond good and evil:

[It is] pregnant with impious absurdity . . . to assert . . . that God's promises convey no right to them to whom they are made. For, "'tis a ruled case,"[T. D.] says, "in the Schools, that God cannot properly be said a debter to His creatures;" and then adds of [his] own, "no, not when He hath passed a promise to them," and pursues this so far as to say "If He should (to suppose an impossibility) . . . break His word, He would be but *mendax, non injustus.* . . ." What dispensation have some men to speak at this rate . . . !![113]

In effect, then, Marvell could not have been completely satisfied by any of the major hypotheses yet developed by Christianity to deal with the problem of evil.

He was not, I think, free from misgivings about some of the corollaries, either. He was required to believe, in order to preserve his orthodoxy, that the moral lapse of the first man warranted a "dreadful vengeance," and that this punishment had in justice to be shared by Adam's descendants. There is no strong evidence that Marvell ever repudiated these beliefs, but there are hints that his confidence in them was not serene. He is disturbed when "the innocent suffers for the guilty."[114] He is indignant at those who would involve others in their personal misfortune—at Tom May, for example:

Must therefore all the World be set on flame,
Because a Gazet writer mist his aim?[115]

Or at the Mower, who will have "Flow'rs, and Grass and . . . all" fall with
him "in one common Ruine" ("The Mower's Song," 21-22). Or even, as
we have seen, at the biblical hero Samson, who in Marvell's view
destroyed a whole populace "to revenge his sight." It is, then, also
possible that in his more skeptical moments Marvell questioned the justice
of the moral and juridical system that allowed, even required that the
wicked carry down "all" with them. He knew and may well have shared
Donne's anxiety over this issue.[116] About the severity of the punishment he
could only wonder. At the end of *The Rehearsal Transpros'd*, he refers to a
story about Pope Julius III, who,

> when he missed a dish of cold peacock, which he had com-
> manded to keep to him, having other new rosted peacocks, he
> vomit out most horrible blasphemy against God. And when one
> of his Cardinals answered, *Let not your Holinesse be offended at so
> light a matter.* He replyed, *If God was so angry for the eating of one
> apple, that he cast out our first parents out of Paradise; wherefore shal it
> not be lawful to me who is his Vicar, to be angry for a peacock, seeing it is
> far greater then an apple?*[117]

The satirist laughs at the pope's rationalization. But the laughter may be
slightly nervous; for it is not inconceivable that at times Marvell felt that
the apple, even though "far greater" than the peacock, in that it could test
man's "moral fibre," had led to a tragedy too great for any man's reason
to be able to justify.

When Marvell does profess himself reconciled to the ways of
Providence, it is not because rational arguments have conquered his
doubts. The intellectual skirmishings of the *Defence of John Howe* do not
really establish its fundamental theses, which are founded, rather, on the
authority of Scripture:

> Whereas that second chapter of Genesis [Marvell must have
> meant the third, also] contains the plain history of good and evil,
> and (not to mention so many attestations to it of the Old and
> New Testament) what other comment needs there, for what
> belongs to good, than that, James i. 17, that it is from God only,
> "that every good giving, and every perfect thing descendeth?"
> And, as to evil, that of St. James is sufficient conviction, cap i. v.
> 13.14, "Let no man say when he is tempted, I was tempted of
> God. God cannot be tempted with evil, neither tempteth He any
> man; but every man is tempted when he is drawn aside by his
> own lusts and enticed."[118]

The "conscience" of the "examining Christian" also bears witness (against Danson's and Calvin's "frightful" doctrine that God predestined the fall of Adam and Eve)[119] to the fact that moral evil and its consequences are solely man's responsibility (169). Beyond this point Marvell is not willing to go. Nowhere does he firmly endorse any rational grounds for God's permission of evil, choosing instead to accept the utter mysteriousness of a divine decree which no amount of commentary can render more rationally compelling.[120] In an eloquent sally against Parker, he draws the line where speculation must end and the will make its decision:

> You do hereby seem to imagine, that Providence should have contrived all things according to the utmost perfection, or that which you conceive would have been most to your purpose. Whereas in the shape of Mans body, and in the frame of the world, there are many things indeed lyable to Objection, and which might have been better if we should give ear to proud and curious Spirits. But we must nevertheless be content with such bodies, and to inhabit such an Earth as it has pleased God to allot us. And so also in the Government of the World, it were desirable that men might live in perpetual Peace, in a state of good Nature, without Law or Magistrate, because by the universal equity and rectitude of manners they would be superfluous. And had God intended it so, it would so have succeeded, and he would have sway'd and temper'd the Minds and Affections of Mankind so that their Innocence should have expressed that of the Angels, and the Tranquility of his Dominion here below should have resembled that in Heaven. But alas! that state of perfection was dissolv'd in the first Instance, and was shorter liv'd than Anarchy, scarce of one days continuance. And ever since the first Brother Sacrificed the other to Revenge, because his Offering was better accepted, Slaughter and War has made up half the business in the World, and oftentimes upon the same quarrel, and with like success. So that as God has hitherto, in stead of an Eternal Spring, a standing Serenity, and perpetual Sun-shine, subjected Mankind to the dismal influence of Comets from above, to Thunder, and Lightning, and Tempests from the middle Region, and from the lower Surface, to the raging of the Seas, and the tottering of Earth quakes, beside all other the innumerable calamities to which humane life is exposed, he has in like manner distinguish'd the Government of the World by the intermitting seasons of Discord, War, and

publick Disturbance. Neither has he so order'd it only (as men endeavour to express it) by meer permission, but sometimes out of Complacency.[121]

What bitter medicine for Marvell to swallow as a cure for his "proud and curious" spirit! God does not think highly of the categorist's ideal, but Marvell can give no reasons why the Lord should not. God had, Marvell believed, assured the "security of good angels by [a] determining influence," and could have done the same for Adam and Eve.[122] Although God could have "sway'd and temper'd the Minds and Affections" of men so that they would not have fallen from perfection, he simply "intended" that Elysium be set at hazard; and now, after the loss of Paradise, he hurls his thunderbolts, sometimes even "out of Complacency." From this point of view, the dreadful vengeance, the errors of spring, and the great iron nail that split the axel-tree of Nature were not necessary, but the effects of an inscrutable purpose. When contemplating such mysteries, even so reasonable a theologian as Jeremy Taylor gave over attempts to understand:

> Whose reason can give an account why, or understand it to be reasonable, that God should permit evil for good ends, when He hates that evil, and can produce that good without that evil? and yet that He does so we are taught by our religion. Whose reason can make it intelligible, that God who delights not in the death of a sinner, but He and His Christ and all their angels, rejoice infinitely in the salvation of a sinner, yet that He should not cause that every sinner should be saved; working in him a mighty and a prevailing grace, without which grace he shall not in the event of things be saved . . . ? Why does not He work in us all to will and to do, not only that we can will, but that we shall will? for if the actual willing be anything, it is His creation. . . . Why . . . , human reason cannot give a wise or a probable account.[123]

Marvell offers no justification for evil, for he can think of none. Like Job he submits; but whereas Job had the benefit of an epiphany which awed him and reconciled him to God's will, Marvell must, it seems, stand alone and uninspired like Shylock before the bar of justice and declare "I am content" for want of a better alternative.

Marvell's options were not broader because the categorist in him would not allow them to be. Furthermore, his temperament may have alerted him to some of the theoretical inconsistencies in the theodicies available to him. But the fact remains that, however narrow his field for decision, he did choose to "let God be true and *just* to His word, and every man (that saith otherwise) a lyer."[124] What did this resolution accomplish? Did it "solve" for Marvell the problem of evil? Did it win for his mind the "standing Serenity" which he looked for in the world but could not find, or the *ataraxia* of the Epicurean and Skeptic connoisseur? Did it change his values where it could not accommodate them? Marvell wrote poems in which categorical and paradoxical conceptions of value are clearly at war.[125] Does the outcome provide a pattern for his truce with God? These questions must be approached in a more extensive study of the process by which Marvell became a "Resolved Soul."

4

The Imbalance of Contradiction

To be in both worlds full
Is more then God was, who was hungrie here.
Wouldst thou his laws of fasting disannul?
  Enact good cheer?
Lay out thy joy, yet hope to save it?
Wouldst thou both eat thy cake, and have it?

George Herbert, "The Size"

For good grows wild and wide,
Has shades, is nowhere none;
But right must seek a side
And choose for chieftain one.

G. M. Hopkins, "On a Piece of Music"

But who shall so forecast the years
  And find in loss a gain to match?

Tennyson, *In Memoriam*

There has been little general agreement about the character of Marvell's resolutions, especially of those to be found in his poetry. Critics who consider his poems impersonal naturally seek in them simply a fitting, artistic conclusion, the resolution of a game. Critics who allow that the poems in some way speak Marvell's mind tend to be divided among those who believe that his firmest resolve is to make none—"the poems examine without judging, weigh without deciding";[1] those who see him achieve a personal intellectual synthesis that provides him with the "security of . . . untroubled belief";[2] and those who feel that his resolutions come primarily from a stoic will, in the exercise of which he exults—"Marvell's favorite story [is that] temporal life necessarily incurs corruption; perfection cannot hold; fate demands sacrifice and sacrifice becomes beautiful."[3] As I have indicated, I do not find any of these views wholly satisfactory. I believe that Marvell's writings reflect his genuine concerns and point to personal resolves, but that he makes his decisions nervously, reluctantly, and often in the dark. The clash of categorical and paradoxical principles comes to some sort of conclusion, as can be seen in Marvell's political and religious choices. To what extent these determinations signal that the issues are, in the strict sense of the word, "settled" is quite another question.

The results of a choice can sometimes be clarified by an understanding of its causes, and such is the case with Marvell's rejection of part of the categorical ideal. His poetry suggests that his motives, although complex, were not all hopelessly mystifying; and while a search for them is bound to be speculative, there is enough evidence to keep conjecture plausible. The following discussion cannot offer a perfectly chronological picture of a developing awareness, because some of the poems discussed are not datable. What I can say about "development" (there is a modest case to be presented on the subject) will be said in the next chapter. A strict chronology, however, is not of crucial importance to an understanding of the resolutions to be described. Since they are much more achievements of will than triumphs of reason, they are liable to be approached then receded from, made then unmade. Marvell can and does move from side to side the weights that upset the balance of contradiction—perhaps, as Annabel Patterson has proposed, in a "pattern of alternating commitment and retreat, of rash involvement followed by self-doubt or apology, of changes of mind and direction."[4] While it is not possible to assign each move an exact time and place, his writings provide clues to large patterns of choice, the elements of which can be defined even when chronology is violated.[5]

If we read the lyrics as episodes in Marvell's "quarrel with himself,"[6] we can sense that he describes in some of them a perfection that is most desirable but doomed, and therefore promises himself, like his admired Ben Jonson, that "hence-forth, all his vowes be such, / As what he loues may neuer like too much."[7] Marvell esteems highly the exquisite fastidiousness of the Drop of Dew, its yearning for the Fullness of Being, its impatience with the impure and provisional. He realizes, however, as most idealists do, that nowhere are dewdrops allowed to sit tremulously poised on "sweat leaves and blossoms green," the "World excluding round" as they wait to be dissolved (23, 29). The mowers are in the fields with their scythes.

This realization is most poignantly expressed in "The Nymph

complaining for the death of her Faun," a lament for the helplessness of innocence, for the loss of pure, spontaneous beauty, goodness, and joy before forces which make their destruction inevitable. In what Marvell may have intended to be an Ovidian aetiological myth, purporting to explain how the statue of a nymph and her pet came to be in a particular garden or wilderness, we receive from the girl herself the story of her rude introduction to evil. She has suffered the inconstancy of the swain Sylvio, she reveals; and, after transferring all her affection to the fawn which her false lover had given her, she has seen "Wanton Troopers" ride by and kill it, gratuitously. The loss of the animal is enough to make the Nymph resolute for death, for by dying she can join her pet, her only reason for living, in "fair *Elizium*" (107). She had, in fact, hoped to enjoy something like Elysium in her own garden, as she reveals in a description of her games with the deer:

> I set myself to play
> My solitary time away,
> With this: and very well content,
> Could so mine idle Life have spent.
> . . . .
> I have a Garden of my own,
> But so with Roses over grown,
> And Lillies, that you would it guess
> To be a little Wilderness.
> And all the Spring time of the year
> It onely loved to be there.
> Among the beds of Lillyes, I
> Have sought it oft, where it should lye;
> Yet could not, till it self would rise,
> Find it, although before mine Eyes.
> For, in the flaxen Lillies shade,
> It like a bank of Lillies laid.
> Upon the Roses it would feed,
> Until its Lips ev'n seem'd to bleed:
> And then to me 'twould boldly trip,
> And print those Roses on my Lip.
> But all its chief delight was still
> On Roses thus its self to fill:
> And its pure virgin Limbs to fold
> In whitest sheets of Lillies cold.
> Had it liv'd long, it would have been
> Lillies without, Roses within.

[37-40, 71-92]

This categorist's paradise has both purity (lilies) and intensity (roses), but its reds and whites are the intensities neither of martyrs nor of blushing lovers.[8] The worldly-wise may find it ominous that the lips of the fawn "ev'n seem'd to bleed," and smile knowingly at the Nymph's escape from frustrated passion into a compensatory world where lilies are "cold" and roses only things of beauty.[9] But the Nymph herself is not bothered by such considerations. For her the fawn has become nothing less than an embodiment of the highest values: its virginity (89) is innocence, not what in a human being would be triumphant virtue, and its symbolic whiteness is unalloyed; its affection is love that neither demands nor offers violence; its occupation is "play," joyous activity good in itself, without need of further justification.

The Nymph lacks sturdiness, but she is not simply a frail, timorous, mindless waif. She learns from her first ordeal that the fairest hopes may play one false, as the fawn may her:

> Had it liv'd long, I do not know
> Whether it too might have done so
> As Sylvio did: his Gifts might be
> Perhaps as false or more than he,
>
> [47–50]

and she is brave enough to let her attachment develop anyway. She has the strength and the kindness to forgive the cruel men who killed her deer:

> I'me sure I never wisht them ill;
> Nor do I for all this; nor will:
> But, if my simple Pray'rs may yet
> Prevail with Heaven to forget
> Thy murder, I will Joyn my Tears
> Rather then fail.
>
> [7–12]

Although she has been judged "myopically self-regarding,"[10] her grief is not wholly self-centered, but occasioned by the destruction of a good that she knows exists apart from her and before which she can efface herself:

> I blusht to see its foot more soft,
> And white, (shall I say then my hand?)
> NAY any Ladies of the Land.
>
> [60–62]

The Nymph may be naive, but her naiveté is in some ways disarming, certainly not altogether unattractive, for it is a generous simplicity whose inability to survive even the wise must keenly regret.

And why must the Nymph—her ideal with her—be destroyed? Most obviously because men are malicious and she has no will to fight. Ultimately, however, because "Heavens King," who "keeps register of every thing" (13-14), numbering every hair,[11] makes simple innocence vulnerable and allows it to be destroyed. Heaven's King goes further, as the Nymph, speaking of her pet's murderers, unwittingly reminds Christians who enjoy the benefit of a revelation unknown to her:

> Though they should wash their guilty hands
> In this warm life-blood, which doth part
> From thine, and wound me to the Heart,
> Yet could they not be clean: their Stain
> Is dy'd in such a Purple Grain.
> There is not such another in
> The World, to offer for their Sin.
>
> [18-24]

There *was* to come into the world "such another," and he was to shed his blood so that guilty men might wash their hands in it and be clean. That is to say, God was to keep his "register" somehow balanced by demanding that the destruction of innocence be atoned for by the destruction of the greatest innocence. Whether this be paradox or absurdity the Nymph is not capable of judging. Her simple moral code—"I cannot be / Unkind t'a Beast that loveth me" (45-46)—indicates that she does not think in paradoxical terms. Her limitations are obviously not the poet's however, and Marvell must certainly be aware of the incongruity in the Nymph's untroubled thought of a sacrificial animal of atonement while she complains of the slaughter of her spotless fawn.

Marvell sees the problem, but if disturbed, he registers no explicit protest. Content to let the situation speak for itself, he allows the Nymph to hint at his anxiety in her references to a Providence whose benevolence is far less simple and straightforward than her own, allows to operate on its own the irony that Diana (104), the divinity who endorses the Nymph's love of purity, is also the bloody goddess of the hunt.[12] As many readers have sensed, Marvell imbues the poem with with "overtones," classical and biblical, which, taken in sum, fail to constitute a well-denoted meaning.[13] Through such a procedure he can suggest a disquiet of mind and conscience too vague to be marshalled into defiance. Thus allusion to the death of Silvia's stag in the *Aeneid* (7. 475ff.) raises at least the remote suggestion of supernatural participation in the taking of life and the subversion of peace. The picture of the dying Nymph's metamorphosis into a second Niobe (at first sight perplexing, since Niobe in Ovid is punished for criminal pride) may bring to mind the non-Ovidian, ultimately blameless heroine whose potentially scandalous treatment by the gods incited Plato to theodicy:

> If a poet writes of the sufferings of Niobe . . . , either we must not permit him to say that these are the works of God, or, if they are of God, he must devise some such explanation of them as we are seeking: he must say that God did what was just and right . . . ; but that God being good is the author of evil to any one, that is to be strenuously denied. . . . Such a fiction is suicidal, ruinous, impious.[14]

Reminiscence in Marvell's poem of the Song of Solomon,[15] as well as reference to Providence, a redeemer, and redemption, may set the ingenue by ironic contrast in a world diminished because deprived of revelation; yet the plight of innocence, even delicate, naive, unenlightened, pagan innocence, calls to heaven for explanation and redress—for remedies whose actual sovereignty in the Christian era is not in the poem placed above question. These tremors of faith, however, none of them clearly defined, can be perceived only in the work's resonances, for the poet's explicit intention is to animate a pathetic scene:

> O help! O help! I see it faint:
> And dye as calmely as a Saint.
> See how it weeps. The Tears do come
> Sad, slowly dropping like a Gumme.
> So Weeps the wounded Balsome; so
> The holy Frankincense doth flow.
> The brotherless *Heliades*
> Melt in such Amber Tears as these.
>   I in a golden Vial will
> Keep these two crystal Tears; and fill
> It till it do o'reflow with mine;
> Then place it in *Diana's* Shrine.
>   Now my Sweet Faun is vanish'd to
> Whether the Swans and Turtles go:
> In fair *Elizium* to endure,
> With milk-white Lambs, and Ermins pure.
> O do not run too fast: for I
> Will but bespeak thy Grave, and dye.

[93–110]

We see from the Nymph's words, actions, and situation that her ideal is too fragile and that her response to the forces of evil moiling about her in the forest is inadequate. But if Marvell cannot accept her as a model for action, it is only because he sees that, for whatever reason, the categorist's flower is too delicate to take root in earth, not because he finds the Elysian vision in itself simplistic, ignoble, or perverse. He gives us no reason to doubt that the fawn is holy, as the Nymph claims (94ff.); and though the Nymph's tearful farewell is melodramatic and perhaps too self-consciously sacrificial (111ff.), it neither obliterates our sense of her truly noble qualities nor annuls her naive wisdom. Marvell himself, here as elsewhere poet of Elysium, cherishes the whiteness of the fawn's "purest Alabaster" (120), and therefore cannot blame the Nymph for being in love with it.

Like Desdemona's "monumental alablaster," however, this surpassing excellence cannot, except in Elysium, survive outside the cold pastoral of art; and survival is a most important value for the categorist, who is not consoled for loss by the grandeur of sacrifice. If survival is the point, we may see little wrong with the Nymph's intention to run into the eternal day of Elysium, where she may live according to her heart without interference. Nothing is "wrong" with it—at least, not here. Questions of conscience are taken up in other poems. The fact is, however, that only "in Story" do characters die pining for a categorically perfect world: "Men have died from time to time, and worms have eaten them, but not for love,"[16] not even for love of paradise. Marvell is neither a nymph nor a drop of dew, able to live for a moment in a sparkling fiction and then evanesce smoothly into eternity, however much he is predisposed to dream about doing so. His ties to earth are too strong: among them, the desperate, instinctive will to live, which all men share, and the uncertainties that make wholehearted commitment to any ideal seem to the skeptic rash (may not "vast eternity" be but a "Desart"?). The Nymph's way, creating new difficulties to replace the ones it avoids, will not *work*. When goodness is too weak to stand up for itself, it can inspire at once admiration, sympathy, and contempt in the same observer. Just so does the Nymph lose some of Marvell's respect even as she represents values dear to him. Furthermore, if survival is such a crucial issue for a categorical idealist, he should not seek in the plight of innocence *casus belli contra divos*, for, to paraphrase Dr. Johnson, one who wrestles with the gods struggles with adversaries not subject to casualty. A man anxious about the problem of evil must carefully reserve his judgments, raising questions, perhaps, but stopping short of the wrong answers.

While contemplating the splendor of Elysium, then, Marvell finds it necessary at times to bite his lip, to ask himself where is the good in the vision for all the good in it. He must remind himself that hopes are forever being disappointed, even the grandest ones, and he must tell himself that his only recourse is a discreet public silence and strong patience. This process of accommodation is also at work in "Bermudas."

I have already called attention to this poem's vision of "eternal spring," which is presented in a chorus sung by fervent English Protestants, fugitives from religious persecution, who approach the island in their rowboat. We can assume that they have just left the main ship, now anchored off the rocky, inhospitable coast, and are anxious to set foot for the first time on an island about whose virtues they have been generously—if not always accurately—informed. In anticipation, they describe for themselves a second Eden, where beauty and pleasure are not at odds with devotion, worship taking the form of praise and thanksgiving instead of sacrifice. Although such an ideal has appeared to some too static, too delicious for a true wayfaring and warfaring Christian to harbor, and has prompted a search for ironies that would prove a toughminded poet's dissent from the embarrassing fancies of sybaritic refugees,[17] there is no good reason to doubt that Marvell approves of the content of a song which he calls "holy" as well as "chearful," the notes of which he sounds with his own voice in other poems. It matters little that the "eternal Spring" of Bermuda actually served—according to the report of Capt. John Smith— to stunt the growth of vegetation; little that the island was not indeed a wonderful haven from intolerant churchmen.[18] Surely Marvell could sympathize with the dreams of devout lovers of the finality of Elysium, even if waking might register the shock of disappointment. The poet must show himself aware, however, of the difference between sleep and waking, and he does so in the usual subtle ways. First, through a parenthetical "perhaps" which the singers themselves cannot avoid when they consider in all honesty how little predictable God's ways have turned out to be:

> Oh let our Voice his Praise exalt,
> Till it arrive at Heavens Vault:
> Which thence (perhaps) rebounding, may
> Eccho beyond the *Mexique Bay*.

[33–36]

Then, again, through the hazy suggestiveness of allusion. It has been pointed out that "Bermudas" invites comparison with Waller's "The battle of the Summer Islands" (1645), in which there are descriptions and phrases that Marvell's poem echoes.[19] If, as seems likely, Marvell had Waller's mock-heroic lines in mind in composing his own piece, he may have intended more than verbal parallels. The "Summer Islands" recounts a battle that furnishes a very obvious moral. The islanders, hearing that a pair of whales has been spotted, immediately rush to "Behold with glad eyes a certain prey."[20] They

> Dispose already of the untaken spoil,
> And, as the purchase of their future toil,
> These share the bones, and they divide the oil.
> So was the huntsman by the bear oppressed,
> Whose hide he sold—before he caught the beast!
>
> [2.35–39]

And of course the "certain prey" proves too elusive to catch. Marvell's boatmen row with almost as firm a conviction of success; but, after all, they are still "in the . . . boat" (37) and have no guarantee that paradise lies at the end of the journey. Marvell's Puritan acquaintance John Oxenbridge had not found the Bermudas entirely hospitable,[21] and must have told him that one could not expect to find there conditions no man had seen on earth since Adam. Visions of perfection are worth entertaining even if the ideal is unattainable, as Marvell well knew; but when men begin to move towards an imaginary landscape to capture the wind, when they begin to think and act as though in paradise or near it, they invite the condescending smile of an idealist like Marvell, who is yet pragmatic enough to sense that he has to compromise and take another way. Marvell watches the "falling Oars" in a silence both knowing and regretful, enjoying the "holy and . . . chearful Note," but unable this time to join in.

Capitulation to what is usually called "reality" may seem like a relatively simple resolve, and in concept it is. If Marvell had had no strong loyalties, he could have walked a straight line to surrender. His emotional and intellectual attachment to categorical principles, however, was too intense to make rejection of them an easy decision. Otherwise his attitude toward the Nymph's catastrophe would have been more cavalier; his partiality toward the men bound for Bermuda would have been less pronounced; and, I suggest, the interior debate that preceded his first attempt to deal in a poem with the problem of Cromwell would have been much less anguished.

"An Horatian Ode upon Cromwel's Return from Ireland" is a pressing attempt on Marvell's part to come to terms with a "force" (26) beyond coping with in a metaphysical debate, a furious energy that runs roughshod over his categorical principles and drives him toward a resolution. That this decision is expressed in the tranquil, reflective accents of an Horatian ode does not mean that he makes it, as has been said, "*sine ira et studio.*"[22] A rage for the kind of order one can master may well develop in response to a sense of helplessness before an overpowering confusion. The issues at stake as Marvell contemplates what "angry Heavens flame" has wrought are at bottom the very ones that preoccupy and often confound him in poem after poem, paragraph after paragraph. It would indeed be strange if he were suddenly able to become for a moment indifferent about questions that usually engage his most intense feelings.

The ode begins with a proclamation that the time has come for war:

The forward Youth that would appear
Must now forsake his *Muses* dear,
    Nor in the Shadows sing
    His Numbers languishing.
'Tis time to leave the Books in dust,
And oyl th' unused Armours rust:
    Removing from the Wall
    The Corslet of the Hall.

And Cromwell's response is swift:

So restless *Cromwel* could not cease
In the inglorious Arts of Peace,
    But through adventrous War
    Urged his active Star.
And, like the three-fork'd Lightning, first
Breaking the Clouds where it was nurst,
    Did thorough his own Side
    His fiery way divide.

[1–16]

I do not see how Marvell could have written these words with composure. His admission that war is a practical necessity in a flawed universe is not altogether surprising, for the poems of resolution already considered reveal submissions to practical necessities. But he goes further and declares the arts of peace "inglorious" (10), and war "adventrous" (11); and this must have been most difficult for the categorist in him to do. The rest of the ode gives evidence that these adjectives are not wholly ironical. Feeling that they must carry their literal and obvious meanings, he must, at the same time, realize their distance from his ideals.

If the necessity pressing upon Marvell were only practical, we might be justified in raising the ghost of Machiavelli,[23] in attributing to Cromwell or to his panegyrist the same earthbound, expediential outlook as that pragmatic political scientist had. The poem does not bear out, however, the contention of some critics that it "lacks the providential dimension in any religious sense."[24] The poet does not speak as a dévot, but the expediency to which he yields, Cromwell's "three-fork'd Lightning," comes from Heaven (26); and Heaven's God is here just as real—and just as much a source of anxiety—as he is for Marvell in other contexts. When Marvell acknowledges a quarter of the way through the poem that

> if we would speak true,
> Much to the Man is due,
>
> [27-28]

he as much as states that he has not yet been concerned with Cromwell's personal *virtu*. It is the *divine* lightning which Cromwell represents, creating the kinds of division that God has always wanted, always mystifying men like Marvell, who cannot easily justify its use.

> Burning through the Air he went,
> And Pallaces and Temples rent.[25]
>
> [21-22]

The picture resembles one in Lucan's *Pharsalia*, which Marvell had in mind (both in the original and in Tom May's translation)[26] as he was writing his ode:

> [Caesar] loves that ruine should enforce his way;
> As lightning by the wind forc'd from a cloude
> Breakes through the wounded aire with thunder loud.
> . . . .
> Not *Joves* owne Temple spares it. . . .
>
> [May's *Pharsalia* (3rd ed., 1635),
> 1.144ff.]

It is also likely that Marvell had at least in the back of his mind a passage from the *De rerum natura,* which he knew so well:

> If Jupiter and the other gods shake the shining regions of heaven with appalling din, if they cast fire whither it may be the will of each one, why do they not see to it that those who have not refrained from some abominable crime shall be struck and breathe out sulphurous flames from breast pierced through, a sharp lesson to mankind? Why rather does one with no base guilt on his conscience roll in flames all innocent, suddenly involved in a tornado from heaven and taken off by fire? . . . Why does [Jupiter] shatter holy shrines of the gods, and even his own illustrious habitations, with the fatal thunderbolt . . . ?[27]

Lucretius came to the conclusion that the gods were not responsible for the lightning, because they were above such senseless violence. Marvell knew that his God was not so fastidious. Deity could not work a contradiction and allow "penetration" (42) (the simultaneous occupation of the same place by two physical objects), however deeply Marvell, like Touchstone, cherished vague, irrational hopes of the compossibility of opposites.[28] But the rents in Nature's garment were more than logical necessities. The young Cambridge student's first published words, in a Latin parody of an Horatian ode, refer to the havoc purposely wrought by *Juppiter Fulgurator,* enigmatically called *"pater":*

> Jam satis pestis, satis atque diri
> Fulminis misit pater, & rubenti
> Dexterâ nostras jaculatus arces
> Terruit urbem.[29]

The Lord of Hosts loved "Courage" (17) in men, even though in its sometimes shattering effects, like lightning, it was no distinguisher of persons or causes:

> 'Tis all one to Courage high
> The Emulous or Enemy.
>
> [17-18]

It is perfectly in accord with God's character, then, although not easy for Marvell to accept, that he should use Cromwell to "ruine the great Work of Time" (34); and since the great soldier is something more, even, than a force of nature ("Nature . . . must make room / Where greater Spirits come" [41-44]), " 'Tis Madness to resist or blame" him (25) and what he stands for. If this be Machiavellianism, it is not of the most common sort.

Marvell's acquiescence to Cromwell and to God may seem like the decision of an unflinching realist, and to some extent it is. The studied calm with which he presents his Hobbesian reflections is only one of many signs of his determination not to be dismayed:

> Though Justice against Fate complain,
> And plead the antient Rights in vain:
> . . . Those do hold or break
> As Men are strong or weak.
>
> [37-40]

But the calm is not that of a mind at peace. Having read Lucan, Marvell knew the sentiments of a poet who was obsessed with the thought that the gods were wont to confer "legality upon crime" ("*Ius . . . datum sceleri canimus*"),[30] and who could hardly restrain his outrage over it:

> If no other way to Neroes reigne
> The Fates could find, if Gods their Crownes obtaine
> At such deare rates, and Heav'n could not obey
> Her *Iove,* but after the sterne Gyants fray;
> Now we complaine not, gods, mischiefe and warre
> Pleasing to us, since so rewarded, are;
> Let dire *Pharsalia* grone with armed Hosts,
> And glut with blood the Carthaginian ghosts;
>
> . . . .
>
> Warres rage is threatened; the sword's power all right
> Confounds by force: impietie shall beare
> The name of Virtue, and for many a yeare
> This fury lasts, it boots us not to crave
> A peace: with peace a master we shall have.
>
> [May's *Pharsalia,* 1.33–39, 666–68]

Though Marvell could not, as Lucan did, push his discontent into rebellion, he was aware of the terms of indictment and could not refute
them point by point. He resolves to take Cromwell's and Heaven's side
because it is "Madness" to do otherwise, but on that side there is no
freedom from apprehension or bitterness. There could hardly be when
Fate was at odds with Justice. "That memorable Hour / Which first
assur'd the forced Pow'r" has to be remembered because it was too
traumatic for anyone to forget; it does not have to be loved. Knowing that
Marvell was not shy of lodging metaphysical protests (he wrote the elegy
for Lord Hastings not very long before the "Horatian Ode"), we should
not be quick to attenuate the enigma he defines, thinking that in the ode
"Justice" is simply "the limited vision of human law that must give way
before the divine will."[31] Marvell had too much respect for the claims of
transcendental principles to allow an arbitrary force, even if it were a
divine will, to flout them without inciting resistance.[32] Not disposed to
overestimate the accuracy of man's "limited vision" of these principles,
he nevertheless felt strongly enough about threats to their integrity to
write of his concern.

It has been said that the author of the "Horatian Ode" believes
"more in men than in parties or principles," or, less extremely, that he is
"far more interested in persons than in theories."[33] These views, reflecting an understandable modern bias, arise from a notion that the poet's
attitudes toward Cromwell and Charles I are the poem's central concern.
My sense is rather that Marvell's genuine passion is for principles and
theories, to which a bewildering world and its mysterious ruling forces

seem to do violence, and that he finds the actors in the political drama merely interesting in comparison. He does not speak with the ardor of a political partisan, as though he believed in the absolute equation of Justice and the monarchical order, or in the divine right of the king. We should not expect to see evidence of such clear, convinced allegiance in a man who heretofore had given in his writings only hints of party-fervor,[34] and in his actions (according to all available evidence) no sign at all. But Marvell loved Justice, however provisionally a political institution with its "antient Rights" (38) might embody it. And he could not fail to be troubled by an historical crisis in which "greater Spirits," not *better* Spirits, triumphed (44), "helpless Right" yielding to "forced Pow'r" (66). He could not help asking himself whether the claims of the monarchy— which, he suggests, are grounded in "Nature" (41)—were so weak and objectionable that a people should wage civil war and execute a king to suppress them. Ancient rights "*do* hold or break / As Men are strong or weak." *Should* they?

If the only sanction for Cromwell's actions, the one which that Christian warrior himself appealed to,[35] was the blessing of Heaven made visible in success, Heaven might be questioned—even, up to a point, impugned. Or one might at least object that throughout history God has made use of human "scourges" (like Nebuchadnezzar or Tamburlaine) who are themselves wicked and doomed to eventual destruction, in order to punish the godly who have strayed.[36] Yet Marvell the categorist was so attached to ends that he could be tempted to believe that success, in a world where problems of value were murky and God's ways maddeningly unfathomable, should tame criticism when one's honesty could not allow protests to be silenced. Nature must make room (43). It has already given way—to a Fate that is "happy" (72) insofar as it promises through Cromwell to magnify England and thwart the despotic Catholic powers:

> What may not then our *Isle* presume
> While Victory his Crest does plume!
>   What may not others fear
>   If thus he crown each Year!
> A *Caesar* he ere long to *Gaul*,
> To *Italy* an *Hannibal*,
>   And to all other States not free
>   Shall *Clymacterick* be.

> [97–104]

The prospect of such a consummation may not be a reason for Marvell to choose the destiny he cannot avoid, but it may be a motive.

Marvell's retreat from reason, or at least from rational metaphysics, is not unrelated to his concomitant concern in the ode with "personalities." Much has been made of the poet's "complex" attitude towards the royal victim and the Wars' and Fortune's son. It is supposed to be a mark of Marvell's wisdom that he can show a compassionate appreciation of the king (53-64) while recognizing in Charles's adversary Cromwell an unimpeachable personal virtue (30), the gentle creativity of a gardener (25-32), the fierce, awe-inspiring destructiveness of a bird of prey (91), and a selfless obedience (83ff.)—in short, qualities of *both* Lucan's Caesar and Pompey.[37] No one should doubt Marvell's perceptiveness. But questions about personality are not the ultimate tests of his powers of insight. Complexities of character can be easier to deal with than the terrifying simplicities of philosophy. Marvell does, of course, confront metaphysical, moral issues, offering what many see to be a cautious, balanced (but not very extensive) presentation of opposing rights and claims, and, as I believe, finally abandoning speculation about the right for prudential choice. His interest in personalities, which seems intense in the same measure as his desire for moral enlightenment is hopeless, may be attributed to his need for fact before the uncertainty of value. If he speaks of Charles and Cromwell with the detachment of a scholar or of a theatergoer, he does so because when he asked for the egg of truth he was given the scorpion of history, which he has resolved to live with as best he can.

The ode's ending indicates how strained and regretful that resolution is. The poet exhorts Cromwell to preserve peace, or more precisely, "Pow'r," by threat of the sword:

> But thou the Wars and Fortunes Son
> March indefatigably on;
>   And for the last effect
>   Still keep thy Sword erect:
> Besides the force it has to fright
> The Spirits of the shady Night,
>   The same *Arts* that did *gain*
>   A *Pow'r* must it *maintain*.

[113-20]

This proposal comes from one who was later to observe that a "good Cause" (and he does not in the ode go so far as to call Cromwell's cause "good") "signifys little, unless it be as well defended."[38] The poet's advice here cannot be single-minded. Behind it lurks his memory that the nation's "happy Fate" was augured by a "bleeding" head (69), signifying both preeminence and its price, an omen that applies not only to the events of the recent past but to prospects for the future: Cromwell is readying for the campaign in Scotland and for who knows what other battles. The sword will be kept erect and used by a new "*Caesar*," a second "*Hannibal*" (101–2); but the ancient leaders were memorable for their defeats as well as for triumphs. Most significantly, the poet's final address to Cromwell has behind it an exhortation (overlooked by interpreters of the ode) which Lucan had put into the mouth of Pothinus, a shameless amoralist who urged the assassination of Pompey:

> Justice and truth have many guilty made:
> Faith suffers, Ptolomey, when it would ayde
> Whome fortune hates; joyne with the gods, and fate,
> And fly the wretched, love the fortunate:
> Profit from honesty differs as far
> As does the sea from fire, earth from a star.
> Crownes lose their power, whilst only good they doe.
> Respect of right all strength does overthrow.
> 'Tis mischiefes freedom, and th'uncurbed sword,
> That does to hated crownes safety afford.
> No cruell actions, unless throughly done,
> Are done secure; let him from court be gone,
> That would be good; nothing but feare shall he,
> That is asham'd a tyrant deem'd to be.

[May's *Pharsalia*, 8.484ff.]

It might seem sensible to claim that this text shows Marvell's professed obeisance to Cromwell to be wholly ironical. Surely the poet could not in all sincerity imply that Pothinus' doctrine was his own. As difficult as it is for us to acknowledge, however, Marvell means what he says. Although he does not draw the alternatives between good and evil as starkly as did Lucan's Egyptian courtier, he sponsors with full awareness an expediency that seems to him no less ignominious for being "fated." He does so partly because he yearns for the ends to be achieved through questionable means, and partly because by risking a dishonorable stance, he may protest to Heaven its creation of a dilemma in which a man can submit to destiny only by choosing to his shame.

As has been said about Euripides, another poet who was troubled by the actions of the gods, Marvell is "baffling because himself baffled."[39] It is Marvell's concern for the uncertain status of principles that keeps him at a distance from the persons, parties, and institutions that incarnate cherished values all too imperfectly. We should not be astonished, then, that in "Tom May's Death," a poem that he probably wrote only a few months after the "Horatian Ode,"[40] the poet allows the ghost of Ben Jonson to heap scorn upon the Parliamentary party by referring with contempt to "*Spartacus*" (74) and to "*Brutus* and *Cassius* the Peoples cheats" (18);[41] whatever Marvell's own feelings may be, he makes no official judgments in his own person. Nor should we read any genuine personal enthusiasm or newly hardened political philosophy into his flattery of the Commonwealth official Oliver St. John soon thereafter.[42] Preoccupation with the transcendental, impatience with the proximate and provisional (even in his political writing the otherworldly lyricist speaks his mind), are conducive to flexible stances and, often, to inconsistency.

The position Marvell takes in the "Horatian Ode" follows from a choice he made "in his own cabinet" and kept hidden. Unlike the "forward Youth" of whom he speaks (1ff.), Marvell did not forsake his Muses dear and oil the rusty armor he had never worn. His decision was made at a special moment, willfully, and at too high a cost to conscience to preclude all backsliding (he could not have been unsympathetic to the notions of Ben Jonson's ghost) or to remain without some kind of further justification. After writing the "Horatian Ode," Marvell goes neither to war nor into government, whither untroubled certitude would have directed him, but to Appleton House, where he will learn to make destiny his choice with less bitterness.

Upon Appleton House is a rambling poem—"chatty," Legouis calls it; [43] and although many critics have judged it a "well-articulated whole,"[44] its unclassical proportions (almost two hundred of the 776 lines are devoted to the episode involving the nuns) and its loose principle of progression (an imaginary ambling from point to point in a landscape, with stops to admire elegances and curiosities and to dwell on "significances") suggest that Marvell's main concern was not with the exactions of form. The poem is, in part, the "dramatization of . . . [a] choice,"[45] but the debate does not have clean contours. Marvell needs leisure and space to work his way emotionally through contradictions that he cannot resolve by force of argument. Since from the beginning he knows what his conclusion will be, his tone is not desperate; yet the arch Clevelandism and the casual fantasizing do not hide the clash of principles that makes for inquietude in an *"easie Philosopher"* (561) whose unruffled manner, it will be seen, is not always a straightforward indicator of his feeling.

The ostensible purpose of *Upon Appleton House* (and this relates it to the tradition of "country house poem")[46] is to extol the greatness of Lord Thomas Fairfax and his family, both directly and through a tribute to the moral qualities embodied in their estate. Insinuating itself into the running compliment, however, often dominating it, is Marvell's private musing about the categorical-paradoxical complication. Thus while Lord Fairfax receives in eulogy the meed of his virtue, Marvell is struggling for himself with virtue's definition.

At first it seems that, as the Psalm says, "righteousness and peace have kissed," for the temperate beauties of Nunappleton are offered as the perfect expression of Lord Fairfax's moral character (1–80). Then comes the story of the "Suttle Nunns" (inhabitants of the site before the dissolution in 1542) who had captivated Isabel Thwaites, a sixteenth-century ancestor of the Fairfax family, and the issues are engaged. One of the nuns tries to entice Isabel into the convent by picturing for her what the order considers to be the beauty of holiness and by assuring her that she can contribute eminently to that holy splendor.

'Our *Orient* Breaths perfumed are
'With insense of incessant Pray'r,
'And Holy-water of our Tears
'Most strangly our Complexion clears.

'Not tears of Grief; but such as those
'With which calm Pleasure overflows;
'Or Pity, when we look on you
'That live without this happy Vow.
'How should we grieve that must be seen
'Each one a *Spouse,* and each a *Queen;*
'And can in *Heaven* hence behold
'Our brighter Robes and Crowns of Gold?

'When we have prayed all our Beads,
'Some One the holy *Legend* reads;
'While all the rest with Needles paint
'The Face and Graces of the *Saint.*
'But what the Linnen can't receive
'They in their Lives do interweave.
'This Work the *Saints* best represents;
'That serves for *Altar's Ornaments.*

'But much it to our work would add
'If here your hand, your Face we had:
'By it we would *our Lady* touch;
'Yet thus She you resembles much.
'Some of your Features, as we sow'd,

'Through ev'ry *Shrine* should be bestow'd.
'And in one Beauty we would take
'Enough a thousand *Saints* to make.

. . . .

'I see the *Angels* in a Crown
'On you the Lillies show'ring down:
'And round about you Glory breaks,
'That something more than humane speaks.

'All Beauty, when at such a height,
'Is so already consecrate.

[109-36, 141-46]

This is categorical sanctity, bringing a heaven out of season down to earth. As in Dorinda's Elysium, where every nymph is a queen of May, in the nuns' cloister everyone is a "*Spouse,* and each a *Queen.*" There is no competition here—and no violence. Since "those wild Creatures, called Men" are excluded (101-2), love is only a soft affection, whose loveliness must be compared to objects beautiful without alloy:

'Each Night among us to your side
'Appoint a fresh and Virgin Bride;
. . . .
'. . . You may lye as chast in Bed,
'As Pearls together billeted.
'All Night embracing Arm in Arm,
'Like Chrystal pure with Cotton warm.

[185-86, 189-92]

The "shining Armour white" of the "Virgin Amazons" (105-6) has never been dented or stained because it has never seen use: the "yoke" the nuns desire is "soft" (159),[47] the "Tryal" they undergo "neither Costs, nor Tyes" (196). They have no reason to court sacrifice, for they profess a both/and philosophy which refuses to surrender either of two "incompatible" values to necessity:

'Here Pleasure Piety doth meet;
'One perfecting the other Sweet.
'So through the mortal fruit we boyl
'The Sugars uncorrupting Oyl:
'And that which perish while we pull,
'Is thus preserved clear and full.

[171-76]

Indeed their God shows himself sympathetic to this idea, determining, unlike the bridgegroom in the Gospel, that of the two brides who await him, "Neither should be left behind" (188).[48]

Isabel had listened to the proposals that were made to her, and the "*Nuns* smooth Tongue . . . suckt her in" (200), but Marvell is at pains to show that he is not won. His resolve against the convent's categorical program seems absolute as he associates himself with the declaration of William Fairfax (Isabel's rescuer) that in the cloister "vice infects the very Wall" (216). What Marvell would consider vice is evident in the nuns' hypocrisy (205) (they are wooing the heiress Thwaites with offers of special privileges for the money she may bequeath them);[49] evident in their idolatrous "superstitions" (260); evident in their homosexuality (185-92) (which they present to the naive Isabel as mere sisterly love). But it is not so clear after all that Marvell represents the more basic categorical attitudes—the both/and philosophy, the love of Elysian perfection—as unambiguously vicious in themselves. We cannot doubt that the poet is set on condemning the cloister's "holy leisure" (97) and the principles that support it. Yet, as some critics have recognized,[50] Marvell reveals a fascination with what he denounces, describing the nuns' subtle assault on Isabel with that expert knowledge of a temptation which comes from intimacy with it. One might go further and say that Marvell *had* to portray the nuns as crassly sinful in the more usual ways, for he had to differentiate their way of life from Lord Fairfax's retirement (which was easy enough to do) and (a much more difficult task) to establish that the nuns' categorical ideals were somehow more reprehensible than the ones he has to acknowledge in the rest of the poem as his own. The story of Isabel Thwaites, then, marks the beginning, not the end, of the debate of categorical and paradoxical principles.

As his attention moves from the house out onto the grounds of Nunappleton, Marvell immediately encounters the flower forts which Sir Thomas Fairfax (an ancestor of the current owner) had planted (283ff.),[51] and, ambiguous symbols that they are, they evoke in him a complex response. The flowers left to themselves would no doubt have been appropriate adornments for Elysium, but the warrior hero who laid out the garden "in sport" (285) gave them a paradoxical significance ill-suited to a pastoral paradise. "With five Bastions [he] it did fence, / As aiming one for ev'ry Sense" (287-88). Thus one is faced with the anomalies of "Silken Ensigns" (294), "fragrant Volleys" (298), a condition "still middle betwixt War and Peace."[52]

In meditating on the scene, Marvell does little to resolve the ambiguous meanings, taking up themes as momentous as those in Genesis, and just as bewildering:

O Thou, that dear and happy Isle
The Garden of the World ere while,
Thou *Paradise* of four Seas,
Which *Heaven* planted us to please,
But, to exclude the World, did guard
With watry if not flaming Sword;
What luckless Apple did we tast,
To make us Mortal, and The Wast?

Unhappy! Shall we never more
That sweet *Militia* restore,
When Gardens only had their Towrs,
And all the Garrisons were Flowrs,
When Roses only Arms might bear,
And Men did rosie Garlands wear?
Tulips, in several Colours barr'd,
Were then the *Switzers* of our *Guard.*

The *Gardiner* had the *Souldiers* place,
And his more gentle Forts did trace.
The Nursery of all things green
Was then the only *Magazeen.*
The *Winter Quarters* were the Stoves,
Where he the tender Plants removes.
But War all this doth overgrow:
We Ord'nance Plant and Powder sow.

And yet their walks one on the Sod
Who, had it pleased him and *God,*
Might once have made our Gardens spring
Fresh as his own and flourishing.

[321–48]

Some have seen in these lines a tactful criticism of Lord Fairfax's
retirement and a "summons to involvement,"⁵³ but I do not see Marvell
here admonishing and exhorting out of a sense of superiority. By what
right or privilege could he criticize, who had himself withheld commitment and avoided danger while the Lord General suffered wounds on the
battlefront?⁵⁴ And what specific cause might the as yet uninvolved poet
urge the retired soldier actively to promote? Up to this point in his life,
Marvell had not, as far as we know, positively espoused any political
platform; nor does he reveal in this poem, even when he speaks of a proud
prelate (366) or refers obliquely to the late civil wars (420–22), anything

more than a vague, albeit impassioned, regret that England falls short of Elysian perfection. He does not, either, possess the security of certitude about the religious issues that his rhetorical questions invoke: "What luckless Apple . . . ?" "Shall we never more . . . ?" It is a mysterious God, not likely to mitigate this puzzlement, who has endorsed a choice proceeding from "Conscience, that Heaven-nursed Plant" (355). Since Marvell could not doubt that Lord Fairfax's moral scruples about the execution of the king and about the war with Scotland were sincere motives for retirement, since Marvell considered obedience to informed conscience obedience to God,[55] he could not find fault with the Lord General without also reproaching Providence. Although Marvell was not unwilling to question the ways of God and, as I think likely, is in this passage disturbed by a divine decision which he cannot understand ("had it pleased him and *God* . . ."), he is not so sure of his ground that he can dispense advice.

A lover of Elysium himself, Marvell desires a world in which the "*Gardiner* [has] the *Souldiers* place." But it is conscience that urges the spiritual warrior Fairfax to disdain a quest for the categorical end—the achieved, permanent condition—in favor of the paradoxical act which will keep Paradise, or something resembling it, in abeyance; and the poet must stand up for conscience:

> *Conscience,* that Heaven-nursed Plant,
> Which most our Earthly Gardens want.
> A prickling leaf it bears, and such
> As that which shrinks at ev'ry touch;
> But Flowrs eternal, and divine,
> That in the Crowns of Saints do shine.

> [355-60]

Is Marvell here, then, making a simple choice of the paradoxist's ethic, in a mood completely different from the one he displayed in "The Picture of little T. C."? In that poem he wished to "disarm" the roses of their thorns; now he finds value in a "prickling leaf." This is a leaf, however, that he wants to touch and not to touch, for at every touch it "shrinks." His feelings are wistful about flowers that are beautiful and fragrant, yet martial, and yet again harmless. It is as though he were groping toward a compromise "middle condition," or a synthesis, which (whatever the dialecticians say) he knows is not possible, for he will entertain similar thoughts again and, finally, dismiss them. Thus Marvell shows himself genuinely confused as he considers the irony of Lord Fairfax's situation: a man who has the power to hasten the coming of Elysium (though necessarily by violent means) refuses to do so on moral grounds; and the decision has the effect of creating for its maker a private categorical paradise which of itself is beyond criticism by the paradoxist who sees his "morality" flouted. The moral sacrifice becomes the sacrifice of a noble end. As the artillery of flowers points at "proud *Cawood Castle*" (363), threatening the wicked "Ambition of its Prelate great" (366), while in fact the guns are impotent, Marvell listens to the silence, and his only reaction is silence in return. Clearly he has not yet made a decision of his own.

From the gardens Marvell passes to a scene of at least as much uncertainty, an "Abyss" of "unfathomable Grass" (369-70), where "none does know / Whether he fall through it or go" (379-80). The ruling spirits of the "Meadows" are not the gentle shepherds of pastoral but "tawny Mowers" with their scythes, who, like fiercely paradoxical "Israelites," "divide" the "Grassy Deeps" (389-91), and provide an occasion for the debate to continue.

> With whistling Sithe, and Elbow strong,
> These Massacre the Grass along,
> While one, unknowing, carves the *Rail,*
> Whose yet unfeather'd Quils her fail.
> The Edge all bloody from its Breast
> He draws, and does his stroke detest;
> Fearing the Flesh untimely mow'd
> To him a Fate as black forebode.

> But bloody *Thestylis,* that waites
> To bring the mowing Camp their Cates,
> Greedy as Kites has trust it up,
> And forthwith means on it to sup:
> When on another quick She lights,
> And cryes, he call'd us *Israelites;*
> But now, to make his saying true,
> Rails rain for Quails, for Manna Dew.

> Unhappy Birds! what does it boot
> To build below the Grasses Root;
> When Lowness is unsafe as Hight,
> And Chance o'retakes what scapeth spight?
> And now your Orphan Parents Call
> Sounds your untimely Funeral.
> Death-Trumpets creak in such a Note,
> And 'tis the *Sourdine* in their Throat.

Or sooner hatch or higher build:
The Mower now commands the Field. . . .

[393-418]

"Bloody *Thestylis*" acts, in effect, as a paradoxical God's spokeswoman, discovering a rationale for the blade's massacre of helpless innocence, claiming that for the new "*Israelites*" the bloody stroke is providential. The laws of the Lord of Hosts positively require that the Mower command the field. Marvell, however, does not fully participate in the "Triumphs of the Hay" (426), though he can look on in some amusement at the dance of the mowers in their "wholsome Heat" and the "Females fragrant as the Mead" (427-29). There is something "Greedy" (403) about Thestylis, something almost rabid in her eagerness to bring good out of evil, and it is obvious that the poet does not approve of her or her philosophy. His voice is (for this poem) uncommonly bitter as he asks, "What does it boot / To build . . . ?" (409-10).[56]

Marvell does not linger on these thoughts. Letting the haystacks recede, those "Hills for Soldiers Obsequies" (440), he welcomes a purified scene,

A new and empty Face of things;
A levell'd space, as smooth and plain,
As Clothes for *Lilly* strecht to stain.
The World when first created sure
Was such a Table rase and pure.

[442-46]

A bloody spectacle yields to a picture whose sanative properties the spectator would love to take advantage of, if he could just persuade his imagination to dwell upon the unparadoxical beauty swelling up into his attention at this happy moment. But the scene cannot go unchallenged. One who in these latter days envisions "a Table rase and pure" cannot easily put aside thoughts of the sanguinary business enacted on the level spaces of this world, in "the *Toril,* Ere the Bulls enter at Madril" (447-48). It may be wise, then, to look upon things from a height that creates a non-tragic perspective. The large fields become "A Landskip drawn in Looking-Glass" (458); the cattle seem like "Fleas" (461); and the flood which covers the meadow, unlike its biblical analogue, serves only to conclude the "pleasant Acts" of an entertainment (465), yielding paradoxes that are amusing and harmless (473-80).

Still in search of security, the poet leaves the high points of vantage for shelter within, attempting to "Take Sanctuary in the Wood," a "green yet growing Ark"—"while it lasts" (481ff.). The wood is not, in fact, a sanctuary perfectly secure against the troubling thoughts that have followed Marvell around on his tour. He encounters at first a scene that makes him think fondly of a categorical paradise where music springs from sheer joy. His nightingale, no Procne or Philomela with a history steeped in violence, does not need a thorn in its flesh to make singing sweet:

> The *Nightingale* does here make choice
> To sing the Tryals of her Voice.
> Low Shrubs she sits in, and adorns
> With Musick high the squatted Thorns.
> But highest Oakes stoop down to hear,
> And listning Elders prick the Ear.
> The Thorn, lest it should hurt her, draws
> Within the Skin its shrunken claws.
>
> [513–20]

The image is attractive, but the poet cannot stop here and allow himself to be fascinated. In spite of himself, he is moved to seek a "Sadder, yet more pleasing Sound," that of the stock-doves, artists of Paradox who turn some unknown and unfathomable tragedy to music (521-28). At this crucial point, he may have to admit after all that the sound is more pleasing *because* sadder. Marvell seems in a mood to give in. As the doves moan unto the elms, providing fit accompaniment for the scenes that follow, he looks with apparent calm, even nonchalance, at living emblems of paradoxical violence. Sacrificial violence:

> The *Heron* from the Ashes top,
> The eldest of its young lets drop,
> As if it Stork-like did pretend
> That *Tribute* to *its Lord* to send.
>
> [533–36]

And the violence of crime and punishment, which is a work of Providence:

> But most the *Hewel's* wonders are,
> Who here has the *Holt-felsters* care.
> He walks still upright from the Root,
> Meas'ring the Timber with his Foot;
> And all the way, to keep it clean,
> Doth from the Bark the Wood-moths glean.

He, with his Beak, examines well
Which fit to stand and which to fell.

The good he numbers up, and hacks;
As if he mark'd them with the Ax.
But where he, tinkling with his Beak,
Does find the hollow Oak to speak,
That for his building he designs,
And through the tainted Side he mines.
Who could have thought the *tallest Oak*
Should fall by such a *feeble Strok'*!

Nor would it, had the Tree not fed
A *Traitor-worm*, within it bred.
(As first our *Flesh* corrupt within
Tempts impotent and bashful *Sin*.)
And yet that *Worm* triumphs not long,
But serves to feed the *Hewels young*.
While the Oake seems to fall content,
Viewing the Treason's Punishment.

[537–60]

It is astonishing how coolly Marvell describers these scenes—the last, especially, which is reminiscent of the Body's protest against the injustice of being made "fit" for sin and punishment.[57] Here there is little sign of resentment, the poet now professing to admire the neatness of a Providence that will have nothing in the physical or moral ecology go to waste. This happy insouciance will have to be accounted for. For the moment, however, the poet must be followed, for he now moves silently from Nature resistant and violent back to Nature yielding, embracing, pacific: categorically aesthetic (561ff.).

He knows this Nature's "Language" (569–71). It teaches him in its green "Temple" (510) from its mystic book all he needs to know—even what "*Palestine* ere said" (581). But if Palestine's doctrine was harsh, holding sacred the altar and the gibbet, the "*easie Philosopher*" will not advert to it now, for he imagines himself on the edge of Elysium:

And see how Chance's better Wit
Could with a Mask my studies hit!
The Oak-Leaves me embroyder all,
Between which Caterpillars crawl:
And Ivy, with familiar trails,
Me licks, and clasps, and curles, and hales.

Under this *antick Cope* I move
Like some great *Prelate of the Grove,*

Then, languishing with ease, I toss
On Pallets swoln of Velvet Moss;
While the Wind, cooling through the Boughs,
Flatters with Air my panting Brows.
Thanks for my Rest ye *Mossy Banks,*
And unto you *cool Zephyr's* Thanks,
Who, as my Hair, my Thoughts too shed,
And winnow from the Chaff my Head.

How safe, methinks, and strong, behind
These Trees have I incamp'd my Mind;
Where Beauty,[58] aiming at the Heart,
Bends in some Tree its useless Dart;
And where the World no certain Shot
Can make, or me it toucheth not.
But I on it securely play,
And gaul its Horsemen all the Day.

[585–608]

"How safe, *methinks* . . . ." Then arises a sudden, nearly indefinable qualm: Marvell feels this world too loose; he wants to feel "strong" (601), and therefore needs to experience *some* resistance, some "tough" branches (647) to support him without galling, some "Silken Bondage":

Bind me ye *Woodbines* in your 'twines,
Curle me about ye gadding *Vines,*
And Oh so close your Circles lace,
That I may never leave this Place:
But, lest your Fetters prove too weak,
Ere I your Silken Bondage break,
Do you, O *Brambles,* chain me too,
And courteous *Briars* nail me through.

[609–16]

Here is Marvell's most desperate attempt at the synthesis I spoke of earlier.[59] He wishes to be nailed with "courteous" briars, crucified yet not crucified, staked forever (612), but to Elysium!

The effort is hopeless. Although Marvell can conceive of an Eden with "no *Serpent*" (629), the prospect remains a dead hypothesis. The poet must put away his idle thoughts and "idle Utensils" (650) at the appearance of young Maria Fairfax, for " 'Twere shame that such judicious Eyes / Should with such Toyes a Man surprise . . ." (653-54). Having been lulled into contentment by his categorist's fancy, he blushes when he thinks of Maria, who forces "loose Nature" to "recollect" itself (657-58), who, herself raised under the "*Discipline* severe / Of *Fairfax*" (723-24), in turn "streightness on the Woods bestows" (691). The girl, it is true, gives the Nunappleton world "Beauty" and "sweetness" (690, 692), but these qualities are compounded of sterner stuff than their categorical equivalents. Maria reigns as princess of a paradoxical miscrocosm, in which sacrifice is held noble and creative:

> Hence *She* with Graces more divine
> Supplies beyond her *Sex* the *Line*;
> And, like a *sprig of Mistelto,*
> On the *Fairfacian Oak* does grow;
> Whence, for some universal good,
> The *Priest* shall cut the sacred Bud;
> While her *glad Parents* most rejoice,
> And make their *Destiny* their *Choice.*

[737-44]

As the Fairfaxes "rejoice" in making their stoic resolve *(ducunt volentem fata, nolentem trahunt),* [60] Marvell duly praises them. Indeed, his own resolution, an acceptance of Nature "cut" (742) down the middle, must pattern itself on theirs. The "sacred Bud," he must admit, exists to be severed (742). Appleton House itself with its "doors so strait" has reminded him of the divine law prescribing that men must "strain themselves through *Heavens Gate*" (31-32), "hacking and hewing" their spirits so that their glorified bodies might fit. [61] Yet there is a hint of recalcitrance in the poet's voice as he allows sacrifice to be offered "for some universal good" (741): "for *some* universal good or other, whatever it is," he is tempted to say, perhaps mindful of the stock-doves, whose mourning "for some Cause unknown" also defies explanation (525). He resists the temptation, pays a final tribute to the girl whose paradoxical "Order" (766) constitiutes what must be "*Paradice's only Map*" (768), and is ready to stop dreaming: "Let's in."

If the Nymph shows Marvell that her approach to Elysium will not work, the woods of Nunappleton prove to him that the categorist's program cannot, for reasons not wholly known to him, fully satisfy his conscience. What is he to make of the psychological need—undeniably accompanying his moral assessments and decisions—for the barrier, the thorn, or the knife? What is he to do in the face of the impassable Fact, indifferent to any objector's outrage, that in this world to be quarantined from all evil is to become impotent for much good? Marvell cannot deal with these problems by resorting, as has been suggested,[62] to faith in a kind of "rotation-method," according to which belief, life, as represented on Achilles' shield, is properly a series of successive moments each with its own appropriateness or "decorum"—now war, now peace; now sacrifice, now enjoyment; now activity, now retirement.[63] Such a scheme may prove a good practical expedient, but it offers no true solace for a metaphysical ache that originates in the need to know the *why* of things and their justness. Not even a paradoxist would consider rotation a synthesis of opposites.[64] And if other evidence about Marvell's cast of mind is to be believed, he was not one to rejoice unhesitatingly in a decorum based on a paradoxical coincidence of light and darkness, gain and loss. In other words, he could not avoid renunciation simply by making a proper strategic choice, by keeping opposites in balance, or by paradoxically resolving contradictions. In all likelihood, he believed that a "double Heart" was too often a symptom of a "vain Head" ("A Dialogue between the Soul and Body," 10). He had, then, to choose at some point between pastoral and martial values; and he could not let himself accept too easily the notion that the gardens of repose are holy, even when they are only baiting-places, or that their habitués are saints. Sometimes when he desires to visit and abide in them he feels embarrassed, like the "easie Philosopher" caught with his toys by Maria Fairfax, and he might then parody himself, as he does in "The Garden."[65]

The speaker in "The Garden" is recognizable as the same man who walked as the "great *Prelate of the Grove*" on the Nunappleton estate:

> Ripe Apples drop about my head;
> The Luscious Clusters of the Vine
> Upon my Mouth do crush their Wine;
> The Nectaren, and curious Peach,
> Into my hands themselves do reach;
> Stumbling on Melons, as I pass,
> Insnar'd with Flow'rs, I fall on Grass.
>
> ["The Garden," 34–40]

Like the categorist who speaks in other poems, he eschews red-hot "Passions heat" (25) for the cool, "green Shade" (48) of gentler pleasures; he has hopes of a "flight" (55) toward a world of absolute purity; and he does not see that the journey need be rugged or costly. The important difference is that in the "The Garden," the speaker is portrayed as shortsighted and a little silly.

The lover of the garden's "delicious Solitude" belittles the efforts of striving, energetic souls because their "incessant Labours" win for them but little shade from narrow garlands, crowns but from "some single Herb or Tree" (1–8). One would like to think that such notions, which are either preposterous—ignorantly arrogant—or deliberately comic, serve merely to display the speaker's facetious wit. There is little doubt that he wishes to sound like a man who can speak with condescending humor about the foolish of the world, laborers and lovers. The same tone of lighthearted superiority informs the Latin companion-piece to this poem. But a delicate dramatic irony is also at work, inviting us to ask what lies behind the recluse's cleverness and drollery, behind, even, such solemn protestations as:

> Fair quiet, have I found thee here
> And Innocence thy Sister dear!
> Mistaken long, I sought you then
> In busie Companies of Men.
>
> [9–12]

This apostrophe sounds and is more pompous than wise. Why should the seeker of fair quiet search for it in, of all places, busy companies of men? And why must he absurdly play the dendrophile?

> No white nor red was ever seen
> So am'rous as this lovely green.
> Fond Lovers, cruel as their Flame,
> Cut in these Trees their Mistress name.
> Little, Alas, they know, or heed,
> How far these Beauties Hers exceed!
> Fair Trees! where s'eer your barkes I wound,
> No Name shall but your own be found.
>
> [17–24]

If this strange metamorphosis of sexual passion and the recluse's later expressions of misogyny (57–64) are only jests, if he knows that Apollo did not chase Daphne "Only that She might Laurel grow" (30), then we may ask what is the point of the humor in a poem whose speaker is bound for what he considers genuine Neoplatonic ecstasies. If we allow the speaker to be aware of his exaggerations, which he trusts will be understood as such by the cognoscenti who can appreciate the value of his retirement, we should also demand to know from him the norm against which hyperbole can be measured. We learn from him, indeed, that his true love is not a larch or a geranium; it is himself. He faces a difficult task (an impossible one, I would say) in trying to persuade us that such a love, as he conceives of it, is noble, and that in his advocacy of it the humor is not ultimately at his own expense.

"What wond'rous Life in this I lead!" he exclaims in all ingenuousness, expressing a delight in the pleasures of sense that in most cases would be unexceptionable. In the present instance, however, we might almost see the happy man hugging himself in a congratulatory rapture as he utters these words, unaware of the comic figure he cuts when he stumbles and falls, with dripping mouth and garments ready to be stained, onto a ground rife with fruit. There is no Maria Fairfax here to make his face burn with embarrassment.

As he moves on to more intellectual pleasures, which he acknowledges to be higher, he takes himself, his utterances, and his visions quite seriously:

> Mean while the Mind, from pleasure less,
> Withdraws into its happiness:
> The Mind, that Ocean where each kind
> Does streight its own resemblance find;
> Yet it creates, transcending these,
> Far other Worlds, and other Seas;
> Annihilating all that's made
> To a green Thought in a green Shade.
>
> Here at the Fountains sliding foot,
> Or at some Fruit-trees mossy root,
> Casting the Bodies Vest aside,
> My Soul into the boughs does glide:
> There like a Bird it sits and sings,
> Then whets, and combs its silver Wings;
> And, till prepar'd for longer flight,
> Waves in its Plumes the various Light.

[41–56]

Since, however, mystics themselves have seen the necessity for some kind of discernment of spirits—"Believe not every spirit, but try the spirits whether they are of God: because many false prophets have gone out into the world" (1 John 4:1)—the experiences of the garden's visionary ought to be put to the test. His character as revealed in the rest of the poem should at least render his perspicacity suspect, so that when he rhapsodizes about the annihilation of "all that's made / To a green Thought in a green Shade," we might wonder whether he were not trying to discover profundity in a pleasant green blur, the garden-equivalent of white-on-white.[66] In any case, the fundamental criterion in the discernment of spirits is the rule that "by their fruits ye shall know them"; and the spirit which moves the garden's mystic turns him toward a rather vain preoccupation with self. Whereas the mystically inclined Drop of Dew spent its time gazing up to heaven, was "*there* in Love" (32), the bird-like soul in "The Garden" is fascinated with the "Light" only as it enhances the beauty of its own plumage: it "whets, and combs its silver Wings" and "Waves in its Plumes the various Light," oblivious to anything else, even to the light's source. Unlike other Neoplatonic contemplators whose ascent heavenward is temporarily stalled at an intermediate level,[67] this soul seems quite content with its present condition. He "certainly wants to go to a still better place some day," Legouis has remarked, "but no less certainly he does not want to go yet"—the cause of this complacent dalliance being not so much (as Legouis claimed) "Nature" as what Nature provides or leads to: self-delight.[68] It is not surprising that this soul should desire to "live in Paradise alone" (64), for, as e.e. cummings has said in a different way, loneliness can be I-ness.

But Marvell will not allow his recluse to escape entirely into himself. The poet forces upon the attention of the speaker (who, after his ecstasy, or his report of it, continues his stroll) signs of the world outside the garden of the mind:

> How well the skilful Gardner drew
> Of flow'rs and herbes this Dial new;
> Where from above the milder Sun
> Does through a fragrant Zodiack run;
> And, as it works, th' industrious Bee
> Computes its time as well as we.
> How could such sweet and wholsome Hours
> Be reckon'd but with herbs and flow'rs!

[65–72]

The solitary ignores the significance of what he sees; the poet does not. Marvell places the floral sundial in the garden to remind himself that gardens changed when Paradise was lost (although the happy mystic believes that he has recaptured Eden [57]): Time will wither the "herbs and flow'rs" of the "fragrant Zodiack," as well as the garden's fruits, with the change of seasons. The "industrious Bee" and the "skillful Gardner" remind Marvell that the garden has been created and kept by the "uncessant Labours" which the leisured recluse has mocked: none of the fruits mentioned in the poem will grow in the gardens of England without cultivation.[69] These facts "prudently upbraid" the recluse's solipsistic "repose."

This reproof must have been directed at the categorist in the poet himself, whose reveries elsewhere are similar to those described in "The Garden" but never so liable to objection. Even in *"Hortus,"* the Latin version, the speaker is less laughable because less pretentious. Speaking in the same arch tone throughout, he neither stumbles in naive wonder nor casts his "body's vest aside" in pursuit of an ecstatic vision. If it is true, as some critics believe, that Marvell wrote the Latin poem first,[70] we might venture the guess that he did not initially intend that his garden-lover be ironically diminished. As the poet wrote in English, however (at a later time perhaps?), and saw possibilities of, positive cause for, parody, he decided to demonstrate by indirection how rich in folly pastoral wisdom and its exponents might be—his wisdom, he himself.

Yet, *abusus non tollit usum.* Marvell was perfectly capable of making a better case for a categorical philosophy, but in "The Garden" he has resolved not to, and the poem itself suggests why. In the Nymph's complaint for the death of her fawn Marvell sees that her categorical ideal is not viable; yet this fact is not absolutely crucial to the silencing of his debate, for he can himself, as he does elsewhere, complain against gods and men for not making the ideal attainable. In *Upon Appleton House* the same ideal evokes in him qualms of conscience and fears of formlessness. These facts are not absolutely crucial either, for the man who wrote "Bermudas" and "On a Drop of Dew," who could conceive of a cause "too good" to be fought for, is surely able to argue questions of conscience on the categorist's side and summon up faith that Elysium is not a formless abyss. The debate, however, has no syllogistic conclusion in sight. To complain and to argue would not only keep Marvell at war with his conscience, the tradition that helped to form it, and his more "virile" energies; it would also enclose him, like the solitary in "The Garden," forever within his own mind. There is an "outside" which requires that debate be cut off and action taken, and which is likely to prove fatal to a categorical idealism. On the outside are politicians, ecclesiastics, wanton troopers, and economic men; Nature split by a great iron nail; and a God with whom one must square accounts. "The Garden" is the poem of a man who knows he has to face them.

Both *Appleton House* and "The Garden" (if it was written at about the same time) suggest that Marvell will approach this brutal world more assured in his compromises than he was before his stay at Nunappleton. After two years with Lord Fairfax, he will in 1653 approach the regicide Bradshaw (through Milton) seeking position in the government; later in the same year, his hope for public employment frustrated, he will emerge as tutor to Cromwell's ward.[71] The author of the encomiastic *First Anniversary of the Government under O. C.*, which appeared in 1655, is not the same angry and divided poet who wrote the "Horatian Ode."[72]

In *The First Anniversary* Marvell is eager for a compromise between categorical and paradoxical values. While indulging his millennial hopes, which look to a world beyond the need for paradox (131–40),[73] he yet applauds the union that Cromwell has created out of opposites (87–98); he speaks with admiration of Cromwell's likeness to fire and storm (233–38, 261–62), of his "pulling down" in order to erect anew (239–47), of his "Troubling the Waters" to make them heal (401–2)—images now approved of by the same poet who seven years earlier had lamented the degeneracy of a society in which "He highest builds, who with most Art destroys."[74] I have already suggested that *The First Anniversary* represents an attempt by Marvell to rescue his categorical principles from hopeless irrelevancy to the world as it is.[75] It may also indicate an increasing admiration for Cromwell the man,[76] as well as an optimistic anticipation that the millennium is really within reach, when the therapeutic sword can be put away. Thus in the *Poem upon the Death of O. C.* (1658), Marvell can reflect with some enthusiasm that the Protector has "put Armes into *Religions* hand" (179). Cromwell has proved to him that he was ultimately "all for Peace" (15). The soldier's vigor was "temper'd with an aire so mild" (235), even with "tendernesse" (204). That this situation is the best one can hope for under an "angry Heaven" that sways unto war (16) Marvell can now accept with more equanimity than before; he can even allow his patriotism (or chauvinism) to profit from the fact. Although his thinking will be somewhat qualified after the Restoration, especially on the question of "*Religions*" arms,[77] it has taken a major turn.

The peace with Cromwell seems to leave angry Heaven lowering in the distance; but in fact Marvell, in whom the categorist was never so repressed as to make him a Promethean, had to come to terms with a paradoxical God just as surely as with God's paradoxical universe. The letter to Sir John Trott, *The Rehearsal Transpros'd*, the poem on *Paradise Lost*, and the *Defence of John Howe,* from which I have already quoted, all indicate that Marvell had by his later years submitted in faith—nervously, but steadfastly—to the God in the whirlwind. There are several poems[78] in which this submission (or an episode along the way to final surrender) is dramatized, and the poet's state of mind at the end of each contest says much about the power of resolution to alter his values and "solve" his deepest religious problems.

"Clorinda and Damon" is a pastoral dialogue in which a shepherd,

newly converted to the cause of Virtue (10) by the Christ-figure "great
Pan" (20),[79] resists the overtures of a shepherdess and persuades her to sing
Pan's praises with him. The temptations Clorinda offers embody the same
values Marvell speaks for in the poems which approve of the "smoothest
way": the lovely flowers without prickling edge (smooth enough to adorn
a shepherd's temples) (6), the cave "cool" and "Safe" (11–12), and a love
without opposition and violence. Damon's refusal of the flowers as
insubstantial (7), his choice of the scorching "Eye" of heaven over the
cave's coolness (12) and of a love founded on renunciation (10), might be
taken to represent Marvell's own acceptance of the paradoxical ethic. But
did Marvell really meet great Pan? The poem hardly vibrates with a
mystical fervor; the meeting referred to was probably an unecstatic
encounter with a God to be seen through a glass darkly in the conscience.
What is remarkable about the experience is that it gives Damon the
power to resist temptation so easily—one is tempted to say, too easily.
Were the shepherd a purely allegorical figure, this would not matter
much. Since Damon is, however, a part of Marvell himself, the rejected
temptations Marvell's own, there is some reason to ask why the conquest
proceeds without a struggle. A partial answer lies, perhaps, in the
Spenserian Chorus which concludes the poem:

> Of Pan the flowry Pastures sing,
> Caves eccho, and the Fountains ring.
> Sing then while he doth us inspire;
> For all the World is our Pan's Quire.

The flowers, caves, and fountains which Damon had rejected glorify the
Lord; and, one feels, they do so in and of themselves, not simply because
they are occasions of virtue, goods one must renounce in order to achieve
a triumph dear to God's heart. Marvell is trying to save as much
categorical value as he can. For those who love God, the poet intimates,
the struggle is not bloody; nor is it costly, for after his test, the virtuous
man still has his treasures—just as Job, when found faithful, received
"twice as much as he had before" (Job 42:10), or, more to the point, as
Abraham "sacrificed" Isaac without ever losing him. The extent to which
these paradoxes resolve Marvell's dilemma is not clear. In the first place,
the concept of "resolution" is a slippery one, the term referring to any
number of processes which lead one to say, "I am content"; and, in the
second, the paradoxes themselves require a large act of faith that can leave
one troubled even after it is made. What is clear is that Marvell has not in
this instance fully complied with the demands of the paradoxical ethic—
not if he proposes that renunciation is ultimately only an illusion.

A similar evasiveness informs "A Dialogue Between The Resolved Soul, and Created Pleasure," in which the poet encourages his Soul to bear its "Shield," press down its "Helmet," and balance its "Sword" (1–10) for a "Combat" that does not define heroism in the usual paradoxical way. Instead of meeting the temptations of Created Pleasure head on, the Soul triumphs by appealing to categorical consolations greater than the ones offered: rejecting "Nature's banquet" for a finer one "above" (14–17); "downy Pillows" for a "gentler Rest" (23); earthly "Perfumes" for "Heaven's and its own" (25, 30); earthly beauty for heavenly (31ff.); earthly wealth, knowledge, and power for higher and more substantial kinds (51ff.). The spirit is hardly sacrificial; the victory comes easily and its end is *"rest"* (77)—which is the aim, after all, of Dorinda, whose desire for the "smoothest way" to Elysium is not wholly absent in this Resolved Soul.

Does Marvell's God approve of such a way? In one poem, at least, "The Coronet," he does not, so that the poet is forced to make the kind of clean and unequivocal choice which is dear to the paradoxist, but not, as the poem reveals, to Marvell himself.

> When for the Thorns with which I long, too long,
>   With many a piercing wound,
>   My Saviours head have crown'd,
> I seek with Garlands to redress that Wrong:
>   Through every Garden, every Mead,
> I gather flow'rs (my fruits are only flow'rs)
>   Dismantling all the fragrant Towers
> That once adorn'd my Shepherdesses head.
> And now when I have summ'd up all my store,
>   Thinking (so I my self deceive)
>   So rich a Chaplet thence to weave
> As never yet the king of Glory wore:
>   Alas I find the Serpent old
>   That, twining in his speckled breast,
>   About the flow'rs disguis'd does fold,
>   With wreaths of Fame and Interest.
> Ah, foolish Man, that would'st debase with them,
> And mortal Glory, Heavens Diadem!
> But thou who only could'st the Serpent tame,
> Either his slipp'ry knots at once untie,
> And disintangle all his winding Snare:
> Or shatter too with him my curious frame:

And let these wither, so that he may die,
Though set with Skill and chosen out with Care.
That they, while Thou on both their Spoils dost tread,
May crown thy Feet, that could not crown thy Head.

Here is the law of the Cross in all its starkness. The flowers of pastoral, a categorist's flowers, gathered and woven into a rich chaplet of exquisite beauty, "debase" Heaven's diadem, the crown of thorns. The aesthetic that excludes paradox is too bound up with an ethic of self-interest, which, as Nature is divided, is opposed to God's interest; and there is little hope for compromise. God could "tame" and "disentangle," thereby forestalling the destruction of categorical values, but Marvell knows from experience that God will "shatter" the beautiful to annihilate the wicked, creating a new, terrible "beauty" that one is compelled to admire despite all reservations. The poet submits: the exhortation to "shatter" is his own—although he cannot help reminding God immediately afterwards, with a note of pleading in his voice, that the flowers were "set with Skill and chosen out with Care." As if in confirmation of this resolution, Marvell in writing the poem creates out of his own pain, or the "deformity" of his spirit, the sweet sadness of an art that can include the very chaos it abhors. The poem bespeaks a strong resolve—I think, from Marvell's heart, but not from his heart of hearts. Beside his dutiful concession, the prayer of Donne seems positively enthusiastic:

Doe not, with a vile crowne of fraile bayes,
Reward my muses white sincerity,
But what thy thorny crowne gain'd, that give mee,
A crowne of Glory, which doth flower alwayes.

[*La Corona*, 1.5-8]

And Donne's meditation on the beauty of the crucified Savior relies on paradoxes that Marvell could never in acknowledging make vivid for himself:

Marke in my heart, O Soule, where thou dost dwell,
The picture of Christ crucified, and tell
Whether that countenance can thee affright,
Teares in his eyes quench the amasing light,
Blood fills his frownes, which from his pierc'd head fell,
And can that tongue adjudge thee unto hell,
Which pray'd forgivenesse for his foes fierce spight?
No, no; but as in my idolatrie
I said to all my profane mistresses,

Beauty, of pitty, foulnesse onely is
A signe of rigour: so I say to thee,
To wicked spirits are horrid shapes assign'd,
This beauteous forme assures a pitious minde.

["Holy Sonnet XIII," 2-14]

So there are two versions of the peace which Marvell concluded with God, each plausibly authentic: one an accommodation, the other a hardly eager but unconditional surrender.[80] Since the poems in which they appear cannot be set in a chronological sequence, there is no way of telling which version, if either, was final. In any case, Marvell probably made each decision with the reservations that a skeptic is likely to have when he takes a necessary risk in a faith at least partially blind (he never did in his theodicy go so far as to use paradox to justify the ways of Providence). A final speculation about how he took this risk may help to explain one more quality of his resolution.

I have referred to the view held by some critics[81] that Marvell plays "games" with ideas as well as with words and thus proves himself detached—one might say, detached in the manner of Santayana's skeptic, who "is not . . . tethered in [his] home paddock, but ranges at will over the wilderness of being,"[82] in love with uninvolvement. While I have objected and found Marvell engagé, I do not wish to deny that his writings show him playing for stakes. Of some games he was not fond: those of "love" and "heroism," for instance, and those in which a player could cheat justice:

In gaming . . . though the cheat may lose for a while, to the skill or good fortune of a fairer player, and sometimes on purpose to draw him in deeper, yet the false dice must at the long run carry it, unless discovered, and when it comes once to a great stake, will infallibly sweep the table.[83]

Marvell's attitude toward the contingent—Time's "useless Course," the "vain Curlings" which only postpone "the latest Day" (*The First Anniversary*)—suggests that the game of history seemed to him at times tedious and otiose. And we may wonder what he thought of the Protestant game of salvation, wherein success was to be achieved neither without "good works" nor because of them, only through grace arbitrarily bestowed, which was a process foreseen, predetermined, and yet just, a reward—but not really—for valor in a spiritual combat that existed not to prove worth (since all worth is given) but to display the divine sovereignty. In mortal contests, however, one can no more refuse to venture than one can excuse himself from history. The game created when skepticism shakes faith without toppling it requires that real bets be placed, as Pascal realized in addressing his famous wager argument for belief in the existence of God to those who were uneasy in their suspension of judgment and concerned about the consequences of their choices:

> "God is, or He is not." But to which side shall we incline? Reason can decide nothing here. There is an infinite chaos which separated us. A game is being played at the extremity of this infinite distance where heads or tails will turn up. What will you wager? According to reason, you can do neither the one thing nor the other, according to reason you can defend neither of the propositions.
>
> Do not, then, reprove for error those who have made a choice; for you know nothing about it. "No, but I blame them for having made, not this choice, but a choice. . . . The true course is not to wager at all."
>
> Yes; but you must wager. It is not optional. You are embark- ed. Which will you choose then? Let us see. Since you must choose, let us see which interests you least. You have two things to lose, the true and the good; and two things at stake, your reason and your will, your knowledge and your happiness; and your nature has two things to shun, error and misery. Your reason is no more shocked in choosing one rather than the other, since you must of necessity choose. . . .[84]

I do not say that Marvell's calculations were as cold-blooded and self-interested as these, but he was "embarked," and, forced to play, he felt the pressure to win. A hypothetical case which he described in the *Defence of John Howe* may well illustrate how he worked through alterna- tives until he could see none left but "action":

> Suppose a man to meet with some afflicting calamity which tends to provoke, among other his passions, that of aversion or hatred. He considers this or that man may have contributed to his calamity: he considers also that God may have had an hand in bringing it upon him: he considers, perhaps, . . . whether to put forth one act of hatred toward God, or whether only to hate the evil itself that afflicts him. . . . At last he is limited to this rather than another action, and apprehending with that prophane

person, 2 Kings vi. 33, "Behold this evil is from the Lord, what shall I wait for the Lord any longer?" he pours out his hatred against God Himself.[85]

Now as Marvell read St. Paul, the "prophane person" who has placed the bet by choosing to disbelieve in God's goodness, though unaware that he is wrong, must pay for making it. For while Marvell recognized that faith cannot be compelled against the certain conviction of the mind,[86] he believed that if "a fundamental truth [be] clearly demonstrated from Scripture, though a man cannot force himself to believe it, yet there is enough to render a man inexcusable to God."[87] This on the authority of Romans 3:

> What if some did not believe? Shall their unbelief make the faith of God without effect? God forbid: yea, let God be true, but every man a liar; as it is written. That thou mightest be justified in thy sayings, and mightest overcome when thou art judged. But if our unrighteousness commend the righteousness of God, what shall we say? Is God unrighteous who taketh vengeance? (I speak as a man) God forbid: for then how shall God judge the world? [3-6]

Since Marvell so understood the rules of the game played for his soul, he tended to play close to the vest. Indeed, many moral theologians would have advised him to do so. "In all questions of general enquiry concerning lawful or unlawful, necessary or not necessary," wrote Jeremy Taylor (whom Marvell read and respected), [88] "the equal probability cannot infer a suspension or an equal non-compliance."[89] That is, to suspend choice is in itself a choice, for which one may be held responsible. And when a decision has to be made about opposing probabilities, *in dubiis juris tutior pars sequenda est*: "If there be a danger on one side only, and a doubt on both sides, there is no question but that side is to be chosen where there is no danger; unless the doubt on one side be contemptible and inconsiderable, and the other not so."[90] The author of *Upon Appleton House,* we might recall, pointedly approved of "the safe but roughest Way" (720). In some games, especially in political ones, Marvell had some room in which to maneuver, and he took advantage of it. In the contest of faith, however, unable to take his fencing master's advice to seize the advantage,[91] he could only do his best within severely limited prerogatives.

The writings which record some of his moves show Marvell composed (even when, as in the "Horatian Ode," he is confused), cautious (except in the satires, which by their very nature proscribe caution), and intense. Yet at the same time he is often facetious. There is humor and playfulness even in his sympathetic description of events tinged with tragedy: the trials of the Mower, the emblematic destructions of animals and trees in *Upon Appleton House,* the death of Charles I in the "Horatian Ode."[92] Marvell's is not the merely self-conscious, gratuitous frivolity of a John Cleveland (although there are superficial resemblances to be found in their works).[93] Nor does he display, as one critic has proposed, the kind of playful pococurantism that enables him "to engage fully, without commitment, in the dance of contradictions which make up experience."[94] What Eliot called the "alliance of levity and seriousness" in Marvell "by which the seriousness is intensified,"[95] and what Marvell himself suggested was an attitude somewhere "betwixt Jest and Earnest,"[96] is much like the serio-comic vision of Pierre Bayle.[97] Marvell and Bayle, thoughtful men both, see too much absurdity in life to approach it with a uniformly dread solemnity. Since their thirst for answers to metaphysical questions is not quenched by the tangy liquors of paradox, and since they need comic, not tragic, solutions—which only faith can provide them—each professes his reconciliation to the universe with a humor that recognizes Incongruity, protests it, but will not in the last analysis defiantly call it Injustice.

If Marvell's self-possession and humor are congenital, they are also indispensable for playing the game well, as, no doubt, he knew. The speaker's "nonchalance" in *Upon Appleton House,* then, is neither factitious nor purposeless; the "easie Philosopher" has the best chance of winning. Marvell must either laugh at himself as in "The Garden," or retreat stiffly and nervously towards defeat. Christopher Hill has said that "humour is for Marvell one way of bearing the unbearable."[98] It is. The tear-shaped Drop of Dew, the "Amber Tears" that come from the Nymph's fawn (100), the tearful "Essence" of the world postulated in "Eyes and Tears"—

> The all-seeing Sun each day
> Distills the World with Chymick Ray;
> But finds the Essence only Showers,
> Which straight in pity back he powers—
>
> [21-24]

all suggest that Marvell shared Virgil's intimation that there are "tears in the nature of things."[99] As consoler of Sir John Trott, Marvell might bring himself to speak paradoxical wisdom, attempting to render suffering "beautiful" and a source of joy: "The Tears of a family may flow together like those little drops that compact the Rainbow, and if they be placed with the same advantage towards Heaven as those are to the Sun, they too have their splendor."[100] But such consolation is official, sounds hollow even in its context. The Book of Revelation promised that God would eventually dry all tears. It seems that Marvell, in this vale of soul-making where the rainbow was not enough, had to wipe away his own for himself.

5

Universal and Particular

But evil on itself shall back recoil
And mix no more with goodness, when at last
Gathered like scum, and settled to itself,
It shall be in eternal restless change
Self-fed and self-consumed; if this fail
The pillared firmament is rottenness,
And earth's base built on stubble.

Milton, Comus

Dimmesdale: "Is it not better than what we
dreamed of in the forest?" Hester: "I know
not! I know not!"

Hawthorne, The Scarlet Letter

"I am . . . subject to be particular," Marvell wrote to a friend, apologizing for his habit of crowding his letters too thickly with fact and circumstance.[1] The apology was, no doubt, *pro forma*, for his correspondents in the provinces were eager for news and must have appreciated his epistolary gazettes. But Marvell did not preoccupy himself with details solely for the benefit of his friends and clients. He was by temperament subject to be particular, acutely aware of what happened around him, alive to mundane realities which he did not always know how to value and which in some ways he, like his Drop of Dew, would have preferred to ignore. The fact-filled letters and satires which he wrote during the Restoration[2] confirm evidence already present in "The Character of Holland" (1653), a poem containing vivid recollections of a tour made in the early 1640s:[3] Marvell was not able to be "careless" of his earthly "Mansion" ("On a Drop of Dew," 4), nor was he inclined to try annihilating all that's made to a thought.

Furthermore, the scenes and events which Marvell observed or participated in, the associations which he sought or welcomed, and the reading to which he devoted so many of his private hours[4] are present in his writings not as unimpassioned memories but as felt experiences, "vital" in both senses of the word. Although this is not the kind of judgment that can be absolutely verified by quasi-scientific proof, the probabilities offered by the facts of Marvell's biography strongly suggest that it is correct. There is a congruence between the particulars of his life and the particulars of his professed thought, and this relationship, already touched upon in the previous chapters, must now be explored in more detail.

Too little is known about Marvell's private life to warrant an extended discussion of his love poetry as a reflection of his personal experiences. Since he died a bachelor,[5] one might guess that he never found in life the uncomplicated and unstrenuous love presented as an imaginative ideal in his pastorals, or that he was never able to be satisfied by the love which "envious fate" kept imperfect. But love is not the exclusive prerogative of the married, and the absence of any substantial biographical evidence about Marvell's amorous attachments makes such conjectures rash. Much more open to biographical scrutiny are his religious and political statements which bear upon categorical and para-doxical themes. On these subjects, his words can be considered against significant circumstances in a life history which, although not available to the critic in all its completeness, has definite outlines and offers many occasions for interpretation.

In the first half of Marvell's life, from his birth in 1621 until the early 1650s, we have only glimpses of him; yet these are enough to suggest how he may have begun to agonize over the meaning of perfection. His father, Andrew Marvell senior, was a Calvinistic minister,[6] a graduate of the Puritan Emmanuel College, and, we can assume, conscientious about fostering a strong distrust of "works" in his son, while teaching him the severe limitations of "virtue" and the predominant responsibility of divine grace for all good actions. The younger Marvell attended Trinity College, whose Puritan spirit was less doctrinaire than that of Em-manuel,[7] and where it might more readily occur to a curious student to ask questions about the rational foundations of his religion's moral order. Such questions must have become urgent for the young Marvell at his conversion by the Jesuits in 1639.[8] He was probably given then, in an abbreviated form, the *Spiritual Exercises* of Ignatius Loyola, which were designed to help the exercitant make a "choice of a way of life."[9] In the

Exercises, Marvell would have been offered propositions such as the following:

> There are two ways of gaining merit from an evil thought which comes to me from without:

> 1. The thought comes to me to commit a moral sin. I resist the thought immediately and it is conquered.

> 2. The same evil thought comes to me and I resist it, and it returns again and again, but I continue to resist it until it is vanquished. This second way is much more meritorious than the first.[10]

The system of values here implied, the antithesis of that agreed upon by Plutarch's Gryllus and Odysseus, is in a way as abhorrent to the Calvinist as it is alien to the categorist. Since such a clash of traditions can often lead one to examine the presuppositions of each, it is quite conceivable that Marvell's meditations about the meaning of virtue were, even at this early stage, searching. If his restlessness is any indication, they were also troubled.

Soon after Marvell's defection, his father rushed to London, rescued him from the Jesuits, and returned him to Cambridge. But the young man did not remain there long, for the elder Marvell died the following year in a boating accident, and the son left the university soon afterwards without taking his M.A. The death of his father (whom he spoke of with reverence in *The Rehearsal Transpros'd*)[11] must have affected Marvell deeply, for he had it in mind over a quarter of a century later when he assured Sir John Trott, "I know the contagion of grief, and infection of Tears, and especially when it runs in a blood."[12] It is possible that with the grief was mingled an anxious, perhaps even an angry perplexity. The Rev. Mr. Marvell was drowned, if we can credit Thomas Fuller, "crossing Humber in a barrow-boat . . . by the carelessness, not to say the drunkenness, of the boatmen."[13] Having read *Lycidas,*[14] an elegy for another shipwrecked clergyman, the young Marvell may have been inspired by that submission to Providence to look upon his father's death with the eye of faith. Yet the accident on the Humber, which was, after all, something of a fiasco, may just as well have struck him as much more absurdly and irremediably tragic than the death of Edward King. God did not in the case of the elder Marvell solemnly call his beloved saint to himself by catching him in the embrace of majestic waves divinely ruled, but abandoned a faithful servant to the petty yet fatal malfeasance of men who could hardly seem executors of a sacred purpose. When, a few years later (1649), Marvell was to write an elegy of his own in honor of Lord Hastings, the poet's thoughts were anything but submissive or holy; and that rebelliousness could well have been nourished by a confused resentment which his father's death had occasioned.[15]

Such resentment had, ultimately, to be controlled. In the letter to Trott, Marvell was to prescribe a regimen for coping with the kind of tragic loss that might set a man brooding over the problem of evil: "You will do well to make use of all that may strengthen and assist you. The word of God: The society of good men: and the books of the Ancients."[16] The writer was here, we may assume, speaking from personal experience; and we may wonder which of the "books of the Ancients" he had over the years consulted himself. While he was most likely referring to the Church Fathers, especially Augustine, he was probably thinking of pre-Christian writers as well. He knew Seneca's *De providentia,* which he recalled in composing "A Dialogue between the Resolved Soul, and Created Pleasure,"[17] and was at least generally familiar with that Stoic philosopher's *Consolationes.*[18] In Seneca's writings Marvell could meditate on a moral philosopher's answer to the problem of evil; in Augustine's, he could consider that solution in the context of the paradoxical Christian aesthetic.[19] Here were assurances from both pagan and Christian authorities that evil could be redeemed, that "fortune" was ultimately not outrageous.

Yet the books of the Ancients might disturb as well as console. Since Marvell was not a man to ignore distressing evidence in his quest for peace of mind, he read and took to heart, as we have noticed, Lucretius and Lucan as well as Seneca. Having considered the Stoic's defence of Providence, he would not have neglected Cicero's criticism of the Stoic position in *De natura deorum.* When he read in Horace that heaven sent thunder and plague upon earth as a punishment for crime,[20] he would not have overlooked the same poet's melancholy observation that "Jove often strikes the good along with the wicked when he is scorned."[21] And if Marvell looked to Genesis, "the word of God," for "the plain history of good and evil,"[22] it is not likely that he would have closed his eyes to Julian the Apostate's heretical opinions about how that history should be interpreted. He considered some of Julian's ideas as they were given in the works of the Fathers,[23] and, while recognizing that the emperor had been a cruel persecutor, judged him nevertheless "a man of great wit."[24]

Inclined, then, to debate the truth, to search for objections to even the most comforting of doctrines, Marvell did not in the years immediately following his father's death appear ready to act according to any firmly held convictions. His grand tour of the Continent in the 1640s was undeniably a retreat from commitment to either side in the Civil War,[25] an escape that was, I suggest, made more from a lack of certitude than from a deficiency of courage. War is, of course, precisely the kind of trauma that may provoke anxious questions about the problem of evil, about the nature of justice and moral obligation, and about specific standards of personal conduct. Once the man of "weak and variable" judgment[26] decided where he must take a stand, he would accept the risks entailed by actions that committed him to religious and political convictions; but in these unsettled years, he had not yet made the decisions, and the risks he allowed himself were mostly intellectual.

Marvell was probably reading Donne in the 1640s, that is, the alternately saucy and solemn, frequently skeptical and adventurous Donne. "Fleckno" (ca. 1645–47) reveals the influence of Donne's *Satyres*.[27] Part of "Thyrsis and Dorinda" may well have been Marvell's response to *Biathanatos*.[28] And *The Progresse of the Soule,* or *Metempsychosis,* which Marvell certainly knew,[29] would, especially in its tentative questioning of Providence, have suited his mood during the time (1641–50) between his father's death and "The Horatian Ode":

So fast in us doth this corruption grow,
That now wee dare aske why wee should be so.
Would God (disputes the curious Rebell) make
A law, and would not have it kept? Or can
His creatures will, crosse his? Of every man
For one, will God (and be just) vengeance take?
Who sinn'd? t'was not forbidden to the snake
Nor her, who was not then made; nor is't writ
That Adam cropt, or knew the apple; yet
    The worme and she, and he, and wee endure for it.
                    [*The Progresse of the Soule,* 101–110][30]

O might not states of more equality
Consist? And is it of necessity
    That thousand guiltlesse smals, to make one
        great, must die.

                                        [Ibid., 328–30]

It may have been at this time also (perhaps during his travels in Italy) that Marvell committed to memory an epigram about Aretino, which he was later to sanctify by using against Samuel Parker.

Qui giace il Aretino
Chi de tutti mal disse fuor d'Iddio
Ma di questo si scusa perche no'l conobbe.

Here lies Aretine,
Who spoke evil of all, except God only,
But of this he beggs excuse, because he did not know him.[31]

Conjectures about Marvell's experiences and his state of mind during these poorly documented years must not, of course, be pushed too far. But at the end of this period, he is heard complaining of the "Jealousies" of Heaven ("Lord Hastings," 22) and describing with consternation the victory of Fate over Justice ("Horatian Ode," 37); he is seen wavering between a reluctant acceptance of the Civil War as an act of God ("Horatian Ode") and an eager denunciation of it as the despicable plot of "*Spartacus*" ("Tom May's Death," 74). The "Poet, Puritan, [and] Patriot" has invited a search for an explanation of his attitudes, even if conclusions can be only tentative.

When Marvell applied for and accepted the tutorship of Maria Fairfax in early 1651,[32] he had passed a point of crisis and was approaching an uneasy accommodation with a paradoxical world and its God. Lord Fairfax, a fierce soldier whose tender conscience disapproved of the execution of the king and could not condone Cromwell's invasion of Scotland, whose flower-forts intrigued Marvell with their symbolic possibilities, was perhaps a figure to inspire a sense of compromise in a man not inclined to ignore the demands of necessity anyway. Marvell's association with the retired Puritan general was not yet a commitment to "restless *Cromwel*" and the concept of *pax quaesita bello*, but certainly a prelude to commitment. The poet's thoughts in *Upon Appleton House* about Providence and its violent ways were, as I have indicated, not entirely devout; but his mood in that poem was essentially tranquil and submissive, reflecting a resolve to limit the free idealism of his categorical imagination by becoming sociable with the steel that severs living buds. His temperamental aversion to paradoxical beauty in art or in moral virtue could not be given free rein if he decided—and he did decide—to participate in the only world he knew. In a poem that celebrates the Fairfacian estate of Bilbrough, Marvell will have the classical perfection of the "circular" line and the "equal" hill prevail for a moment ("Upon the Hill and Grove at Bill-borow," 4, 6). All access is "soft" (17); no path is "rugged" (19); the trees are safe. "No hostile hand durst ere invade / With impious Steel the sacred Shade" (35–36). A lesson is proffered:

Here learn ye Mountains more unjust,
Which to abrupter greatness thrust,
That do with your hook-shoulder'd height

The Earth deform and Heaven fright,
For whose excrescence ill design'd
Nature must a new Center find,
Learn here those humble steps to tread,
Which to securer Glory lead.

[9–16]

Yet the poet cannot blink away a vision of Fairfax that seems to superimpose itself upon the benign sylvan scene:

Much other Groves . . . then these
And other Hills him once did please.
Through Groves of Pikes he thunder'd then,
And Mountains rais'd of dying Men.

[65–68]

The violent image, now intensifying, now fading, is unable to remain fixed and dominant; the poem ends with an emphasis on the general's "Retirement" from rough strife. But Marvell must live with disturbing pictures. Even while honorably flattering his employer, he manages to speak his own true concerns, suggesting thoughts that are leading him to a career away from the sanctuaries of the "happy man." As Fairfax combines in himself the gardener and the soldier—although not at the same time and with problematical consequences—so (in another poem) gentle Bilbrough finds its antithetical complement in wild and rugged Almscliff, whose beauty is "sublime," founded on deformity that may terrify:

Cernis ut ingenti distinguant limite campum
    Montis Amosclivi Bilboreique juga!
Ille stat indomitus turritis undique saxis:
    Cingit huic laetum Fraxinus alta Caput.
Illi petra minax rigidis cervicibus horret:
    Huic quatiunt virides lenia colla jubas.
. . . .
Erectus, praeceps, salebrosus, & arduus ille:
    Acclivis, placidus, mollis, amoenus hic est.

Behold how Almias-cliff and Bilborough's brow
Mark with broad bound the spacious plain below!
Dauntless, on that, the rocky turrets frown,
This, the tall ash adorns with lightsome crown;

There the rough rocks in terrors grim are dressed,
But here, the smooth hill waves a verdant crest.
....
The steep, the rough, the difficult are there;
Here all is sloping, gentle, soft and fair.

> ["Epigramma in Duos montes Amosclivum
> Et Bilboreum," 1-6, 13-14;
> trans. in Grosart]

Nature, says the poet, combines both sets of values in the character of Fairfax—"Dissimilis Domino coiit Natura sub uno" (15)—who is proper lord of each territory. Marvell is straining here, almost, we might say, attempting to will both the concept and the reality of union into existence. Almscliff and Bilbrough were in point of physical fact so far apart that neither could be seen from the other.[33] And as emblems of moral values, of ways of life, they were (again) like parallels that never meet. Fairfax had to abandon one state to achieve the other, just as Marvell, passing the Lord General at the momentary nexus of Appleton House, traveling in the opposite direction, had to leave behind Elysium for the Agora. What then has happened to Marvell's sense, as he expressed it in the "Horatian Ode," that Nature will not allow "penetration"? That idea, along with the habit of mind that made it for him a compelling thought, he now suppresses and will do so again in *The First Anniversary*.[34] He has prepared himself to step from Nunappleton out into the State and establish public, though provisional, allegiances to Cromwell and his Lord of Hosts.

After two years' service with Fairfax, Marvell sought a position in the government as Milton's assistant, but, even with the support of the Secretary for Foreign Tongues himself, he was turned down. He must, nevertheless, have been introduced to Cromwell around this time, for he became tutor to William Dutton, Cromwell's ward, before July of 1653. This employment brought Marvell to Eton and into the house of John Oxenbridge, where he was to compose *The First Anniversary of the Government under O. C.* (1654). Marvell's attempt in that poem to mediate the conflict between categorical and paradoxical values required compromises, submissions, and justifications of the kind he had already undertaken at Appleton House. *The First Anniversary* was published anonymously; but the author of so positive an evaluation of the Protector would have been made known to those who could provide a suitable reward,[35] and Marvell had already shown that he desired the reward of employment by the regime for which he wrote the apology. There is, of course, no way of knowing for certain what scruples and doubts—there were some, surely—lurked beneath the surface of the poem's robust certitudes and qualified hopes. The clear indication, however, from this work, from others, and from his actions, is that during the 1650s Marvell was attempting to make "his peace with things of great account."

He may have been helped in this process by the great Anglican churchman John Hales, who, while living near Eton in the early part of the decade, became his admired friend. In *The Rehearsal Transpros'd* Marvell was to reminisce:

> Mr. *Hales* of *Eaton* [was] a most learned Divine, and one of the Church of *England*, and most remarkable for his Sufferings in the late times, and his Christian Patience under them. . . . I account it no small honour to have grown up into some part of his Acquaintance, and convers'd a while with the living *remains* of one of the clearest heads and best prepared brests in Christendom.[36]

Hales was an independent thinker—a reader of Socinian books, a critical observer of the Synod of Dort (at which he bid "goodnight to John Calvin"), a moderate skeptic who distrusted dogmas and discouraged their multiplication.[37] He would, on the one hand, have sympathized with a sincere man's intellectual hesitancies and confusions, for he believed that

> the nature of truth is such, that if the understanding apprehend it for truth, it cannot but assent to it. No man can force himself to believe what he lists, or when he lists. Sometimes a man knows not what to believe, but finds suspension of his faith, or trepidation of his understanding, not knowing which way to turn. This cannot be called a resisting of the truth, when the truth is unknown, but doubted of.[38]

On the other hand, though he respected the place of reason in theological inquiry,[39] Hales preached that man's prerogative to question the divine goodness must ultimately be limited by his obligation to believe in that goodness, to perform, that is, what is essentially a moral act necessary for salvation. Thus he distinguished heresy from honest error:

> Heresy is an act of the will, not of reason; and is indeed a lie, not a mistake: else how could that known speech of Austin go for true; *Errare possum, haereticus esse nolo?*[40]

And when the divine goodness was in question, Hales would allow error little room. It may offend reason, he says, to think that many times one man's sin ruins a whole country, as Achan's offence turns all Israel to flight; or, as when for the sin of Saul, 2 Sam. XX.I. all the people are like to starve with famine. Thus doth [God] visit, not single persons, but whole nations, with famine and pestilence, with the sword, with fire, with earthquakes, and the like, which, like the rain in the gospel, he makes to fall upon the good and bad.[41]

Men must not, however, be scandalized by what, in this instance, they cannot understand:

What if . . . we were able to render no reason at all of this action of God? ought this to prejudice or call in question the justice of it? . . . How readily ought we to take him at his word, and willingly believe him above, against our reason.[42]

"Yea, let God be true, but every man a liar."[43] Now a Christian may take this fideistic position at the beginning of his spiritual journey, thereby forestalling the doubts and anxieties which a freely active reason can provoke; or he may come to it gradually, after exploring, perhaps fitfully, different avenues of rebellion. Marvell seems to have taken the latter course, and it is not unreasonable to assume that he would have received sympathetic encouragement to renounce lingering doubts from the clear head and prepared breast of Hales.

Marvell may also have discussed with his thoughtful friend the questions about the religious uses of violence which would soon appear in *The First Anniversary*. Hales reveals an awareness similar to the poet's of anomalies in the concept of sacred violence, and at the same time a similar inclination to search for ways to make that concept acceptable to the Christian mind. Hales's "Tract concerning Schism and Schismatics,"[44] for instance, is reducible, as he himself says, to "that precept of the Apostle,—'As yet that far as it is possible, have peace with all men'";[45] and this precept is clearly offered out of a deep love of the "communion" which "is the strength and ground of all society, whether sacred or civil."[46] But the theologian is forced to find a place for a "due Christian animosity," which can create a "necessary separation" in the fabric of peace.[47] However regretful his concessions to the might that establishes right, he does not shrink from making them—seeking all the while the "victory of peace":

Neither was the voice of the church only the voice of Jacob, a soft and still voice, and her actions like unto the hand of Esau, rough, implacable, and indisposed to peace; but in all her oppositions she shewed a sweet and peaceable behaviour. "Good men," said S. Austin, "as far as it is possible, even wage war mercifully." And St. Jerom observes, that the children of Israel went to fight with peaceable hearts; "amidst the swords, and bloodshed, and slaughtered carcases, not minding their own, but the victory of peace."[48]

If Marvell heard such words as these from a true irenicist and a respected friend, he would have been reassured about the right-mindedness of his own attempts, underway at this time, to find a principle of legitimacy for the "Armes [in] *Religions* hand" (*Death of O. C.,* 179). As Hales could see the Israelites sent by God to wage war with peace in their hearts, so Marvell could now look with fewer reservations upon Cromwell as one required by "Heav'n" to "walk still middle betwixt War and Peace" (*First Anniversary,* 243–44), to make the waters of State heal by troubling them (ibid., 402), to annihilate war by waging it (*Blake's Victory,* 159–60)— this Cromwell "whom Nature all for Peace had made" (*Death of O. C.,* 15), who felt more keenly "Each wound himself which he to others delt" (ibid., 198). The casuistry of Marvell and Hales on this subject is neither systematic nor remarkably acute; but clearly the same impulse urges both men to search for justice wherever necessity leaves the slightest room for it, and to hope for peace in every swing of the sword. Association with the "learned and judicious divine" of Eton could have intensified this impulse in Marvell and may, indeed, have given it direction.

At any rate, during the Protectorate, as Marvell dwelt on thoughts of an "angry Heav'n" that swayed "unto War" (*Death of O. C.,* 16), he did so with more complacency than before. Having celebrated in verse the victories of the government, he eventually entered its official service (in 1657) as Latin Secretary to the Council of State. He drew closer to Cromwell and to the Protector's family,[49] becoming convinced, as the elegy on Cromwell's death would reveal, of the soldier's "tendernesse," and hopeful, as he professed in *The First Anniversary,* of the union of "High Grace" with "highest power" in a millennial peace which the soldier might help to establish. Marvell's enthusiasms were becoming focused, even partisan.

It is possible that this new, energetic singlemindedness was principally the result of his increased acquaintance with power through those who wielded it. Participation in authority can heighten one's desire for its legitimacy, and desire often begets acknowledgment. Then too, there was something about Cromwell the man that could excite in Marvell admiration and hope. Not only was the Protector successful; he preached that success was holy, appealing to the categorist's deeply felt intuition about the continuity of values. Like Marvell himself, Cromwell looked at human institutions in self-confessed ignorance about the ideal they should approach and with high-minded unconcern, almost disdain, for the concrete forms government might take. "I can tell you, sirs, what I would not have, though I cannot what I would," Cromwell once told two members of Parliament. And as for constitutional forms, he considered them "but a moral thing . . . dross and dung in comparison of Christ."[50] As we shall see, Marvell knew and accepted in his own character such independence from hallowed means, although the uncertainty about moral choices that this "freedom" gave rise to was not helped in his case by a conviction of direct access to God's intentions.

Not to be overlooked, either, as a major source of inspiration for whatever martial and millennial spirit the *"easie Philosopher"* of Nunappleton came to possess is his friendship with Milton. In all probability, the two men had become acquainted not long before Milton's letter to Bradshaw on Marvell's behalf in 1653;[51] but Marvell soon became a frequent visitor to Milton's house in Westminster, where religion and politics were staple topics of conversation, and eventually the great man's trusted friend. Marvell was among the first to receive a presentation copy of the *Defensio Secunda,* to which he gave somewhat fulsome praise,[52] promising to study it "even to the getting of it by heart."[53] He had, indeed, already taken other words of Milton to heart. As I have indicated, Marvell had read *Lycidas* in his youth; and during the years of political decision that preceded his application for a post in the government, he was certainly conversant with Milton's poetry and prose. The author of *Upon Appleton House* found his *"antick Cope,"* for example, in the *Apology for Smectymnuus,* his "gadding vines" in *Lycidas,* a pattern for his *"Admiring Nature"* in the *Nativity Ode.*[54] If Milton's influence on the decisions made in *Upon Appleton House* seems remote, his effect on the sturdy declarations of *The First Anniversary* is hardly negligible. While the latter poem again reveals the influence of the *Nativity Ode* and of *Lycidas,*[55] it also, and more significantly, incorporates some of the fervent notions of *Areopagitica.* Marvell shares (for the moment, at least) and embellishes Milton's vision of a "perfection" achieved when, "out of many moderat varieties and brotherly dissimilitudes that are not vastly disproportionall arises the goodly and gracefull symmetry that commends the whole pile and structure":[56]

The Common-wealth does through their Centers all
Draw the Circumf'rence of the publique Wall;
The crossest Spirits here do take their part,

Fast'ning the Contignation which they thwart;
And they, whose Nature leads them to divide,
Uphold, this one, and that the other Side;
But the most Equal still sustein the Height,
And they as Pillars keep the Work upright;
While the resistance of opposed Minds,
The Fabrick as with Arches stronger binds,
Which on the Basis of a Senate free,
Knit by the Roofs Protecting weight agree.

[*The First Anniversary*, 87-98]

To endorse this coincidence of opposites, Marvell had to suppress many of his deepest feelings, just as he had to close his eyes to Cromwell's depredations of the "Senate free" (97).[57] But such coercion of emotion and intellect, in part a bow to necessity, is also understandable as service to an ideal. Milton's confidence in that ideal, his oracular vision of a "noble and puissant nation rousing herself" in "these latter ages" to usher in "some new and great period" decreed by Providence,[58] surely helped to foster Marvell's hope that, as he put it in his own words, a "seasonable People" would contribute to the advent of the "latest Day" of God's "mysterious Work" (*The First Anniversary*, 133, 140, 137). And hope covers a multitude of reservations.

David Masson once expressed the opinion that "Marvell's discipleship to Milton . . . [was] perfect and exceptionless to the last."[59] This claim may be true without qualification in respect of the younger man's personal loyalty to a friend whom he venerated; that Marvell would have consistently placed his independent mind in subjection to the wisdom of anyone is not very likely. There were, nevertheless, a good many issues that served to unite the two in intellectual sympathy.[60] Of most interest here are those convictions of Milton that would have made his counsel valuable to the poet and thinker described in this study. Marvell knew, for example, what the author of *Areopagitica* thought about projects for gaining Elysium: "To sequester out of the world into *Atlantick* and *Eutopian* polities, which never can be drawn into use, will not mend our condition; but to ordain wisely as in this world of evil, in the midd'st whereof God hath plac't us unavoidably."[61] Milton's view of war as a means to a "victorious peace" was similar to Marvell's.[62] Both men at one time or another expressed something of a "desperate faith in successful leaders" and were tempted to believe that success marked the approval of Providence.[63] Both were impatient with the strictures of human laws, regretting them as necessary, jealous of the free prerogatives that the law limited. In the *Defensio Secunda,* which Marvell was to have studied so diligently, Milton addressed Cromwell:

> The greater the number, the worse in general is the quality of the laws, which become, not precautions, but pitfalls. You should keep only those laws that are essential and pass others— not such as subject good men with bad to the same yoke, nor, while they take precautions against the wiles of the wicked, forbid also that which should be free for good men.[64]

Similarly persuaded, Marvell wrote: "To the good . . . all law is uselesse"; and, "Law is force, and the execution of that Law a greater Violence; and therefore with rational creatures not to be used but upon the utmost extremity."[65] Each man pursued his inquiry into religion with some intellectual latitude, each uneasy with established traditions, each aware, as Milton said, that "no man is infallible here on earth. . . . So long as all . . . profess to set the Word of God only before them as the Rule of faith and obedience; and use all diligence and sincerity of heart . . . to understand the Rule and obey it, they have done what man can do."[66] Their versions of religious truth were in many ways quite different—Milton being far more positive and systematic in his conclusions, far more willing to accept the paradoxical character of "this world of evil, in the midd'st of which God hath plac't us unavoidably." But both yearned for the prompt coming of the millennium and, however inconsistently at times, advocated religious toleration while saints of different persuasions worked and waited together in semidarkness for the new age to come.

Both visionaries were to suffer, of course, from expectations mocked. Cromwell died, the Commonwealth dissolved, and a king was crowned who seemed to supporters of the Good Old Cause neither noble nor puissant nor divinely moved. Milton's reaction was to turn inwards— as Coleridge has said: "Finding it impossible to realize his own aspirations, either in religion, or politics, or society, he gave up his heart to the living spirit and light within him, and avenged himself on the world by enriching it with [the] record of his own transcendent ideal."[67] Marvell's response to disappointment is not susceptible of description in such majestical phrases. He too felt the need to retire from the ruins of a political and religious ideal; indications are, however, that his retreat was accomplished not by an expansive turning to a "transcendent" reality that could in a paradox turn defeat into victory, but through a process of constriction.

That this is so is not immediately obvious. Marvell did not, after all, retreat from the world into a comfortable and ineffectual solitude. During the period of the Restoration he plunged into parliamentary politics, occasionally into theological controversy, and fought for his reconsidered causes to the end of his life. He did not simply abandon a confident belief for a timid skepticism: his faith in the God and the men of the Commonwealth had from the first been based on reluctant compromises; and in fact his utterances during the Restoration years sound more dogmatic than ever. He began in the 1660s, to be sure, to speak frequently with the crass, narrow certitude of a satirist; but, since he had revealed a similar propensity much earlier in "Fleckno" and "The Character of Holland," his later satirical writings can hardly in themselves be considered as signs of a diminished sensitivity. Nor, in the absence of positive proof, can it be claimed that his rich, lyrical imagination failed him in these later years. It is certain that his sense of humor did not.

Yet Marvell's energetic activity in religious and political causes and his tone of assurance in religious and political statements are not enough to void the impression that, as his hopes and expectations were chastened, he did in some ways contract his vision to suit a smaller, darker universe.

Because his religion had to be repaired, not undermined, he did not revert to wondering how Fate could be at war with Justice, or to contemplating with bitterness the "Jealousies [of] Heaven." He put on, rather, the blinders of faith, which allowed him to see intensely in one direction and to act with purpose. It was a new, determined, even proselytizing fideism which informed his spiritual counsel in the letter to Trott (1667), his acquiescence to a complacently violent Providence in *The Rehearsal Transpros'd* (1673), his subjection of "blind" Understanding to Faith in "On Mr. Milton's *Paradise lost*" (1674), and his championing of the cause of God in the *Defence of John Howe* (1678). Marvell became impatient with rational argumentation, which, he felt, could lead to few certain conclusions about the religious problems that concerned him. He quoted with approval Bacon's exhortation to theologians and religious authorities "not to enter into Assertions and Positions."[68] He read, and recommended to his nephew, Henry Cornelius Agrippa's *De Incertitudine:* "Si . . . p[er]fect[ius] aliq[ui]d desideras oporteret ipsum Cornelium Agrippam de vanitate scientiarum consulere. . . ."[69] He took particular note of respectable opinion that prescribed a safe theological course— heeding, for example, the words of a sermon by Edward Stillingfleet on the subject of "the reason of good and evil":[70]

> Those who find themselves to be free enough to do their souls mischief, and yet continue still in the doing of it, find nothing more ready to plead for themselves, than the unhappiness of mans composition, and the degenerate state of the world. If *God*

had designed (they are ready to say) that man should lead a life
free from sin, why did he confine the soul of man to a body so
apt to taint and pollute it? But who art thou O Man, that thus
findeth fault with thy Maker? Was not his kindness the greater,
in not only giving thee a soul capable of enjoying himself, but
such an habitation for it here, which by the curiosity of its
contrivance, the number and usefulness of its parts, might be a
perpetual and domestick testimony of the wisdom of its Maker?
Was not such a conjunction of soul and body necessary for the
exercise of that dominion which *God* designed man for, over the
creatures endued only with sense and motion? and if we suppose
this life to be a state of tryal in order to a better, . . . what can be
imagined more proper to such a state, than to have the soul
constantly employed in the government of those sensual inclina-
tions which arise from the body? In the doing of which, the
proper exercise of that virtue consists, which is made the
condition of future happiness.[71]

Marvell did not find in these propositions satisfactory answers to the
questions he raised in his own writings about the soul-body relationship,
the shortcomings of Nature, or the complicity of Providence in the Fall. If
he had so accepted them, he would have used such arguments in his own
theodicy. What really impressed him was the urgency of the question
which lay in the middle of and behind all of Stillingfleet's rationalizations:
"Who art thou O Man, that thus findeth fault with thy Maker?" This is
the matter for the peroration of the sermon—matter saved for last
because it must persuade where all other argument fails:

Wherewithal . . . wilt thou be able to dispute with *God?* Wilt
thou then charge his Providence with folly, and his Laws with
unreasonableness? when his *greatness* shall affright thee, his
Majesty astonish thee, his *Power* disarm thee, and his *Justice*
proceed against thee . . . ? Art thou then resolved to put all these
things to the adventure, and live as securely as if the *terrours* of
the *Almighty* were but the dreams of men awake, or the fancies
of weak and distempered brains? . . . Do [the mockers of sin]
design to out-wit infinite Wisdom, or to find such flaws in *God's*
government of the World, that he shall be contented to let them
go unpunished?[72]

"To put all things to the adventure"—Marvell was not willing to play the
game at so great a hazard. He was now inclined rather, to take the

recommendation of Donne, who knew that the quest for "Truth" was rugged, yet felt compelled to advise:

Strive so, that before age, deaths twilight,
Thy Soule rest, for none can worke in that night.

["Satyre III," 83–84]

Marvell's fideism conquered his doubt by dividing (epistemologically, at least) the world which in its wholeness was the doubt's occasion. The poet who hated division began to think compartmentally, like Bacon, whose disjunctive attitude Marvell referred to and commended: "'*habet Religio quae sunt Aeternitatis, habet quae sunt Temporis*, Religion hath parts which belong to Eternity, and parts which pertain to time.'"[73] In such a temper, Marvell warned Samuel Parker to "take heed of hooking things up to Heaven."[74] This admonition was more than a ploy to deflate an extreme Erastian who was ignorant of even elementary distinctions. It was a new proverb which Marvell's experience had taught him to speak and to abide by. He had struggled, after all, with some success, to accommodate himself to "the force of angry Heavens flame" ("Horatian Ode," 26), only to see the light quenched before it could consume the darkness. He could no longer locate with any kind of certainty points where the eternal and temporal intersected, though he believed that such points must exist. Thus he would admire from earth the eternities of "Heaven," impenetrable by and therefore safe from reason, and leave the realm of Universals—"Justice," "Love"—to operate in its own mysterious way.

This is not to say that Marvell could now dispense with the divine "Ordinance"[75] as a sanction for law and government or eliminate Providence from his explanation of human events. On the contrary, he insisted that God upholds the order which makes society possible: "The Power of the Magistrate does most certainly issue from the Divine Authority. The Obedience due to that Power is by Divine Command. . . ."[76] And he affirmed that God directs the flow of history and intervenes, "sometimes out of Complacency," in "intermitting seasons of Discord, War, and publick Disturbance."[77] The universe is no Lucretian "Empire of Atoms," utterly subject to "Chance."[78]

But these truths, though metaphysically secure through faith's guarantee, became for Marvell more difficult of application than ever. During the Civil War and the Commonwealth, he had tried to use the doctrine of Providence to interpret his experience, having seen, so he thought, the movements of God's hand, and having acted at its behest in the cause of a large, definitive ideal: for absolute Justice, for a "Kingdom blest of Peace and Love," for a compromised but plausibly authentic political Elysium. Defeat and disappointment taught him new, more sober, agnostic principles: although God moves and determines events, no one can confidently claim to see that operation; for Providence is essentially "inscrutable," governing in ways that confound man's understanding.[79] Human certitudes about the connections between heaven and earth are limited:

> There is not now any express Revelation, no Inspiration of a Prophet, nor Unction of that Nature as to the declaring of that particular person that is to Govern. Only God hath in general commanded and disposed men to be Governed. And the particular person reigns according to that right, more or less, respectively, which under Gods providence he or his Predecessors have lawfully acquired over the Subject.[80]

Where vision is circumscribed, "natural" explanations are to be sought for—as cause, for example, of "Commotions" against the government:

> In all things that are insensible there is . . . a natural force alwayes operating to expel and reject whatsoever is contrary to their subsistence. And the sensible but brutish creatures heard together as if it were in counsel against their common inconveniences, and imbolden'd by their multitude, rebel even against Man their Lord and Master. And the Common People in all places partake so much of Sense and Nature, that, could they be imagined and contrived to be irrational, yet they would ferment and tumultuate at last for their own preservation.[81]

And natural sanctions are to be urged for laws that God has not clearly endorsed:

> An humane Law can create only an humane obligation; and unless the breach chance likewise to be against some express Divine Law, I cannot see but that the offendor is guilty not to God, but onely to the Magistrate, and hath expiated his Offence by undergoing the Penalty.[82]

It is understandable that Marvell's agnosticism should have led him to a public ethic based on ignorance and limitation. If, he reasoned, laws and creeds cannot infallibly be "hooked up to heaven," men who have power to impose them should be most reluctant to enforce, even to the buffeting of private consciences, their idiosyncratic notions of what the Kingdom of God on earth requires. In the first place,

> men . . . are to be dealt with reasonably: and conscientious men
> by Conscience. . . . Even Law is force, and the execution of that
> Law a greater violence; and therefore with rational creatures
> not to be used but upon the utmost extremity.[83]

Furthermore, since "'we [cannot] by reason make any deduction by way of argument from that which we understand not,'"[84] the "humane extentions" (beyond the simplicities of Scriptural formulations) of heavenly truths into creeds and into laws forcing compliance with those creeds are intellectually dishonest and potentially tragic: "Men, . . . bungling divine and humane things together, have been always hacking and hewing one another, to frame an irregular figure of political incongruity," when instead they should have stayed "within the bounds of [a] saving ignorance by belief according to the Scriptures, untill the last and full manifestation."[85] Like the advocates of religious toleration to whom he refers with great respect—John Hales, William Chillingworth, Jeremy Taylor, and others[86]—Marvell knew the vanity and the dangers of dogmatizing. As an admirer of Cornelius Agrippa, he probably felt less confident than they in the powers of the human mind even when it stayed within its proper domain.

Since "saving ignorance" must diminish expectations, what modest hopes could Marvell legitimately entertain and pursue? That King and Church practice toleration;[87] that laws be enacted for their "utility to the Publick";[88] that the government cast off as much weight of corruption as possible (it is clear from the satires and letters that this hope is quite restrained); that English Protestantism, which once seemed to have the "Beast" of Rome on the run,[89] be simply made safe against the threat of the European Catholic powers. Marvell resigned himself to living with the provisional in a society which, by God's decree, could be "no continuing city" (Heb. 13:14), whose laws were but "Probationers of time."[90] He could no longer look to the divine lightning to establish a definitive Justice, for that great good, it seemed, could come only in secret. "*England*" or "the *Peace*" was now a naked, helpless woman,[91] an earthly image, sought through earthly, even petty, accommodations—that is, through manipulation of those "particulars" which Marvell was so good at recalling, understanding, and acting upon.

Once the Universal was metaphysically secure and isolated in one part of his mind, Marvell could lose himself in the Particular. His letters reveal his interminable and exhausting labor for the not very exalted commercial interests of his parliamentary constituents at Hull (he worked intermittently for seventeen years on a single lighthouse project).[92] He spent a year and a half in the mid-1660s on a trade embassy to Russia and Scandinavia.[93] He tirelessly catalogued and reported political events and gossip to his clients and friends, penned satires at times of high discontent, and eventually wrote in *The Growth of Popery* an often detailed history of the Restoration up to 1677. Challenging selected adversaries in his pamphlets, he defended his principles in rambling, chatty tours through a welter of information and allusion. As a conscientious parliamentarian and loyal subject, he worked on House committees of every kind.[94] As an Englishman disaffected by what he perceived to be his country's drift towards "popery and arbitrary government," he flirted with treason, it seems likely, by becoming involved with a pro-Dutch fifth column that operated in England during the Third Dutch War.[95] Occasionally he rose above the turmoil to consider the results of his efforts, as when in mild despair he asked his nephew, "What Probability is there of my doing any Thing to the purpose?"[96] But he threw himself forward into his work—head down, it seems—until his death, which came suddenly and unexpectedly.

For all his preoccupation with the Particular, however, there was a part of Marvell that could never allow it a real importance. The categorist in him could never look upon "means" as paramount. He once proclaimed, as we have seen, that "To the good . . . / All law is useless" (*Death of O. C.,* 221-22); and there is no indication that he ever retreated from this view, or from its implications (for him, at any rate) that ends could sometimes make means pale into insignificance. If a Buckingham, a Monmouth, or a fanatically Anglican Country Party could further a desirable end, Marvell could accept their contribution.[97] If the king's Declaration of Indulgence seemed at one time, in some ways, of some help to the cause of toleration, Marvell could defend it in print—as he did in *The Rehearsal Transpros'd.* A few months later he may have voted against the same declaration in Parliament—either because *The Rehearsal Transpros'd* represented in the first place a tactical promotion of the "idea of indulgence" rather than a defence of the particular decree,[98] or because he changed his mind and decided that the declaration ultimately ceded too much authority to the monarch. In any event, Marvell condemned the declaration a few years later in *The Growth of Popery.*[99] He could flatter or pillory the king as the occasion demanded;[100] could speak on the floor of the House against a bill for the impeachment of Clarendon while showing the Lord Chancellor no mercy in his satires and working for his downfall in private; could excoriate Arlington "transportedly" for incompetence and then move quickly for forgiveness by supporting parliamentary moves favorable to the king and his secretary of state; could on occasion take the side of the duke of York, whom he despised, against the duke of Buckingham, whose leadership he usually followed as advancing his own principles.[101] Marvell the legislator hid bankrupts in his home to protect them from the law.[102] Marvell the M.P., who fought for his commonalty against the encroachments of the royal power, when he had been part of the authority on the other side, wrote a letter that (as Legouis says) showed him "ready to make short work of the independence of Parliament and the rights of the subject."[103] If in this last instance Marvell was speaking only for Secretary Thurloe, his superior, and not for himself, his conscience was yet sufficiently pliable to allow him to be used as a ready instrument in a campaign against the "Senate free."

What does the suppleness, the lightness and nimbleness, say about his character? It may mean simply that he was a good pragmatic politican. Does it also prove the critics correct when they say that Marvell believed more in men than in parties or principles? I have tried to show that the opposite was true, that men or parties were for him useful or expendable insofar as they furthered, or failed to further, the proper causes. The problem was that the world was not "adequate" to Marvell's principles, so that he found himself hard-pressed to relate them to the intractable facts outside his imaginative ideal. He was not, either, as some have said without realizing it, so detached that one is forced to attribute to him that "Indifference" which, "clad in Wisdom's Guise, / All Fortitude of Mind supplies."[104] He did not walk through life wrapped imperviously in a *nil admirari* but felt the pain that comes when idealism must find its way, fight its way, to commitment and then suffer the shock of confusion and frustration. He did not slip easily or blithely into his final renunciations.

It has been suggested that Marvell was something of a Trimmer.[105] Something of one, perhaps. When we think of him against the model described by the marquess of Halifax in *The Character of a Trimmer* (1684), we can see telling resemblances. Like that idealistic but light-footed exemplar of a political philosopher, Marvell felt no worshipful devotion to ephemeral, instrumental human laws, no unswerving attachment to "factions."[106] Marvell and the Trimmer were also kin in that their few high, ultimate principles, to which myriads of lesser norms might readily be sacrificed, were so exalted, and therefore so general, that loyalty to them might easily be interpreted as mere timeserving. The rarefied might seem no more than vaporous—hence the opprobrium that was soon attached to a character that Halifax presented as an ideal. The trimming spirit was a skeptical spirit, acquiescent but never fully convinced. Halifax professed to be "a Christian in submission," reported Bishop Burnet. "He believed as much as he could, and he hoped that God would not lay it to his charge if he could not digest iron as an ostrich did."[107] Acutely conscious of the flaws in Nature—"When a man looketh upon the rules that are made he will think there can be no faults in the World; and when he looketh upon the faults there are so many he will be tempted to think there are no rules"[108]—the Trimmer sought only amelioration, and that through an expediency which he considered high-minded because eminently sane. "This innocent word *Trimmer* signifieth no more than this," Halifax wrote, "that if men are together in a boat, and one part of the company would weight it down on one side, another would make it lean as much to the contrary; it happeneth there is a third opinion of those, who conceive it would do as well, if the boat went even, without endangering the passengers."[109] In one way or another, Marvell can be associated with all of these sentiments.

There are crucial respects, however, in which his attitudes could not be more unlike those of the self-assured marquess of Halifax. The latter's aristocratic sensibility, his sense of superiority and privilege, his *sprezzatura*, are not to be found in any great measure in Marvell, who, knowing his place, seems to have been outwardly more subservient to men and inwardly more humble before the truth, more riven with doubts, more aware of the difficulty of achieving even a learned ignorance. Where Halifax sought public forums in which to air his certitudes and to exercise his powers, Marvell pursued the anonymity that a man of much intelligence, precarious conviction, and little station needed in order to survive. Halifax, despite his affection for peace, spoke with the man of privilege's coolness about the value of public strife:

> There are winds which are sometimes loud and unquiet, and yet with all the trouble they give us, we owe a great part of our health unto them; they clear the air, which else would be like a standing pool, and instead of refreshment would be a disease to us. . . . These strugglings, which are natural to all mixed governments, while they are kept from growing into convulsions do by a mutual agitation from the several parts rather support and strengthen than weaken or maim the constitutions. . . .[110]

Marvell, although temporarily of this mind in the days of Cromwell, denounced such notions in *The Rehearsal Transpros'd*, remarking that the lack of movement in the "dead calm" of public "Tranquility" is often remedied by forcing citizens to become galley slaves.[111]

Of all the differences between the two men (and more similarities and dissimilarities could be cited), the most fundamental is that which distinguishes the frustrated Renaissance visionary (frustrated by the apparent irrelevance of his visions of Elysium and the failure of his "Republic") from the sensible statesman writing for an age of "reason." Halifax scorned "the frenzy of platonic visions."[112] He placed himself on the side of "Nature, Religion, Liberty, Prudence, Humanity and Commonsense"—the last ideal, as signified by its position in the list, enjoying pride of place.[113] When he referred to "a hidden power in the government, which would be lost if it was defined, a certain mystery,"[114] he meant, probably, a natural law, the essence of which might with profit be left uninvestigated. If Nature or Society fell short of his expectations or hopes, he might be disappointed or grieved; but he would become cynical before he would be scandalized.

Although Marvell was himself moving into the new age with some sympathy for its dearest maxims, he remained too "old-fashioned" to feel comfortable with the developing modern creeds. "Platonic visions" were for him either ravishing attractions or distressing problems, never things contemptible or (even worse) indifferent. His sense that the "mystery" in the state was a divine presence working towards a millennium gave way to a less "enthusiastic" faith in "natural" politics; but the faith was tense, an element of the uneasy peace following a battle. And even late in his life Marvell was engaged with a God beyond Nature, wrestling with him, fearing him, concerned about his "sacred Truths" ("On . . . Paradise lost," 8), and, in a final published work, defending him according to the old way of "saving ignorance by belief" rather than by anticipating the rational, systematic theodicies of the next century.

Halifax seemed devoid of any kind of tragic sense. Marvell saw, as I have said, "tears in the nature of things"—but in the final analysis only the potential for tragedy.[115] He had his "affair with transcendence," inquiring with love and dismay into the absolutes that make tragedy possible. In the face of suffering and injustice he knew pity, fear, and outrage. He did not really believe, however, in the paradoxes of the Greek tragedians, stopped short of the tragic pessimism of the Manichees, and could hardly live with what moderns would call "the absurd." In such a dilemma, saving ignorance was a likely recourse:

> Happy they whom Grief doth bless,
> That weep the more, and see the less:
> And, to preserve their Sight more true,
> Bath still their Eyes in their own Dew.
>
> ["Eyes and Tears," 25–28]

The "Sight more true" is not a capacity for tragic knowledge—these eyes, unlike those of Oedipus and Gloucester, are not bloody—but an access to a truth of feeling experienced in darkness, a truth sufficiently optimistic to make one want to live and work in the world rather than to die fighting it.

Marvell lived, worked, and adapted. Some might say that he allowed himself to be bullied into political and religious positions that were only self-serving. In politics, he did at times, under the pressure of events, hesitate, vacillate, ingratiate, and speak "not without mental reservation." But his motives were almost always complex, and he did prove at personal risk his generous loyalty to his final convictions. In his parliamentary years he took positions that were "neither advantageous nor even safe."[116] Knowing that Sir John Coventry lost part of his nose for so little as making a trenchant remark about the king's sexual habits, he was himself, as the author of *The Rehearsal Transpros'd,* to have his ears threatened and was to experience, it seems, more serious threats still—under the influence of which he may have written in a private letter: "magis occidere metuo quam occidi; non quod Vitam tanti aestimem, sed ne imparatus moriar."[117] The courage that Marvell possessed is all the more remarkable for abiding in one who considered heroism an ambiguous virtue and the highest of causes "too good" to fight for. That a man of agnostic temper should spend himself for particular goals whose value he believed to be provisional, qualified, or in some cases doubtful, is evidence of a special kind of moral stamina indeed.

In religion, Marvell yielded through faith to a mysterious, violent God, choosing thereby to be safe in his "wager." But this was no cowardly surrender without a struggle. As a metaphysical poet and thinker in the most fundamental sense, he tried to push the question, Why? as far as it would go. He consistently refused to accept both a paradoxical theodicy which he could not justify and a voluntaristic theodicy from which he could only recoil in moral revulsion. It appears that he placed his bet only when the game had run its course and was going nowhere. We may be tempted to consider his religious difficulties in the light of an observation by John Stuart Mill:

> The ways of [the Christian's] Deity in nature are on many occasions totally at variance with the precepts, as he believes, of the same Deity in the Gospel. He who comes out with the least moral damage from this embarrassment is probably the one who never attempts to reconcile the two standards with one another, but confesses to himself that the purposes of Providence are mysterious, that its ways are not our ways, that its justice and

goodness are not the justice and goodness which we can conceive and which it befits us to practice. When, however, this is the feeling of the believer, the worship of the Deity ceases to be the adoration of abstract moral perfection. It becomes the bowing down to a gigantic image of something not fit for us to imitate. It is the worship of power only.[118]

But as this statement is an oversimplification of Christianity, so it would be of Marvell's response to his religion. In his least troubled moments of insight, he loved unalloyed Beauty more than Power, unparadoxical Truth more than Enigma. What he settled for was, as he learned over a lifetime of inconclusive debate, the only Beauty and Truth he could know on earth—and, as he ultimately chose to believe, all that he should need to know.

Abbreviations

CW	*The Works of John Milton.* Edited by Frank Allen Patterson.
DNB	*Dictionary of National Biography*
EC	*Essays in Criticism*
ELR	*English Literary Renaissance*
Eud. Eth.	Aristotle, *Eudemian Ethics*
JHI	*Journal of the History of Ideas*
JWCI	*Journal of the Warburg and Courtauld Institutes*
MLQ	*Modern Language Quarterly*
MLR	*Modern Language Review*
MP	*Modern Philology*
Nic. Eth.	Aristotle, *Nicomachean Ethics*
NQ	*Notes and Queries*
P and L	*The Poems and Letters of Andrew Marvell.* 3d ed. Edited by H. M. Margoliouth and Pierre Legouis.
PL	*Paradise Lost*
PQ	*Philological Quarterly*
REL	*A Review of English Literature*
RES	*Review of English Studies*
RN	*Renaissance News*
RT	*The Rehearsal Transpros'd and the Rehearsal Transpros'd, the Second Part.* Edited by D. I. B. Smith.
SCG	Aquinas, *Summa Contra Gentiles*
SEL	*Studies in English Literature, 1500-1900*
ST	Aquinas, *Summa Theologica*
TLS	*Times Literary Supplement*
UTQ	*University of Toronto Quarterly*
YPW	*Complete Prose Works of John Milton.* Edited by Don M. Wolfe et al.

Notes

Chapter 1

1. See Pascal's criticism of Montaigne in *Entretien avec M. de Saci,* printed in the Garnier edition of the *Pensées* (Paris, 1964), pp. 42-43.

2. Ernest Renan, "Henri-Frédéric Amiel," in *Feuilles détachées* (Paris: Calmann Lévy, 1892), p. 396. Renan argues against Amiel's disdainful assessment of *"l'epicuréisme de l'imagination."*

3. I quote throughout this study from the following editions of Marvell's works: H. M. Margoliouth, ed., *The Poems and Letters of Andrew Marvell,* 2 vols., 3rd ed., revised by Pierre Legouis with the collaboration of E. E. Duncan-Jones (Oxford: Clarendon Press, 1971); D. I. B. Smith, ed., *The Rehearsal Transpros'd and The Rehearsal Transpros'd, The Second Part* (Oxford: Clarendon Press, 1971). The rest of Marvell's prose I quote from the final volume of Alexander Grosart's four-volume *The Complete Works of Andrew Marvell* (London: Fuller Worthies' Library, 1875). I take translations of the Latin poems from Grosart and from *The Latin Poetry of Andrew Marvell,* trans. William A. McQueen and Kiffin A. Rockwell, University of North Carolina Studies in Comparative Literature, no. 34 (Chapel Hill: University of North Carolina Press, 1964). I have also consulted the recent editions of the poetry by George de F. Lord (New York: Random House, 1968) and Elizabeth Story Donno (Harmondsworth: Penguin, 1972).

4. *"My Ecchoing Song": Andrew Marvell's Poetry of Criticism* (Princeton: Princeton University Press, 1970), pp. 13, 40, 303.

This apparent absence of consistent "assertion" in a poet's work is to be valued, some critics have claimed. I. A. Richards, for example, has "asserted":

> The amplitude and fineness of the response [to poetry], its sanction and authority . . . depend upon . . . freedom from actual assertion in all cases in which the belief is questionable on any ground whatsoever. For any such assertion involves suppressions, of indefinite extent, which may be fatal to the wholeness, the *integrity* of the experience. And the assertion is almost always unnecessary; if we look closely we find that the greatest poets, as poets, though frequently not as critics, refrain from assertions.

(*Principles of Literary Criticism* [1925; rpt. New York: Harvest Books, n.d.], p. 276.)

5. *The Art of Marvell's Poetry,* 2d ed. (New York: Minerva Press, 1968), pp. 13, 56, 77, 78, 202, 214-15, 213.

6. For surveys of Marvell's reputation, see Pierre Legouis, *Andrew Marvell: Poet, Puritan, Patriot,* 2d ed. (Oxford: Clarendon Press, 1968), p. 224ff. (on occasion I shall refer to Legouis's earlier, unabridged biography, *André Marvell: poète, puritain,*

patriote, 1621–78 [Paris: Didier, 1928]); John Carey, ed., *Andrew Marvell: A Critical Anthology* (Harmondsworth: Penguin, 1969), pp. 17–33, 61–71; Michael Wilding, *Marvell: Modern Judgements* (London: Macmillan, 1969), pp. 10–39; Elizabeth Story Donno, *Andrew Marvell: The Critical Heritage* (London: Routledge & Kegan Paul, 1978).

7. *Correspondence of Gerard Manley Hopkins and Richard Watson Dixon,* ed. C. C. Abbot (London: Oxford University Press, 1935), p. 23.

8. "Andrew Marvell." For a brief critique of the essay and a small survey of its influence, see Carey, *Andrew Marvell,* p. 60ff. I quote from the reprint of Eliot's essay in Carey, pp. 46–58.

9. Carey, *Andrew Marvell,* p. 57.

10. Hence Harold Toliver's *Marvell's Ironic Vision* (New Haven: Yale University Press, 1965); hence Colie's study, despite her claim that the poems are impersonal, of Marvell's "naturally double vision, with the irony resulting therefrom" (*"My Ecchoing Song,"* p. xi). Eliot only hints at Marvell's paradoxical bent: in the definition of "wit" and in the attribution to Marvell of Coleridgean "Imagination," a power which "reveals itself in the balance or reconcilement of opposite or discordant qualities" (Carey, *Andrew Marvell,* p. 52). It is H. J. C. Grierson's Introduction to *Metaphysical Lyrics and Poems of the Seventeenth Century,* published in the same year as Eliot's essay, which specifically identifies paradox as one of the essential features of Marvell's verse (Oxford: Clarendon Press, pp. xxv, xxxvii). Critics have since then tended to assume that the poet who made poems out of paradox must not only have seen it in the nature of things but accepted it as a value.

11. See Eliot, in Carey, *Andrew Marvell,* p. 49; Grierson, *Metaphysical Lyrics,* pp. xxxii–xxxiii. Also, A. Alvarez, *The School of Donne* (1961; rpt. New York: Mentor Books, 1967), p. 84. The play element has now been given a kind of metaphysical and anthropological significance—in Frank J. Warnke's "Play and Metamorphosis in Marvell's Poetry," *SEL* 5 (1965): 23–30, reprinted in William R. Keast, ed., *Seventeenth-Century English Poetry: Modern Essays in Criticism,* 2nd ed. (London and New York: Oxford University Press, 1971), pp. 348–55.

12. Carey, *Andrew Marvell,* pp. 50, 47.

13. This is Toliver's emphasis, especially. It is also much the spirit of J. M. Creaser's "Marvell Effortless Superiority," *EC* 20 (1970): 403–423. Donald M. Friedman, in *Marvell's Pastoral Art* (Berkeley and Los Angeles: University of California Press, 1970), speaks of the "tactics" Marvell employs to come to a "resolution that will signal a victory over inevitable decline and death" (p. 175). And S. L. Goldberg observes that "as a man [Marvell] has to maintain a difficult balance between equally possible but conflicting kinds of fulfillment, . . . but . . . keeping such a balance is almost impossible—almost indeed, a kind of *trick*" [italics mine] ("Marvell: Self and and Art," *Melbourne Critical Review* 7 [1965], in Carey, *Andrew Marvell,* p. 167).

14. Muriel Bradbrook and M. G. Lloyd-Thomas, *Andrew Marvell* (Cambridge: Cambridge University Press, 1940), p. 144; Goldberg, in Carey, *Andrew Marvell,* p. 167; John Press, *Andrew Marvell* (London: Longmans, Green & Co., 1958), p. 19.

15. J. B. Leishman, *On Translating Horace* (Oxford: B. Cassirer, 1956), p. 21.

16. Bradbrook and Lloyd-Thomas, *Andrew Marvell,* p. 73; Christopher Hill,

Puritanism and Revolution (1958; rpt. New York: Schocken, 1964), pp. 336-66, reprinted in Carey, *Andrew Marvell*, pp. 73-102.

17. See especially Maren-Sofie Røstvig, *The Happy Man*, 2d ed., vol. 1 (Oslo: Norwegian Universities Press, 1962) and Ann Evans Berthoff, *The Resolved Soul: A Study of Marvell's Major Poems* (Princeton: Princeton University Press, 1970); also Colie, *"My Ecchoing Song,"* p. 294.

18. John M. Wallace, in *Destiny His Choice: The Loyalism of Andrew Marvell* (Cambridge: Cambridge University Press, 1968), attributes this political philosophy to Marvell in an effort to prove the Royalist sympathizer, the eulogist of Cromwell and Latin Secretary of the Protectorate, and the Member of Parliament a "consistent" man of integrity.

19. See Lawrence Hyman, *Andrew Marvell* (New York: Twayne, 1964), pp. 36, 39, 85; Goldberg, in Carey, *Andrew Marvell*, pp. 166-67; Colie, *"My Ecchoing Song,"* p. 294.

20. Like the decision to go "from contemplation to action." See George de F. Lord, "From Contemplation to Action: Marvell's Poetical Career," *PQ* 46 (1967): 207-24; reprinted in Lord's *Andrew Marvell, A Collection of Critical Essays* (Englewood Cliffs: Prentice-Hall, 1968), pp. 55-73.

21. Carey, *Andrew Marvell*, pp. 76-101. Though see Legouis, *Andrew Marvell*, p. 90n.: "In most of Marvell's nature poetry, or love poetry at that, there is felt little sense of inner conflict; this is restricted to the properly religious poems. . . ."; and Bruce King, "In Search of Andrew Marvell," *REL* 8 (1967): 37: "I see no signs of conflict or confusion in Marvell's outlook." Hill makes the unwarranted assumption that the greatest poems are the earliest.

22. In Carey, *Andrew Marvell*, p. 101.

23. Lives, "Aristides," 7.6.

24. Legouis, *Andrew Marvell*, pp. 4, 8-9.

25. *Brief Lives*, ed. Oliver Lawson Dick (Ann Arbor: University of Michigan Press, 1962), p. 196.

26. See Thomas Fuller's testimony about the senior Marvell in *The Worthies of England* (1662), quoted in Legouis, *Andrew Marvell*, p. 2.

27. *P and L*, 2:324. The story of the wagoner is told in G. Miège's *A Relation of Three Embassies . . .*, pp. 430-31; reprinted in Bradbrook and Lloyd-Thomas, *Andrew Marvell*, p. 154. On Marvell's fight with Thomas Clifford, see Legouis, *Andrew Marvell*, p. 128.

28. See *P and L*, 2:113, 166, 290. Marvell's career, or lack of one, as a speechmaker in Parliament is succinctly summarized by Legouis: "He spoke seldom, but when he spoke he did not quite control himself . . ." (*Andrew Marvell*, p. 138).

29. *P and L*, 2:169.

30. Ibid., p. 324.

31. *Historical Essay [on] General Councils*, p. 127. This passage in context refers to the eternal "salvation" of one's soul. For Marvell, however, keeping one's soul "safe" is not just a matter for eternity.

32. "To a Gentleman . . . ," 15, 17.

33. *P and L*, 2:166.

34. It is even doubtful that Marvell showed them to many of his friends. See Carey, *Andrew Marvell*, pp. 17-18, 190-91, 351.

35. A letter from an anonymous writer in Amsterdam to a friend in England, 1678; quoted in Legouis, *Andrew Marvell*, p. 222. The remark is made in reference to Marvell's "religion." I shall give it this application and a broader one.

36. James Scudamore in a letter to Sir Richard Browne, 15 August 1656. See E. E. Duncan-Jones's letters to the *TLS*, 2 December 1949 and 13 January 1950.

37. 1:42.

38. I do not accept Lord's suggestion, in his edition of the poems (xxxii), that "Tom May's Death" may not be Marvell's. See Legouis's notes in *P and L*, 1:235, 304, 329.

39. For the dating of the two poems, see *P and L*, 1:294–95, 303–4.

40. Pp. 21–22.

41. See Legouis, *Andrew Marvell*, pp. 142–44, 149, 157–58.

42. In his *Historical Essay [on] General Councils*, he mentions "Machiavel" with due contempt (p. 154). I take up later the question of Machiavellianism in the "Horatian Ode."

43. *Mr. Smirke: Or, The Divine in Mode*, p. 73.

44. 2:233.

45. For the best verses in honor of the completion of the Louvre.

46. Trans. McQueen and Rockwell:

These are the double gates of Janus, these are the
   roofs of the Thunderer;
Nor is divinity lacking while Louis is present.

47. 2:203.

48. Smith, in *RT*, p. 374; Legouis, *Andrew Marvell*, p. 108. Legouis is not bent on exonerating Marvell, however. See p. 109. And p. 92: "We cannot but note that this praise of the Commonwealth [in "The Character of Holland"] (written at the end of February 1652/3 or little after) coincides with [Marvell's] first known attempt to obtain official employment."

49. Robert Ellrodt, *L'Inspiration personnelle et l'esprit du temps chez les poètes métaphysiques anglais*, 2 vols., 3 parts (Paris: Corti, 1960), 1.2.131.

50. Goldberg, in Carey, *Andrew Marvell*, p. 167.

51. Bradbrook and Lloyd-Thomas, *Andrew Marvell*, p. 116; and see Margaret Wiley, *The Subtle Knot: Creative Skepticism in Seventeenth-Century England* (Cambridge: Harvard University Press, 1952). (Marvell himself does not figure in Wiley's discussion, but her categories and terminology are certainly appropriate to many recent studies of Marvell's "vision.")

52. It is on the question of Marvell's trust in reason that Wallace and I differ most sharply. See below, chapter 5.

53. *The Varieties of Religious Experience* (1902; rpt. New York: Collier, 1961), p. 165.

54. I am not concerned, then, with presenting a technically and systematically psychoanalytical study.

55. Frank Kermode, Preface to *Andrew Marvell: Selected Poetry* (New York: New American Library, 1967), pp. x, xv.

56. Kermode recognizes this, but rejects the implications for a study of Marvell, a poet who (he quotes Ruth Wallerstein) "accepts elements of symbolic thought imaginatively without accepting them schematically" (*Selected Poetry*, p. xxx.).

57. *The Autobiography of William Butler Yeats* (1916-35; rpt. New York: Collier, 1965), p. 341; "The Artist as Critic: A Dialogue, Part II," in *Plays, Prose Writings, and Poems by Oscar Wilde,* ed. Hesketh Pearson (London: Dent, 1930), p. 48. See Leon Edel, *Literary Biography* (1957; rpt. Bloomington, Indiana: Indiana University Press, 1973), p. 45; Lionel Trilling, *Sincerity and Authenticity* (Cambridge: Harvard University Press, 1972), p. 119.

A theoretical defense of the search for a poet in his poems may be constructed on the basis of Cardinal Newman's essay on "Inference" in *An Essay in Aid of a Grammar of Assent* (1870; rpt. New York: Image Books, 1955).

On some of the problems of literary biography, see Douglas Bush, "John Milton," *English Institute Essays, 1946* (New York, 1947), pp. 5-19; Leon Edel, *Literary Biography,* especially pp. 40-55; M. H. Abrams, *The Mirror and the Lamp* (New York: Norton, 1958), pp. 226-62; Rudolf Gottfried, "Autobiography and Art: An Elizabethan Borderland," pp. 109-34, and Francis Noel Lees, "The Keys are at the Palace: A Note on Criticism and Biography," pp. 135-49, both in *Literary Criticism and Historical Understanding: Collected Papers from the English Institute,* ed. Phillip Damon (New York: Columbia University Press, 1967); R. C. Bald, *John Donne: A Life* (Oxford: Clarendon Press, 1970), pp. 8-9. Wellek and Warren's *Theory of Literature,* 3d ed. (New York: Harcourt, Brace, and World, 1963) contains other bibliographical references.

58. Among the works of some importance to this study, the following can be placed with reasonable certainty at points within the large periods into which Marvell's biography divides itself: "Ad Regem Carolum Parodia," "To His Noble Friend Mr. Richard Lovelace, upon his Poems," "Upon the Death of Lord Hastings," "An Horatian Ode upon Cromwell's Return from Ireland," "Tom May's Death," *Upon Appleton House, The First Anniversary of the Government under O. C., On the Victory obtained by Blake over the Spaniards, A Poem upon the Death of O. C.,* "On Mr. Milton's Paradise lost," most of the satires, and (with the exception of a few letters) all the prose. For the issues involved in the dating of poems and letters, see the notes to the third edition.

Joseph Summers, in *The Heirs of Donne and Jonson* (New York and London: Oxford University Press, 1970), pp. 160-62, suggests that our relative certainty about some dates may be unfounded—without, however, claiming too much for his hypothesis.

59. *My Life and Hard Times,* chapter 8. See Helen Gardner, *The Business of Criticism* (Oxford: Clarendon Press, 1956), p. 122.

Chapter 2

1. *Correspondence* with Dixon, p. 23.

2. And although they differ greatly in some respects, the nuns in Marvell's *Upon Appleton House* and the sister who takes the veil in Hopkins's "Heaven-Haven" have religious impulses in common—as I hope will be made clear in my discussion of Marvell's poem.

3. *The Sermons and Devotional Writings of Gerard Manley Hopkins,* ed. Christopher Devlin, S.J. (London: Oxford University Press, 1959), p. 90.

4. *P and L,* 2:312.

5. Pp. 168–69. I shall take my cue from Grosart and refer to this work as the *Defence of John Howe*.

6. The letter to Sir John Trott, written in 1667, is the earliest document. Marvell was then forty-six. "On . . . Paradise lost" was published over Marvell's name in the second edition of Milton's poem (1674). The *Defence of John Howe* was published anonymously in 1678, the year of Marvell's death.

7. *Defence of John Howe*, p. 229.

8. This is a public statement, published in 1649.

9. Ruth Wallerstein does suggest that in "The Death of Lord Hastings," the "Christian view does not triumph in Christian acceptance" (*Studies in Seventeenth-Century Poetic* [Madison: University of Wisconsin Press, 1950], p. 123).

10. *Defence of John Howe*, p. 170.

11. Some might say that reason has less influence over these convictions than does personal psychology.

12. The categories of the "aesthetic," the "ethical," and the "religious" will remind one of Kierkegaard's "Three Stages on Life's Way," along which one finds "either/or" and "both/and" philosophies. The similarities are obvious, but the dissimilarities, it will be found, are more so. See also Matthew Arnold's "Hebraism and Hellenism." The "aesthetic" and "ethical" strains in Christian theodicy are discussed by John Hick in *Evil and the God of Love* (London: Macmillan, 1966), but Hick does not define the terms and, considering them adequate for his purposes, does not proceed beyond them.

13. 986f–987b.

14. See *Nic. Eth.*, 1151a33–1152b6 and 1128b34–35; Plutarch, *On Moral Virtue*, 445b and 446d.

15. 4.17.

16. See Plato, *Lysis*, 216; *Philebus*, 64e, 66a; Aristotle, *Metaphysics*, 1078a31–1078b6. Here Aristotle also states that goodness is "distinct from" beauty, but his position on the issue is far from consistent. See F. C. Copleston, S.J., *A History of Philosophy*, 9 vols. (1946–   ; rpt. New York: Image Books, 1962), 1.2.100; also the article *"kalos"* by Walter Grundmann in Gerhard Kittel's *Theological Dictionary of the New Testament*, 10 vols., trans. G. W. Bromiley (Grand Rapids: William B. Eerdmans, 1964–76). On a similar inconsistency in Plato, see Copleston, 1.1.283.

17. See *Eud. Eth.*, 1249a9–10: "What is fitting is beautiful"(*to prepon kalon*). Also, the inconclusive discussion of *to prepon* and *to kalon* in the (probably) pseudo-Platonic *Greater Hippias*, 294d–e. Aristotle's ethical theory is often called "aesthetic" because it is widely held that "decorousness" or "fitness" is the closest he gets to "obligation." But see René-A. Gauthier, *La Morale d'Aristote* (Paris: Presses Universitaires de France, 1958), pp. 86–91.

18. *Nic. Eth.*, 1177a25–27; Plutarch, *On Common Conceptions against the Stoics*, 1071b–c. And see Cicero, *On the Chief Good and Evil (De Finibus)*, 4.46:

> [A] point to which I take great exception is that, when you have proved, as you think, that Moral Worth alone is good, you then turn round and say that of course there must be advantages adapted to our nature set before us as a starting point, in exercising choice among which advantages virtue may be able to come into existence. Now it was a mistake to make virtue consist in an act of choice, for this implies

that the very thing that is the ultimate Good itself seeks to get something else.

19. *ST*, 1, q. 39, a. 8.

20. *Philebus*, 66b. Note that "complete" means brought to an "end" (*telos*), which is also "purpose." *Hikanon* means both "sufficient" and "befitting."

21. *Physics*, 246a10-246b10. In the *Nicomachean Ethics*, having defined happiness as "activity in accordance with virtue" and having posited that such activity is the end of life, Aristotle affirms that "nothing can belong to [ideal?] happiness that is incomplete [*ateles*]" (1177b25-26). See also Plutarch, *On Common Conceptions*, 1070b.

22. *Nic. Eth.*, 1128b34-35.

23. Ibid., 1178b8-18. (I have altered Ross's translation slightly.) See also 1154b28-32: "Change in all things is sweet, as the poet says [Euripides, *Orestes*, 234], owing to some badness in us; . . . just as a changeable man is bad, so also is a nature that needs change; for it is not simple [*haple*, single, unmixed] nor good [*epieikes*]."

24. *Philebus*, 59c.

25. *Nic. Eth.*, 1178a20-23. And see Plutarch, *On Tranquility of Mind*, 473-74, where "mixed" good is accepted (as a practical expedient) for what it is worth.

26. *Nic. Eth.*, 1178a9.

27. Ibid., 1177a26-28.

28. For reasons which are given in *Nic. Eth.*, 1177a12-1177b29.

29. Ibid., 1177b29-36. Aristotle does argue (against Plato) that the *idea* of the good is not unitary (*Nic. Eth.*, 1096a11ff.). And since, he claims, we cannot speak univocally of "good" for God and "good" for man (*Eud. Eth.*, 1244b6-23 and 1245b13ff.; *Magna Moralia*, 1212b34-1213a27), a mortal cannot therefore undertake to *imitate* all of God's perfections. Aristotle quotes with approval, however, a line from an unknown sage: "Goodness [in this case, moral goodness] is simple, badness manifold" (*esthloi . . . haplōs, pantodapōs de kakoi* [*Nic. Eth.*, 1106b35]). The good itself has the *property* of wholeness. And his exhortation to his audience that they strive to imitate the divine virtue of contemplation indicates that he did not believe that humanity and divinity were absolutely heterogeneous and incommensurable. At the beginning of the *Nicomachean Ethics*, he is all caution and practicality: the Platonic, absolute good "clearly will not be practicable or attainable by man, but the good which we are now seeking is a good within human reach" (1096b34-36). But by the end of the work, he is calling the "mixed" virtues "secondary" and urging men to strive for the good that is divine.

30. *Phaedrus*, 279b.

31. Ibid., 246a-b. In the *Philebus*, Socrates speaks at some length of the necessity, even the desirability of the "mixed" life for man (61b). But since he equivocates in his use of the term (see Jowett's commentary), the passage need not be discussed here.

32. *Phaedo*, 60c.

33. *Theaetetus*, 176a-b. In the *Symposium* (210-12), Diotima describes the "flight" as a gradual one, proceeding step by step from the appreciation of individual, corporeal beauties to the contemplation of "the very essence of beauty," beauty "entire, pure, and unalloyed" (*eilikrines, katharon, amikton*). This is, of course, one of the seed ideas of Renaissance Neoplatonism.

34. *Nic. Eth.*, 1156b23 and 1099a6.

35. *Sovran Maxims*, 140.

36. See also *Eud. Eth.*, 1249a1-15.

37. Paul Ricoeur, *The Symbolism of Evil*, trans. Emerson Buchanan (Boston: Beacon Press, 1967), p. 323. Ricoeur here summarizes the thesis of Max Scheler's "*Ueber das Tragische.*"

38. In contrast, see Herbert Weisinger's definition of tragedy in *Tragedy and the Paradox of the Fortunate Fall* (London: Routledge & Kegan Paul, 1953).

39. See, for example, Cicero, *On the Nature of the Gods*, 1.19.51 and Plutarch, *On Common Conceptions*, 1065b. In the passage cited, Plutarch argues against the doctrine of the Stoics that evil is necessary for the realization of the good.

40. Hesiod, *Works and Days*, 42-49.

41. *Poetics*, 1452b.

42. See Copleston, 1.2.57-59.

43. Lucretius, *On the Nature of Things*, 5.198-99 and 2.646-51.

44. *On Common Conceptions*, 1067a; and see note 39, above. Aristotle in the *Magna Moralia* (1203b13-26) states that the temperate man, who is free from corrupt or irrational desires, can yet be considered self-controlled on the theory that if he did have such desires he would control them. Aquinas had to deal with the problem in regard to the unfallen Adam and Eve, who could not have possessed the virtues which implied "imperfection" (*ST*, 1, q. 95, a. 3), and in regard to the Divine Goodness, which "contains in its way all virtues" (*SCG*, 1.92) but cannot properly speaking be called "chaste," "repentant," etc.

45. Plato, *Protagoras*, 345bff., especially 352c; Aristotle, *Nic. Eth.*, 1146b8ff. See Copleston, *History of Philosophy*, 1.2.80. Both Plato and Aristotle affirm man's freedom and moral responsibility, but their notion of freedom allows room for knowledge to be determinative. See below, n. 124.

46. *On the Nature of the Gods*, 3.31.76, 78.

47. Plato, *Republic*, 379d-380c.

48. Cicero, *On the Nature of the Gods*, 3.32.79ff.

49. "The Problem of Job," in *Studies in Good and Evil* (New York: D. Appleton, 1898), pp. 8-9.

50. Quoted by Lactantius, *On the Wrath of God*, 13. See also Sextus Empiricus, *Outlines of Pyrrhonism*, 3.9. We shall consider later a way out of the dilemma that is *inconsistent* with these aesthetic principles: the "principle of plenitude."

51. On the limited powers of the God of Plato and Plutarch, see W. C. Greene, *Moira: Fate, Good and Evil in Greek Thought* (Cambridge: Harvard University Press, 1948), p. 297ff., 369.

The denial of God's omnipotence has seemed to many an acceptable way out of the problems of theodicy. It is the Manichaean solution. See also David Hume, *Dialogues Concerning Natural Religion*, ed. Norman Kemp Smith (2d ed., 1947; rpt. Indianapolis: Bobbs-Merrill, n.d.), 11.203; J. S. Mill, "Nature," ed. George Nakhnikian (Indianapolis: Bobbs-Merrill, 1958), pp. 27-29.

52. Plato, *Timaeus* (and Greene's commentary in *Moira*, pp. 303-5); Plutarch, *Isis and Osiris*, 369a-e. (I have changed the translation slightly.)

53. See above, n. 33.

54. See Røstvig, *The Happy Man*, vol. 1.

55. See, for example, Friedman, *Marvell's Pastoral Art*, pp. 93-100; Patrick Cullen, *Spenser, Marvell, and Renaissance Pastoral* (Cambridge: Harvard University

Press, 1970); and two essays by Paul Alpers: his Introduction to *The Singer of the Eclogues: A Study of Virgilian Pastoral* (Berkeley, Los Angeles, and London: University of California Press, 1979) and "*Lycidas* and Modern Criticism," *ELH* 49 (1982): 468–96.

56. "The Oaten Flute," *Harvard Library Bulletin* 11 (1957): 147.

57. *As You Like It*, 3.2.13ff.

58. Ibid., 2.1.5. The dictum of Duke Senior, however, "Sweet are the uses of adversity" (2.1.12), is not on the face of it a categorical one.

59. Ibid., 2.1.16–18.

60. The term—originated, it seems, by Leibniz—can cause confusion. If evil is the absence of *due* perfection, finite beings, who in their finiteness lack perfections not really due them, do not experience an "evil" deficiency.

61. *Epistles*, 90.44–46. Temptation is, of course, something relative. The same object may attract one person, repel another, leave another indifferent. Aristotle said that the temperate man needs the means or opportunity (*exousias*) for indulgence, "otherwise how can he or the possessor of any other virtue show that he is virtuous?" (*Nic. Eth.*, 1178a29–34.) But, by Aristotelian definition, the temperate man's opportunity for vice is not at all a temptation, for the vice is not at all attractive to him.

62. See above, n. 18.

63. See, for example, Cicero, *On the Chief Good and Evil*, 3.36; Diogenes Laertius, *Lives of the Eminent Philosophers*, 7.101. The position taken by Kant, that the only "good without qualification" is a "good will," is not as simple as this Stoic doctrine. See the *Groundwork of the Metaphysic of Morals*, trans. H. J. Paton (New York: Harper & Row, 1964), p. 61.

64. Some would say that without such disjunctions, there is no choice at all, no freedom. Kant held that without a disjunction between the good and the pleasurable there is no "duty." (Hence God does not perform his duty: his will is not "good" but "holy.") Difficulty does not *make* an action good, but is the sign that one acts purely out of a sense of duty rather than for one's self-interest. (See the *Groundwork*, pp. 18–19, 64–65, 81, 107.)

65. That is, the Stoics considered trial an indispensable condition of virtue, which is in their most common definition activity in accordance with nature, or activity in accordance with reason. (See Diogenes Laertius, *Lives*, 7.86–87.)

66. Seneca, *On Providence*, 4.4–5. Contrast Castiglione, *The Courtier*, 4.17.

67. Diogenes Laertius, *Lives*, 7.102. Not all Stoics were so ready to dismiss as indifferent everything but virtue. Some of them subdivided "things indifferent" (*ta adiaphora*) into "things preferred" (*ta proegmena*) and "things rejected" (*ta apoproegmena*) (ibid., 105).

68. Seneca, *On Providence*, 1.i.

69. See Cicero, *Tusculan Disputations*, 3.16.34.

70. Seneca, *On Providence* 4.6.

71. The Stoics in their pantheism (see Diogenes Laertius, *Lives*, 7.137–39, 148) were the ultimate monists.

72. See Cicero, *On the Chief Good and Evil*, 2.73; Seneca, *On the Happy Life*, 9.4; *On Mercy*, 1.i; *Epistles*, 81.20 and 87.24–25; Marcus Aurelius, *Meditations*, 9.1, 42.

73. *On Providence*, 6.6. This very principle could be used by skeptics to try to undermine God's defense. See, for example, Sextus Empiricus, *Against the Physicists*, 1.152ff. (*Adversus Mathematicos*, 9.152ff.): "If the Divine exists . . . it possesses

all the virtues. But it does not possess all the virtues unless it possesses both continence and fortitude, and it does not possess these virtues unless there are certain things which are hard for God to abstain from and hard to endure . . . , which is an absurd thing to say about God." (See n. 44, above.)

74. Cicero, *On Duties,* 1.6.19.

75. See Seneca, *On Providence,* 4.4–5; see above, p. 00.

76. "The Stoics say that the wise man will take part in politics . . . since thus he will restrain vice and promote virtue" (Diogenes Laertius, *Lives,* 7.121).

77. The "Hymn to Zeus," 14.

78. Lucan, *Pharsalia,* 9.404.

79. *Nic. Eth.,* 1105a8; and see above, n. 16.

80. See Seneca, *On Leisure,* 3.2–5; Plutarch, *On the Contradictions of the Stoics,* 1033f ff.

81. See Arthur O. Lovejoy, *The Great Chain of Being* (Cambridge: Harvard University Press, 1936), *passim.*

82. *Timaeus,* 29e–30a, 30d.

83. See Lovejoy, *Chain of Being,* p. 25.

84. See Seneca, *On the Happy Life,* 9.4; Plutarch, *On Common Conceptions,* 1065d.

85. Diogenes Laertius, *Lives,* 7.100.

86. In addition to the chapters on Romanticism in *The Great Chain of Being,* see M. H. Abrams, *Natural Supernaturalism* (New York: Norton, 1971), chapters 3 and 4 especially.

87. It is difficult to determine just what is the opposite of the paradoxical. Lionel Trilling has spoken of the opposition between "categorical" and "dialecti-cal" modes of thought (*Sincerity and Authenticity,* p. 76); and, given my sense that the paradoxist is inclined to transcend high boundaries (often by means of "dialecti-cal" thought), while his opposite is inclined to keep them fast and insurmountable, I think that "categorical" well expresses a contrast with "paradoxical."

88. Thus both kinds of value rely on conjunction. But paradoxical values (and this is of course the paradox) involve conjunctions of "goods" that have been created through disjunctions.

89. *The Ages of the World* (1811), trans. F. de Wolfe Bolman, Jr. See Abrams, *Natural Supernaturalism,* p. 173.

90. See Lovejoy, *Chain of Being,* pp. 302–3; Abrams, *Natural Supernaturalism,* pp. 185–86.

91. A similar point can be made about dissonance in an analogy with music. The opposite of harmony would be inept singing, not the dissonance which "disappears" in *concordia discors.*

92. "Crazy Jane Talks with the Bishop"; *Faust,* 1.1766–74, 1780–84 (trans. C. F. MacIntyre [New York: New Directions, 1949]); Matt. 6:22.

93. This point is forcefully made by Samuel Johnson in his review (1753) of Soame Jenyns's "Free Enquiry into the Origin of Evil." The review is reproduced in Richard B. Schwartz, *Samuel Johnson and the Problem of Evil* (Madison: University of Wisconsin Press, 1975), pp. 98–112.

94. "Dilate" is the word used by Spenser in his "Cantos of Mutabilitie" to describe the change that is compatible with the "stedfastnes" without which this universe would be "vaine." (*Fairie Queene,* 7.7.514, 517; 8.7.)

95. See Aristotle, *Nic. Eth.,* 1154b26–27: "There is not only an activity of

motion, but also an activity of immobility, and there is essentially a truer pleasure in rest than in motion."

96. See Plutarch, *On Common Conceptions,* 1065e–f.

97. "A Song in Storm."

98. Matt. 10:34; John 14:27; Matt. 11:12.

99. The neo-Stoics of the Renaissance recognized this problem. See Justus Lipsius, *Of Constancie:* Man's will is free, yet "God is within us the authour of every motion" (1.20). See the translation of Sir John Stradling (1594), ed. Rudolf Kirk (New Brunswick, N.J.: Rutgers University Press, 1939), pp. 120–23.

100. In the following survey of Christian approaches to the problem of evil, I am concerned primarily with the state of theodicy up to Marvell's day. Occasional references to post-Renaissance theodicies are meant to throw light backward, and should not be judged as an attempt to push this analysis towards a comprehensive commentary on the state of the question.

101. See N. P. Williams, *The Ideas of the Fall and of Original Sin* (London: Longmans, Green and Co., 1927), chapters 1–3; J. Martin Evans, *Paradise Lost and the Genesis Tradition* (Oxford: Clarendon Press, 1968), chapters 1–2.

102. See Williams, *Ideas of the Fall,* pp. 43–44.

103. *Against the Galileans,* 93e.

104. *On the Merits and Forgiveness of Sins,* 2.35. See Evans, *Genesis Tradition,* p. 96. This is Milton's view. See *PL,* 4.428; 9.1070–72.

105. Rom. 5:12.

106. *Imperfectus liber,* 1.3: "Everything which is called evil is either sin or punishment for sin."

107. Ezek. 18:2.

108. There is, of course, no *single* Christian doctrine. I try to limit my discussion to tenets which the major Christian faiths have in some measure shared, and when I cannot, I try to point out the significance of the differences.

109. To argue that the goodness of God and the goodness of man are only analogically comparable is to ignore the fact that theodicy is only undertaken in the first place on the assumption that divine and human "goodness" are in some respect univocal.

110. Roman Catholic doctrine, although itself divided on the theology of grace between Thomism and Molinism, gives man a share in "meritorious acts"; but the share is not as great as that desired by the Stoic, who would consider the trial, therefore the virtue, vitiated by the kind of divine interference described by Aquinas: "God does not justify us without ourselves, because whilst we are being justified we consent to God's justice by a movement of our free choice. Nevertheless this movement is not the cause of grace, but the effect; hence the whole operation pertains to grace" (*ST,* 1-2, q. 111, a. 2). Both Thomists and Molinists agree that God's grace works infallibly. Thomists believe this is so because grace is *intrinsically* efficacious, in which case, it is difficult to see where a moral agent undergoes any real "trial" at all. Molinists hold that grace is *extrinsically* efficacious, operating infallibly because God gives it to those whom he foresees will accept it. (See *The Catholic Encyclopedia* [New York: R. Appleton, 1909] and *The New Catholic Encyclopedia* [New York: McGraw-Hill, 1967], articles on "Grace" and "Molinism.") This theory allows for more of a trial, as does Arminianism, the Reformation theology condemned as heterodox by the Protestant Synod of Dort (1619) but followed in some respects by Milton. Arminianism

postulated that "sufficient grace" (necessary to salvation) was offered by God to all souls yet did not work infallibly and could be freely rejected. (See Dennis Danielson, *Milton's Good God: A Study in Literary Theodicy* [Cambridge and New York: Cambridge University Press, 1982], pp. 66–75.) Even with the libertarian theologies, however, problems remain. Is one who accepts grace with difficulty more virtuous than one who accepts it with ease? (In *ST*, 1, q. 95, a. 4, Aquinas wrestles with the problem of "whether the actions of the first man were less meritorious than ours" because our good works are more difficult to perform.) Who is the source of the strength or generosity by which one accepts grace, God or man? And why are some men not strong or generous enough? If God is able to foresee free actions (the Socinians, for example, denied that he could [see Danielson, p. 156]), why did he not create only those men who, he foresaw, would cooperate with grace and be saved?

111. The blessed cannot sin because "it is impossible that whoever sees [God] in His essence should not love Him" (*ST*, 1, q. 60, a. 5).

112. Augustine, *On Rebuke and Grace* (*De Correptione et Gratia*), 33; *SCG*, 3.71.

113. *SCG*, 3.34, 17, 37. See Aristotle, *Nic. Eth.*, 1094a ff., especially 1095b32: "Even virtue proves on examination to be too incomplete [*atelestera*] to be the End."

114. *Institutes of the Christian Regligion*, 1.15.8. See also 3.24.13 and Luther's *The Bondage of the Will*, trans. J. I. Packer and O. R. Johnston (Westwood, N.J.: Revell Press, 1957), pp. 204, 208.

115. Danielson's discussion of Milton's free-will theodicy is detailed and systematic. See *Milton's Good God*, especially pp. 58–163.

116. A contemporary theologian like John Hick (*God of Love*), who does not believe in the historical fact of the fall, would not claim that all evil results from sin, but would maintain that all evil is made possible by conditions that are necessary for "soul-making."

117. See Danielson, p. 134. The discussion (pp. 132–54) of "compatibilist" and "incompatibilist" views of freedom and necessity is relevant here. Danielson finds the definition of freedom to be a significant part of God's defense, not a challenge to Providence.

118. See below, n. 124.

119. Augustine, *On Rebuke and Grace*, 33. See also Aquinas, *ST*, 1, q. 62, a. 8: "There is greater liberty of will in the [beatified] angels, who cannot sin, than there is in ourselves, who can sin."

120. The assertion of apologists like Milton that the continuum-model applies to God, the balance-model to man *in via* (see Danielson, p. 150), seems gratuitous, except insofar as it is necessary to the free-will defense. The validity of this double standard should be proved antecedent to theodicy. Aquinas (see nn. 119, above, and 124, below) speaks of freedom according to both models, but he does not in his theodicy rely ultimately on the free-will defense.

121. See Williams, *Ideas of the Fall*, especially p. 360ff.; Evans, *Genesis Tradition*, especially pp. 86–99; Hick, *God of Love*, *passim*.

122. See Augustine, *City of God*, 14.10.

123. Ibid., 12.7; *On Free Will*, 3.18.49.

124. See Augustine, *City of God*, 14.10.

Aquinas's "intellectualism" turns the problem of the fall into the most vexed of questions. In his view, the will of man is not free in its choice of an ultimate end (which is happiness, or God, "in whom alone true happiness consists") but only in its choice of means to the end (*ST,* 1, q. 82, a. 2). Furthermore, the will can tend to nothing except under the aspect of good (ibid.). Thus man chooses even evil *sub ratione boni,* because it *seems* good. (It is often human "Concupiscence" or passion that "deceives"; but for Adam and Eve before the fall concupiscence was no problem.) In an important sense, then, sin is or results from a mistake (the Greek *hamartia,* used in the New Testament to mean "sin," is a "missing of the mark")—an error rendered possible because, short of the Beatific Vision which brings "certitude" to the human intellect, man cannot see the "necessary connection" that some things have with (as necessary means to) his final end. Hence "the will does not desire of necessity whatever it desires," and is capable of choosing wrongly. But is that "freedom" made possible by *ignorance* such a valuable gift? And if will must follow intellect (except in the case of incommensurables, where the intellect cannot judge one thing better than another), what moral opprobrium can attach to an errant choice? Is it ultimately man's responsibility that he lacks the knowledge that would preclude sin? Should he be punished because he cannot see "necessary connections"?

The theory, to be advanced by William James (*Principles of Psychology,* chapters 11 and 26), that the human will has the ability to give or refuse *attention* to knowledge which is otherwise determinative would make man responsible for the knowledge which he did or did not *use.* Such a notion, however, is difficult to square with Aquinas's doctrine concerning the Beatific Vision, for this vision provides knowledge which *must* be used by the will. (Although, see *ST,* 1-2, q. 10, a. 2.) Besides, James's theory does not deal definitively with the question. Why does one give or refuse attention? For a reason? If so, we are back to the problem of determinative knowledge.

It should be said that none of the theologies called "maximal" by intellectual historians ascribes to Adam and Eve truly maximal knowledge, the Beatific Vision. Nevertheless, it is legitimate to wonder why Adam and Eve's very great knowledge—they were "unable to be deceived" (*ST,* 1, q. 94, a. 4)—combined with their other astonishing gifts—they possessed "all the virtues" and were created with their "reason subject to God, the lower powers to reason and the body to the soul" (*ST,* 1, q. 95, a. 1 and 3)—did not prevent their choice of an irrational, inherently unattractive evil.

125. See Williams, *Ideas of the Fall,* especially pp. 189-200; Evans, *Genesis Tradition,* especially pp. 78-86; Hick, *God of Love,* especially p. 262ff.

126. Irenaeus, *The Demonstration of the Apostolic Preaching,* 12; see Evans, *Genesis Tradition,* p. 78.

127. From one point of view, the "fall" was upward. Man sinned in growing up too quickly. See Williams, p. 195.

128. "O truly necessary sin of Adam, which was annulled by the death of Christ! O fortunate fault, which merited so great a redeemer as this." The formulation is from the *Exultet* of the Roman Catholic Church's Easter Liturgy.

129. Duns Scotus, however, believed that the Incarnation came about as a result of a free and loving choice of God, and was not demanded as the price of sin. See *Opus Oxoniense,* 3.20.1.

130. *Treatise on the Love of God* (1616), 2.5. See Arthur Lovejoy, "Milton and the Paradox of the Fortunate Fall," in *Essays in the History of Ideas* (Baltimore: Johns Hopkins University Press, 1948), p. 294.

131. *Beames of Divine Light* (1639), 1.12. See C. A. Patrides, "Adam's 'Happy Fault' and XVIIth-century Apologetics," *Franciscan Studies* 23 (1963): 241. See also Lipsius, *Of Constancie*, 2.7.

132. Joshua Sylvester, *Bartas his Devine Weekes and Workes* (1605), 1st Day, 2nd Week, II, p. 318.

133. "God has wondrously established the dignity of human nature and even more wondrously has renewed it." From the Offertory of the Roman liturgy. For some references to this theme, see Patrides, "Adam's 'Happy Fault.'" One might also consider in this connection the seventeenth-century debate between Godfrey Goodman and John Hakewill on whether God is more glorified by the decay of the world or by its preservation. See Victor Harris, *All Coherence Gone* (Chicago: University of Chicago Press, 1949).

134. Rom. 11:32. Compare John 9:23: "And Jesus' disciples asked him, saying, Master, who did sin, this man or his parents, that he was born blind? Jesus answered, Neither hath this man sinned, nor his parents: but that the works of God should be made manifest in him." But see below, n. 140.

135. *King Lear*, 4.6.73-74; the "Chorus Sacerdotum" in Fulke Greville's *Mustapha* (1609).

136. *Commentary on Genesis*, 3.1; see also *Institutes*, 3.23.8.

137. A theodicy cannot make use here of the casuist's "principle of double effect" (see Aquinas, *ST*, 2-2, q. 64, a. 7, and *The New Catholic Encyclopedia*, s.v. "Double Effect, Principle of"). According to this principle, one may legitimately perform an action from which both good and bad effects will follow, if the act itself is morally good or indifferent; and if the agent merely permits, does not positively will the bad effect; and if the good effect is brought about by the action, not by the bad effect; and if the good effect is of significant value in itself. Aside from the question whether the permission of a preventable sin is evil in itself, as the *felix culpa* has been interpreted, the good effect, God's greater glory, is not produced directly by God's permission of the fall, but, in violation of the principle, through the bad effect itself, man's sin.

138. Perhaps the solution to this problem lies in positing that God, who, in the terms of the Scholastics, is "complete act," does not really change in himself; but as his creatures change, they perceive and experience his goodness according to their changed conditions—just as men see the same light differently as it shines on different materials. (See Henry More, *Divine Dialogues* [1668], 2, 1713 ed., p. 154.) But then it hardly seems sensible to call the fall fortunate for "increasing" God's glory.

139. *PL*, 12.477-78.

140. A problem that St. Paul had to contend with. See Rom. 5:20-6:1.

141. *PL*, 5.493-503. Milton actually combines maximal and minimal theologies. See Evans, *Genesis Tradition*, pp. 85-94.

142. *PL*, 11.88-89.

143. Ibid., 12.469-78. For essays dealing with the *felix culpa* in *Paradise Lost*, see Arthur E. Barker, *Milton: Modern Essays in Criticism* (London: Oxford University Press, 1965), pp. 336-67; and Danielson, *Milton's Good God*, pp. 202-27.

144. *Against Heresies*, 3.20.2; see Hick, *God of Love*, pp. 218-19.

145. 1 Tim. 2:4.

146. *Contra Celsum*, 3.38. For the issue in Marvell's day, see Ralph Cud-

worth's *The True Intellectual System of the Universe* (1678), 4 vols. (London: J. F. Dove, 1820), 4:182.

147. Expressed so powerfully (though on different premises from those of this discussion) in Book Five of *The Brothers Karamazov*.

148. *Contra Celsum*, 6.55. The idea must have upset Origen a great deal, for he taught the doctrine of universal salvation. Note that "orderly arrangement" introduces the aesthetic theme.

149. For a survey of Augustine's theodicy, especially in its "aesthetic" aspects, see Hick, pp. 43–95; also Régis Jolivet, *Le Problème du mal d'après St. Augustin*, 2d ed. (Paris: G. Beauchesne et fils, 1936).

150. See *City of God*, 11.22.

151. *On Free Will*, 3.9.26.

152. *ST*, 1, q. 48, a. 2. It is clear that the "perfection" of which Aquinas speaks is aesthetic. "The chief beauty would be taken away from things if the order resulting from distinction and disparity were abolished" (*SCG*, 3.71).

153. *City of God*, 11.23; *On Free Will*, 3.25.44.

154. Exod. 15:11; Heb. 1:9; Gal. 2:20; 1 Tim. 2:4; Job 34:19.

155. The problem of infinity, for example. Hick argues, as did Dr. Johnson before him (see above, n. 93): "Whilst [the principle] might explain why the world contains a variety of kinds, it cannot, without a modification that would disqualify it for theistic use, explain why it contains *only* the particular selection of kinds that it in fact contains out of the infinite realm of the possible." Hick also objects to the formula, What can fail sometimes will. See *God of Love*, pp. 85, 102–103.

156. See Lovejoy, *Chain of Being*, chapter 3.

157. Aquinas, *SCG*, 3.71.

158. *An Explanation of the Grand Mystery of Godliness* (1660), 6.11.

159. See n. 137, above.

160. Rev. 1:16.

161. Augustine, *City of God*, 14.28. God renders the competition more violent by implanting in man what in rabbinical doctrine was called the *yezer-ha-ra* ("evil imagination"): an impulse or, alternatively, a disposition toward sin which man had to control in order to be virtuous. The rabbis believed the *yezer* to be the cause of Adam's fall; St. Paul taught that it was the effect—the rabbinical doctrine being, therefore, more strictly paradoxical. See Williams, *Ideas of the Fall*, p. 150ff.

162. The doctrine of election has proved a scandal to many. See, for example, Julian the Apostate's terse challenge (*Against the Galileans*, 100c) or J. S. Mill's eloquent complaint in "Utility of Religion," ed. George Nakhnikian (Indianapolis: Bobbs-Merrill, 1958), p. 75.

163. John 12:24.

164. There is the heroism of Christ to be taken into account. But it is more than perilous to assert that Adam's sin and consequent redemption were essential to the perfection of God or the God-Man.

165. Augustine, *Sermones*, 297.1.

166. *Samson Agonistes*, 293–305.

167. Matt. 5:48.

168. Citations will be made from the third edition, 4 vols. (Rotterdam, 1720), and from an English translation of the second edition, *The Dictionary Historical and*

Critical of Mr. Peter Bayle, 5 vols. (London, 1734-38). Bayle's thoughts on the problem of evil are widely and profusely scattered throughout the *Dictionary*. Some of the more important articles are: "Manicheans," "Marcionites," "Origen," "Paulicians," "Prudentius," "Pyrrho," "Rufinus," "Xenophenes."

169. "Paulicians," remark E.

170. Ibid., E and G.

171. "Pyrrho," B.

172. "Paulicians," E.

173. Ibid., F.

174. "Manicheans," D; "Paulicians," F.

175. "Marcionites," F.

176. See his *Réponse aux questions d'un provincial*, in *Oeuvres diverses*, reproduced in 4 vols. (Hildesheim: Georg Olms, 1966), 3 (1727): 680ff., 662, 666.

177. "Marcionites," F; "Paulicians," E.

178. "Paulicians," M.

179. Ibid.; and see "Marcionites," G. Not "*all*" divines would concur.

180. "Manicheans," D; "Paulicians," F.

181. "Paulicians," E, at n. 21.

182. *Dictionary*, "Explanation III, 'Concerning the Sceptics,'" iv.

Many of Bayle's readers have been so impressed by the energy which poured into his skepticism that they have doubted the sincerity of his fideistic professions of loyalty to the Gospel. For a modern assessment of the biographical evidence on the subject of Bayle's religious views, see Elizabeth Labrousse, *Pierre Bayle*, 2 vols. (The Hague: Nijhoff, 1963-64).

One does not always find Bayle consistent on the questions of fideism. He can proclaim, for example, that the storm of reason is rightly avoided for the peaceful haven of faith ("Explanation III," ii) and at the same time declare that it is the violence done to reason that enhances faith:

> The merit of faith is enlarged in proportion as revealed truth, which is the object of it, exceeds all the powers of our understanding; for the more the incomprehensibility of this object increases by the numerous maxims of the natural light which oppose it, the more we must sacrifice to God's authority a stronger repugnance of reason, and consequently we show ourselves more obedient to God, and give a greater proof of our respect, than if a thing was moderately difficult to believe. [Ibid., v.]

183. William Empson claims that Marvell in fact secretly married his housekeeper, Mary Palmer (see "Natural Magic and Populism in Marvell's Poetry," in R. L. Brett, ed., *Andrew Marvell: Essays on the Tercentenary of his Death* [Oxford: Oxford University Press, 1979], pp. 49-50). I have not seen the evidence which Empson has promised to publish.

184. I refer later in this study to various statements on the problem of evil with which Marvell was familiar. The search for such statements is not absolutely crucial, however, for Christian theodicy produced no original arguments of major significance between Augustine's day and Marvell's. (See, for example, Friedrich Billicsich, *Das Problem des Uebels in der Philosophie des Abendlandes*, 3 vols. [Wien: A. Sexl, 1936-59]; A. D. Sertillanges, *Le Problème du mal*, 2 vols. [Paris: Aubier, 1948-51]; Hick, *God of Love*.) A seventeenth-century Christian had clearly defined

and relatively uniform doctrines by which to judge his experience, by which to intensify or assuage his apprehensions about the workings of Providence. Even the diverse and complicated interpretations of the story of the fall (see Evans, *Genesis Tradition*) were, for the most part, attempts to accommodate the Biblical narrative to traditional theologies.

Chapter 3

1. "Senec. Traged. ex Thyeste Chor. 2." The original is from lines 391–403:

Stet quicumque volet potens
aulae culmine lubrico;
me dulcis saturet quies;
obscuro positus loco
leni perfruar otio,
nullis nota Quiritibus
aetas per tacitum fluat.
sic cum transierint mei
nullo cum strepitu dies,
plebeius moriar senex.
illi mors gravis incubat
qui, notus nimis omnibus,
ignotus moritur sibi.

2. Poem CCXL in *The Collected Poems of Sir Thomas Wyatt,* ed. Kenneth Muir and Patricia Thompson (Liverpool: Liverpool University Press, 1969).

3. "Meditation 13" in *Devotions upon Emergent Occasions,* ed. Anthony Raspa (Montreal and London: McGill-Queen's University Press, 1975), p. 69. See also *The Second Anniversarie,* 241ff., where Donne admires the "Electrum" (alloy of gold and silver) formed of Elizabeth Drury's noble body and soul. Not all alloys are admirable, of course. See *The First Anniversarie,* 178, 345.

4. Verse letter "To Sir Henry Goodyere," 29–32, in W. Milgate, ed., *The Satires, Epigrams, and Verse Letters* (Oxford: Clarendon Press, 1967). My quotations from Donne's poetry are taken from this edition, from Milgate's edition of *The Epithalamions, Anniversaries, and Epicedes* (Oxford, 1978), and from Helen Gardner's editions: *The Divine Poems* (Oxford, 1952) and *The Elegies and the Songs and Sonnets* (Oxford, 1965). I retain the traditional numbering of the "Holy Sonnets".

5. Letter "To Sir Henry Goodyere," 1609. In *John Donne: Selected Prose,* ed. Helen Gardner and Timothy Healy (Oxford: Clarendon Press, 1967), p. 137.

6. *A Litanie,* 208–209, 136–44.

7. *LXXX Sermons,* xiii; *Fifty Sermons,* xvii; ibid. Quoted from *The Sermons of John Donne,* 10 vols., ed. E. M. Simpson and G. R. Potter (Berkeley and Los Angeles: University of California Press, 1953–62), 9:217; 10:185–86.

8. See *LXXX Sermons,* xxii; Simpson and Potter, 7:373–74.

9. See "A Hymne to God my God, in my sicknesse," 30.

10. See above, p. 35. I quote Milton's prose from the Yale *Complete Prose Works,* ed. Don M. Wolfe et al. (New Haven, 1953–), and where noted from the Columbia *Works,* ed. Frank Allen Patterson (New York, 1931–38). I quote his

poetry from the edition of Merritt Y. Hughes (Indianapolis and New York: Odyssey Press, 1957).

11. *Areopagitica; YPW,* 2:514.

12. Ibid. And *De Doctrina Christiana; YPW,* 6:352–53.

13. I take it that Milton would find some grounds for agreement with Aristotle, who defined happiness as activity in accordance with virtue (*Nic. Eth.,* 1098a16–17).

14. See John M. Steadman, *Milton's Epic Characters* (Chapel Hill: University of North Carolina Press, 1968).

15. *The Reason of Church Government,* 2.1; *YPW,* 1:802. See Jer. 15:10.

16. See *PL,* 6.845 and Ezek. 10:14.

17. *Areopagitica; YPW,* 2:527–28.

18. See *A Documentary History of Primitivism and Related Ideas in Antiquity* (Baltimore: Johns Hopkins University Press, 1935), passim. On the "golden age," see Harry Levin, *The Myth of the Golden Age in the Renaissance* (New York: Oxford University Press, 1969).

19. *Works and Days,* 112–19.

20. See Evans, *Genesis Tradition,* p. 247ff. As an example of the Christianization of the myth of the golden age, Evans quotes Samuel Pordage's description of Eden:

> Then was the golden age indeed, Earth gave
> Nor Weeds, nor Thorns, but cloath'd in liv'ry brave
> Had a perpetual spring; continual green
> In ev'ry place, on ev'ry tree was seen:
> No dainty Flower, which art makes now to flourish,
> But then the Earth did naturally nourish.
> A constant verdure it retain'd, and then
> With thousand flowers spotted was the green:
> Each tree at one time bore both fruit, and flower;
> Each herb to heal, but not to hurt had power.

(*Mundorum Explicatio* [1661], 1.57. Evans, p. 247; and see also pp. 115–16, 124.)

21. Ibid., p. 248.

22. See *PL,* 4.624–32.

23. *Les Poètes métaphysiques anglais,* 1.2.138. "For Crashaw," says Ellrodt, "as for Dante, Paradise is light and fire, the intense heat of noon. Marvell's Paradise knows only the dawn: . . . only 'cool winds' blow there" (ibid.). See the passage from "Thyrsis and Dorinda" below.

24. P. 167.

25. This poem has been excluded from the canon of Marvell's works by Lord on the grounds that its subject matter seems anomalous (Marvell would not have written a poem which seems to advocate suicide) and that it has been removed from the so-called "Bodleian MS" (see *P and L,* 1:232–35, 247–48). Whatever the provenance of the poem (see below, chapter 5, n. 27), I find the theme and manner most characteristic of Marvell's work. If he did not compose all or any of it, he probably copied it and/or put it among his papers because, I would say, he found it a piece so like the products of his own imagination.

26. See *Upon Appleton House,* 424ff.

27. Compare "Thyrsis and Dorinda," 43–44, with *PL,* 9.908, 959–99.

28. Cicero (*Tusculan Disputations*, 1.34) refers to the story of Cleombrotus, who jumped from a city wall into the sea after reading Plato. Milton consigns this notorious suicide to the Paradise of Fools (*PL*, 3.471–73). For further references see Legouis, *Andrew Marvell*, p. 42n.

29. See above, p. 15.

30. Marvell was quite familiar with the *De rerum natura* (see the indices to *P and L* and *RT*). Another of Marvell's favorites was the "atheist" Pliny, who, along with Lucretius and the satirist Lucian, was ranked among the foremost enemies of religion by Christians of the Renaissance (see George T. Buckley, *Atheism in the English Renaissance* [Chicago: University of Chicago Press, 1932], chapter 1).

31. *On the Nature of Things*, 2.7–8; 4.1058ff.; 5.1105ff.; 6; 5.198–99.

32. See above, p. 5.

33. J. B. Leishman (*The Art of Marvell's Poetry*, p. 165ff.) lists a number of analogues to this poem and to "The Picture of little T. C. in a Prospect of Flowers," tracing themes from the *Greek Anthology* to the writings of seventeenth-century poets in support of his contention that Marvell is simply working out a traditional topic. I maintain that here, as elsewhere, the *topos* need not and does not hide Marvell's own sentiments. For one thing, Marvell's emphasis is different from the traditional one. In none of the selections which Leishman gives (in only one, at most) is "young love," "Sportings . . . as free / As the Nurses with the Child," considered a positive ideal, as it is in Marvell's poems. Furthermore, nowhere in his writings does Marvell give genuine and unalloyed praise to "adult" love, love difficult and costly, while he has much to say against it (on "To His Coy Mistress" and "The Definition of Love," see below). I do not mean to suggest that Marvell was himself passionless or sexless (it was his enemies who labeled him a eunuch and thereby, perhaps, occasioned his defense of "an Eunuch; a Poet"), only that he held a nonviolent imaginative and philosophical ideal, a categorical one which extended into the realm of love.

34. A prostitute. See *P and L*, 1:258.

35. I take it that "my poor lover" (11) is the equivalent of "the poor hero of my tale," though conceivably the speaker could be a cynically detached woman to whom the lover had been attracted.

36. Among the critics who have found parody in the poem are Victoria Sackville-West (*Andrew Marvell* [London: Faber and Faber, 1929], p. 44); Pierre Legouis (*Andrew Marvell*, p. 32); Harold Toliver (*Marvell's Ironic Vision*, pp. 164–65); Rosalie Colie ("*My Ecchoing Song*," pp. 48–51); Paulina Palmer ("Marvell, Petrarchism and '*De gli eroici furori*,'" *English Miscellany* 24 [1973–74]: 19–57).

37. The son of Oileus rather than the son of Telamon. "The lesser Aias is the one hero for whom Homer ever shows any personal dislike" (H. J. Rose, *A Handbook of Greek Mythology*, 2d ed. [London: Methuen, 1933], p. 236).

38. See the *Odyssey*, 4.499ff.; the *Aeneid*, 1.41–45.

39. Stanza VII reminds me of Bottom's "raging rocks / And shivering shocks" (*A Midsummer Night's Dream*, 1.2.33–34).

40. Bradbrook and Lloyd-Thomas (*Andrew Marvell*, p. 29) and Colie ("*My Ecchoing Song*," p. 110ff.) emphasize the poem's debt to emblem literature.

41. The line may, of course, be read differently.

42. See *P and L*, 1:255.

43. 3.984ff. The translation is slightly altered.

44. See Palmer, "Marvell, Petrarchism and '*De gli eroici furori*'"; Maren-Sofie

Røstvig, "*In ordine di ruota:* Circular Structure in 'The unfortunate Lover' and *Upon Appleton House,*" in *Tercentenary Essays in Honor of Andrew Marvell,* ed. Kenneth Friedenreich (Hamden, Conn.: Archon, 1977), pp. 245–67. I refer to Bruno's poem in the translation of P. E. Memmo, Jr., *Giordano Bruno's The Heroic Frenzies,* University of North Carolina Studies in the Romance Languages and Literatures, 50 (Chapel Hill: University of North Carolina Press, 1964).

45. Compare Bruno, p. 145, with "The unfortunate Lover," 5–8. See Palmer, "Marvell," p. 41.

46. P. 187.

47. P. 208.

48. Ibid., pp. 203, 202.

49. Ecclus. 49:1; see *P and L,* 1:256. Annabel Patterson (*Marvell and the Civic Crown* [Princeton: Princeton University Press, 1978], pp. 23–25) makes a case for "A political level of meaning in *The Unfortunate Lover*" by finding a "topical analogy," current after 1649, between Josiah and Charles I, and by suggesting an allusion to this analogy in the last stanza of Marvell's poem. If the allusion is there, it is, as Patterson recognizes, an ironic one.

50. See 2 Kings 24:29; 2 Chron. 35:23.

51. Berthoff is the most optimistic. See *The Resolved Soul,* pp. 88–106.

52. See also below, p. 70ff.

53. See "Daman the Mower," 10, 27–28. Only in "The Fair Singer" is love's "conquest" welcome, and it is welcome only because "sweet," the effect of "Harmony." The fair singer is thus very much like "The Gallery"'s tender shepherdess.

54. John Wallace, in *Destiny His Choice,* does not see inconsistency in Marvell's positions. Legouis takes issue with Wallace on this question in a review (*Études Anglaises* 21 [1968]: 414–15). Wallace's contentions are important, however, and must be referred to again.

55. *The Growth of Popery,* p. 283.

56. *RT,* 1:107, 2:285, 1:83.

57. *RT,* 2:232.

58. See "Scaevola Scoto-Brittannus." Against Lord's contention that the poem is not Marvell's, see *P and L,* 1:419.

59. See "Bludius et Corona." On Marvell's connections with Blood, see Legouis, *Andrew Marvell,* pp. 143–44.

60. *P and L,* 1:301.

61. Invasion did not have to be imminent for Marvell to support military action to "repell" it. See, for example, Legouis, *Andrew Marvell,* p. 153ff., concerning Marvell's hostility toward France.

62. *RT,* 2:232.

63. As the sea.

64. An excellent study of "*le temps et l'espace*" in Marvell's poetry is Ellrodt's in *Les Poètes métaphysiques anglais,* 1.2.114ff. I cannot entirely agree with Wallace's approach to the time-theme in *The First Anniversary* (*Destiny His Choice,* p. 109). I do not think that Marvell finds time "useful." What Wallace calls "millennial time" is in Marvell's eyes, I feel, an escape from time.

65. Patterson, *Marvell and the Civic Crown,* p. 88. See also Wallace, *Destiny His Choice,* chapter 3.

66. Patterson (*Marvell and the Civic Crown,* chapter 2) has argued that Marvell is unusually responsible in his handling of the conventions of panegyric.

67. See especially pp. 15–44, 346–94.

68. See J. A. Mazzeo, "Cromwell as Davidic King," in *Reason and Imagination* (New York: Columbia University Press, 1962), pp. 29–55; Wallace, *Destiny His Choice,* pp. 106–40; Warren Chernaik, "Politics and Literature in Marvell," *Renaissance and Modern Studies* 16 (1972): 25–36; Stephen Zwicker, "Models of Governance in Marvell's 'The First Anniversary,'" *Criticism* 16 (1974): 1–12; A. J. N. Wilson, "Andrew Marvell's 'The First Anniversary,'" *MLR* 69 (1974): 254–73; Annabel Patterson, "Against Polarization: Literature and Politics in Marvell's Cromwell Poems," *ELR* 5 (1975): 251–72; Nicholas Guild, "Marvell's 'The First Anniversary of the Government Under O. C.,'" *Papers on Language and Literature* 11 (1975): 242–53. See also Legouis's commentary on the poem in *P and L,* 1:320ff.

69. Cicero, *Philippics,* 8.1.4. See *P and L,* 1:325.

70. *RT,* 1:135.

71. As he did. See Legouis, *Andrew Marvell,* pp. 145, 198–99.

72. *RT,* 1:135.

73. See Legouis, *André Marvell,* pp. 21–22.

74. *A Reproof to the Rehearsal Transpros'd* (1673), p. 445.

75. *RT,* 1:89.

76. *RT,* 2:294–95. See Mark 11:15; John 2:14–16.

In praising the martyrdom of Captain Douglas, the "Loyal Scot," Marvell empties the death-scene of violence and turns it into an art-work:

Like a glad lover the fierce Flames hee meets
And tries his first Imbraces in their sheets.
His shape Exact which the bright flames enfold
Like the sun's Statue stands of burnisht Gold:
Round the Transparent fire about him Glowes
As the Clear Amber on the bee doth Close;
And as on Angells head their Glories shine
His burning Locks Adorn his face divine.
But when in his Imortall mind hee felt
His Altred form and sodred Limbs to Melt,
Down on the Deck hee laid him down and dy'd
With his dear sword reposing by his side,
And on his flaming Planks soe rests his head
As one that Huggs himself in a Warm bed.

[43–56]

Marvell condemns the "armed Bands" who "Did clap their bloody hands" at the execution of Charles I; the King, like Douglas, had "bow'd his comely Head, / Down as upon a Bed" ("Horatian Ode," 55–56, 63–64). In the *Historical Essay [on] General Councils,* Marvell acknowledges that "martyrs for reason" are "manly," but then declares that men would be "more . . . so for reason religionated and christianized" (p. 126). The *Essay* is basically a plea *against* martyr-making.

77. *Historical Essay [on] General Councils,* pp. 154, 143.

78. *RT,* 1:111. In the midst of these remarks Marvell makes the observation

that "difficulty . . . make[s] more . . . honourable." But he is talking about the superiority of the government of men to the government of sheep, so I would take it that "difficulty" here refers more to complexity than to troublesomeness. In any case, it is the kind of platitude one might use simply to win a point.

79. *RT,* 2:190. Compare 1:118: "I do not think it will excuse a Witch, to say, That she conjur'd up a Spirit only that she might lay it."

80. *RT,* 2:234.

81. Matt. 9:13; see *RT,* 2:249.

82. *Defence of John Howe,* p. 218. Also, *The Growth of Popery,* p. 250.

83. See above, p. 41ff.

84. See "The Mower against Gardens."

85. "The Definition of Love," 11. See also n. 89, below.

86. For Simon Magus's "sickle," see *RT,* 2:325.

87. "Upon an Eunuch; a Poet," 2.

88. "A Dialogue between the Soul and Body," 43. See also *The Growth of Popery,* p. 281: "Men . . . have always been hacking and hewing one another, to frame an irregular figure of political incongruity."

89. *RT,* 2:230. There is also Hooker's "nail" (ibid., p. 256). The hammer and nail have been traced back to Horace (*Odes,* 1.35.17-20). I do not believe that Marvell derives comfort from the fact that wedges or nails fasten as well as divide (see Berthoff, *The Resolved Soul,* p. 99). Marvell admits once that "Sudden Parting closer glews" ("Daphnis and Chloe," 16), but his tone is quite ironical, his observation being part of a witty critique of the love-making that relies on masculine siege and feminine resistance. See above, pp. 57-58.

90. Two of the recent York Tercentenary Lectures on Marvell have addressed topics allied to the ones under discussion here: Christopher Ricks's "'It's own resemblance'" discusses the "self-inwoven simile" in Marvell ("its own tear," "mine own Precipice," etc.) and its appropriateness to such themes as "self-division." John Carey's "Reversals Transposed: An Aspect of Marvell's Imagination" considers "restrictions" and "reversals" in the poetry. See C. A. Patrides, ed., *Approaches to Marvell* (London: Routledge & Kegan Paul, 1978), pp. 108-54. For a treatment (about which I have important reservations) of the "dividing" and "excluding" mentality of Puritanism, see Patrick Crutwell, *The Shakespearean Moment* (1954; rpt. New York: Modern Library, 1960), chapter 5. R.I.V. Hodge (*Foreshortened Time* [Cambridge: D.S. Brewer, 1978]) studies Marvell's "dialectical" habit of mind against the background of Ramist logic's disjunctive syllogisms. Robert Heilman, in "Tragedy and Melodrama," *Texas Quarterly* 3 (1960): 36-50, discusses the "dividedness" requisite for tragedy.

91. *A Johnson Reader,* ed. E. L. McAdam, Jr., and G. Milne (New York: Modern Library, 1966), p. 273.

92. *Upon Appleton House,* 45-46. Scarcely any Christian thinker would deny the axiom (stated, for example, by Aquinas, *ST,* 1, q. 25, a. 3) that God cannot work a contradiction. See *RT,* 1:63: "Mr. *Bayes* . . . has face enough to say or unsay any thing, and 'tis his priviledge, what the School-Divines deny to be even within the power of the Almighty, to make Contradictions true."

93. On the *topos "natura non mater sed noverca,"* see Lovejoy and Boas, *Primitivism,* pp. 245, 397.

94. In contrast, consider George Herbert's attitude in "The Pulley," where

"the God of Nature" dispenses to man all "the world's riches" except one, "rest," which the Creator keeps back only to enrich his creature further.

95. A philosopher who accepted the principle of plenitude would object that a tulip should not be both sweet and fair, for then it would not be a tulip; and the world is better off for containing some flowers whose fragrance does not match their beauty.

96. Aristotle's declarations that "all art . . . aim[s] at filling up nature's deficiencies" (*Politics*, 1337a2), that "art partly completes what nature cannot bring to completion, and partly imitates her" (*Physics*, 199a15), are commonsensical enough. Since the Mower seems to have no appreciation at all of this view, he may be seen as somewhat blindly fanatical. (For critical opinions to this effect, see Toliver, *Marvell's Ironic Vision*, pp. 104–106; Colie, *"My Ecchoing Song,"* p. 38: "Taken seriously, the Mower is insane"; Peter Berek, "The Voices of Marvell's Lyrics," *MLQ* 32 [1971]: 148–49.) And there is surely a dramatic irony in the complaint of a destroyer, who "massacres" the fields (*Upon Appleton House*, 394), against mere alteration. The Mower makes some legitimate points, however, and cannot be dismissed. Much alteration *is* adulteration (25). By the law of nature neither the Mower nor the gardener can have right wholly on his side. I do not think that Marvell relishes this fact, seeing in it a complexity that enriches existence. He laments it.

97. "Meditation 12" from *Devotions upon Emergent Occasions*.

98. See More, *Divine Dialogues*, 2.94ff.; Cudworth, *True Intellectual System*, 5, vol. 4, 164ff. Here is a sample from Cudworth:

Atheists can be no fit judges of worlds being made well or ill, either in general, or respectively to mankind, they having no standing measure for well or ill, without a God and morality, nor any true knowledge of themselves, and what their own good or evil consisteth in. This was at first but a froward speech of some sullen discontented persons, when things falling not out agreeably to their own private, selfish, and partial appetites, they would revenge themselves, by railing upon nature (that is Providence), and calling her a stepmother only to mankind, whilst she was a fond, partial, and indulgent mother to other animals; and though this be elegantly set off by Lucretius, yet is there nothing but poetic flourish in it all, without any philosophic truth . . ." [pp. 166–67].

99. "Chorus Sacerdotum," 1, 6.

100. *A Free and Impartial Censure of the Platonick Philosophy*, 2d ed. (1667), pp. 195–96. Compare Milton's statement in *Areopagitica* (above, p. 50).

101. Leishman (*The Art of Marvell's Poetry*, p. 216) says that "the poem as we have it is almost certainly incomplete," adducing evidence from manuscript additions to a copy of the 1681 folio, in which the last four lines of the fourth stanza are scratched and the words *"Desunt multa"* written below. In view of the rather abrupt transition in the final stanza from the first ten to the last four lines, the contention seems reasonable. But in any case, the structure of the poem requires that the body have the last say, and it is hardly likely that the body's complaints, or the soul's, could have been invalidated in a "complete" poem.

102. 1:111–12. This dictum is not really contradicted in the poem, for the body admits to the rule of a "Tyrannick" soul, who shapes it as would an architect. The

poem supplements the prose statement by emphasizing that in some ways soul is also dependent on body; the prose supplements the poem by pointing out that the soul is only a deputy architect.

E. E. Duncan-Jones proposes that in this poem Marvell may have recalled a saying of Themistius Rhetor, referred to by Cowley in a note to *Davideis,* that "the soul is the architect of its own dwelling place." (See *NQ* 3 n.s. [1956]: 383.) My reading is not incompatible with this suggestion.

103. L. N. Wall has noted some of the resemblances between this work and Marvell's poetry. See *P and L,* 1:249–50.

104. Pp. 4–5.

105. See above, p. 29.

106. It had been promised of Jesus, whose power was greater than that of a mere human physician, that "a bruised reed shall he not break . . . till he send forth judgment unto victory" (Matt. 12:20). Marvell, who believed that "to bruise a broken Reed is inhumane" (*RT,* 2:284), must have wondered how a violent God of paradoxical bent could keep this promise.

107. See the *Aeneid,* 7.761ff.

108. One might object against this reading of "Lord Hastings" that the author would never have published under his own name a work that could be considered blasphemous. Are not the complaints in fact conventional? Would not the poet's publisher and his readers assume that the bitter words were not to be taken literally as an indictment of Providence? In reply it might be said that the prospect of such an attitude in his audience might well have encouraged the poet to speak his true mind without fear of inquisition. It was easy enough for him to hide behind the imprecision and triteness of such terms as "gods" and "stars," while flinging at "heaven" reproaches that were really fiercer than usual, but not so far from conventionality as to be dangerous.

109. *RT,* 1:86–87. One may say that this attitude stems from the Puritan's distrust of "works." Whatever the source of his motives, it is clear that Marvell prizes the final state more than the process by which the end is attained.

110. *RT,* 2:263–64. While not as extreme as Aristotle's statement in *Nic. Eth.* 1178b7 (see above, pp. 16), Marvell's shares in the same spirit.

111. See Aquinas, *SCG,* 1.92–93.

112. *Defence of John Howe,* p. 167.

113. Ibid., p. 229. See also p. 225.

114. *RT,* 1:112.

115. "Tom May's Death," 59–60. Marvell actually gives the question broad significance by having the ghost of Ben Jonson, who asks it, allude to the fall of the angels and of Adam and Eve:

But the nor Ignorance nor seeming good
Misled, but malice fixt and understood.

[55–56]

116. See below, p. 130. And see Donne's first "Elegie":

Shall they be damn'd, and in the furnace throwne,
And punisht for offences not their owne?

[19–20]

Donne is of course witty here, witty in regard to a problem about which he could not afford to be too serious, as *Metempsychosis* indicates.

117. J. Welsch, *Popery Anatomized*, 2d ed. (1672), pp. 382–83. Quoted by Smith in his edition of *RT*, pp. 404–405. Marvell's reference to the anecdote is in *RT*, 2:326.

118. Pp. 168–69.

119. Pp. 189, 225–29.

120. In the *Defence of John Howe*, however, Marvell seems somewhat inconsistent, for after condemning "disquisitions" on the "causes" of good and evil (p. 168), he proceeds to give his approval to John Howe's disquisition (p. 170). Actually, Marvell defends Howe for "reducing" disputing parties "within the due limits of Scripture and saving knowledge," that is, for removing such obvious and intolerable scandals to reason as Danson's while preserving the Scriptural mystery in its integrity *as* a mystery. Marvell's own modest ratiocinations in the *Defence* are to the same purpose.

121. *RT*, 2:231–32.

122. *Defence of John Howe*, pp. 225–26. See Calvin, *Institutes*, 3.23.4; and Henry More, *Divine Dialogues*, 2.157–58:

> Wherefore for the general it is fit, that God should deal with free Creatures according to the freedom of their nature: But yet, rather than all should go to ruine, I do not see any incongruity but that God may as it were lay violent hands upon some, and pull them out of the Fire, and make of them potent, though not irresistible Instruments of pulling others out also. This is that Election of God for whom it was impossible to fall, as it is also morally impossible for others that have arrived to a due pitch of the Divine Life.

123. *Ductor Dubitantium* (1660), 2 vols., ed. the Rev. Alexander Taylor (London: Longman, 1855), 1.2.62–63. Part of the *Whole Works* in 10 vols. (1850–55).

124. *Defence of John Howe*, p. 229. See Rom. 3:4.

125. Thus showing the temptations of "Elizium" in the sharpest relief.

Chapter 4

1. Friedman, *Marvell's Pastoral Art*, p. 13.

2. Bradbrook and Lloyd-Thomas, *Andrew Marvell*, p. 116; Christopher Hill, "Society and Andrew Marvell," in Carey, *Andrew Marvell*, p. 102.

3. Berthoff, *The Resolved Soul*, p. 45.

4. *Marvell and the Civic Crown*, p. 10.

5. I probably depart from a chronological treatment by considering "Bermudas" before the "Horatian Ode" and *Upon Appleton House*—for the sake of a conceptual clarity in a sometimes murky biographical picture.

6. See Hyman, *Andrew Marvell*, p. 104.

7. "On My First Sonne," 11–12.

8. See Friedman, *Marvell's Pastoral Art*, pp. 108–9, 143.

9. On the latter point, see Hyman, *Andrew Marvell*, pp. 23–25.

10. Colie, *"My Ecchoing Song,"* p. 89.

11. Matt. 10:30; see *A Poem upon the Death of O. C.*, 2.

12. See Friedman, *Marvell's Pastoral Art*, p. 111.

13. See, for example, E. S. LeComte, "Marvell's 'The Nymph Complaining for the Death of Her Fawn,'" *MP* 50 (1952): 97-101; Karina Williamson, "Marvell's 'The Nymph Complaining': A Reply," *MP* 51 (1954): 268-71. Both articles are reprinted in Carey, *Andrew Marvell*, pp. 274-87.

14. *Republic*, 379c-80a. Plato had in mind the *Niobe* of Aeschylus, frag. 156. See also Plutarch, *On Common Conceptions*, 1065e.

15. See Williamson, in Carey, *Andrew Marvell*, p. 283.

16. *As You Like It*, 4.1.108.

17. See especially R. M. Cummings, "The Difficulty of Marvell's 'Bermudas,'" *MP* 67 (1969-70): 331-40; Tay Fizdale, "Irony in Marvell's 'Bermudas,'" *ELH* 42 (1975): 203-213. At the opposite extreme is Toliver's view that in such poems as "Bermudas," Marvell "heal[s] the broad fissure of nature and grace" (*Marvell's Ironic Vision*, p. 100).

18. See Legouis, *Andrew Marvell*, pp. 95-96; Rosalie Colie, "Marvell's 'Bermudas' and the Puritan Paradise," *RN* 10 (1957): 75-79. Also, Cummings and Fizdale, in the articles cited above. The most balanced consideration of questions of irony in the poem is that of Philip Brockbank in "The Politics of Paradise: 'Bermudas,'" in Patrides, *Approaches to Marvell*, pp. 174-93.

19. *P and L*, 1:246. There is good reason to date "Bermudas" about 1653, when Marvell lived in the house of John Oxenbridge, who had, like Marvell's rowers, suffered from "Prelat's rage" and twice visited the islands. See *P and L*, 1:246, 338.

20. Canto 2.34; quoted from Thorn Drury's two-volume edition (London: George Routledge and Sons, 1893).

21. See Legouis, *Andrew Marvell*, p. 96. When, at the Restoration, Oxenbridge was finally exiled from England for good, he settled in Massachusetts, not in Bermuda.

22. Ibid., p. 14. (In offering this view, Legouis has to admit that in the "Horatian Ode" Marvell speaks this way "for the only time in his life.") The critics are legion who see in the poem what Cleanth Brooks has called "Olympian detachment" ("Marvell's 'Horatian Ode,'" *English Institute Essays* [1946]: 127-58, in Carey, *Andrew Marvell*, p. 198), indicated by the coolly "ironical" way in which Marvell treats Cromwell. In his reply to Brooks, Douglas Bush ("Marvell's 'Horatian Ode,'" *Sewanee Review* 60 [1952]: 363-76, in Carey, pp. 199-210) judges Marvell neither uncommitted nor ironical. And so the controversy has gone. I cannot agree with Brooks that the ode is merely "diagnostic," eventuating in "contemplation" (p. 195). Marvell is pressing himself to make a decision and is hardly detached. "March indefatigably on" is a genuine exhortation, not a mere exclamatory or contemplative sigh. On the other hand, I believe that Marvell struggles with an ironic awareness which he can hardly repress.

23. See J. A. Mazzeo, "Cromwell as Machiavellian Prince in Marvell's 'Horatian Ode,'" *JHI* 21 (1960): 1-17; also Hans Baron's brief corrective, "'An Horatian Ode' and Machiavelli," ibid., 450-51.

24. Mazzeo, p. 9. See also Legouis, *Andrew Marvell*, p. 17; *P and L*, 1:301.

25. See also *A Poem upon the Death of O. C.*, 265-66.

26. See *P and L*, 1:295ff.; R. H. Syfret, "Marvell's 'Horatian Ode,'" *RES* 12 n.s. (1961): 160-72; John S. Coolidge, "Marvell and Horace," *MP* 63 (1965): 111-20, in Lord, *Andrew Marvell*, pp. 85-100.

27. 6.387ff. See also Pliny, *Natural History*, 2.144.

28. See above, p. 22.

29. The poem "Ad Regem Carolum Parodia," published in Marvell's sixteenth year, is based on Horace, *Odes*, 1.2. Marvell's stanza is translated by McQueen and Rockwell:

Already the father has sent enough of plague
and enough of his dire Thunderbolt [or lightning, *fulminis*];
striking our citadels with glowing hand,
he has terrified the city.

For other references in Marvell's writings to the god of thunder and lightning, see "Dignissimo suo Amico Doctori Wittie," 18; "Eyes and Tears," 34–40; *Upon the Death of O. C.*, 69, 265; *The Last Instructions to a Painter*, 356; *RT*, 2:231.

30. 1.2. See also, for example, 1.263–65; 2.1ff.; 2.43–44; 2.59–63; 2.98; 2.304–5; etc. The gods themselves are criminals: 8.799–800.

31. Douglas Bush, "Marvell's 'Horatian Ode,'" in Carey, *Andrew Marvell*, p. 207. Bush recognizes, however, that "Justice" here "*may* be absolute justice" (italics mine).

32. See above, p. 79.

33. Margoliouth and Legouis, *P and L*, 1:295, 297.

34. Commentators have of late tended to downplay suggestions of "Royalist" commitments in such early works as the poems on Lovelace, Hastings, and May (see, for example, Patterson, *Marvell and the Civic Crown*, p. 17; Christopher Hill, "Milton and Marvell," in Patrides, *Approaches to Marvell*, p. 4; Nicholas Guild, "The Contexts of Marvell's Early 'Royalist' Poems," *SEL* 20 [1980]: 125–36). The elegy for Francis Villiers is utterly partisan on the Royalist side, but its attribution to Marvell is not certain (see *P and L*, 1:432–35, for a summary of the evidence for Marvell's authorship).

35. See Christopher Hill, *God's Englishman* (1970; rpt. New York: Harper Torchbooks, 1972), pp. 136, 246–50. Hill finds that "by the 1650's . . . [Cromwell's] doctrine of providences [had] slipped over easily into a theory of justification by success."

36. See Isa. 28:15, 18; and especially Jer. 25.

37. See, for example, the articles on the ode by Brooks, Syfret, and Coolidge.

38. *P and L*, 2:324.

39. Greene, *Moira*, p. 174.

40. On problems of attribution and dating, see *P and L*, 1:294–95. For a view opposed to Hilton Kelliher's contention that "*Tom May's Death* incorporates a thorough rejection of May's classicizing bent that sorts ill with the recent 'Horatian Ode'" (*Andrew Marvell* [London: The British Library, 1978], p. 40), see Coolidge, "Marvell and Horace," in Lord, *Andrew Marvell*, pp. 86–88.

41. "Spartacus" may refer to the earl of Essex or Lord Fairfax or Cromwell. See Donno, *The Complete Poems*, p. 243. "Brutus" and "Cassius" may be references to Fairfax and Cromwell. See Kelliher, p. 40.

42. May died in November 1650. "In Legationem Domini Oliveri St. John" was written early in February or March of 1651. See *P and L*, 1:308.

43. *Andrew Marvell*, p. 63.

44. Legouis (ibid.) refers to some of these readings (by Kenneth Muir, D. C. Allen, M.-S. Røstvig, and Joseph Summers) and disagrees with them. Other studies of the poem's "unity" include those of Edward Tayler, *Nature and Art in*

Renaissance Literature (New York: Columbia University Press, 1964), pp. 150-54; Harold Toliver, *Marvell's Ironic Vision,* pp. 113-29; Kitty Scoular, *Natural Magic* (Oxford: Clarendon Press, 1965), pp. 120-90; M. J. K. O'Loughlin, "This Sober Frame: A Reading of 'Upon Appleton House,'" in Lord, *Andrew Marvell,* pp. 12-42; John Wallace, *Destiny His Choice,* pp. 232-57; Ann Berthoff, *The Resolved Soul,* pp. 163-97. Rosalie Colie, *"My Ecchoing Song,"* pp. 181-294, and Donald Friedman, *Marvell's Pastoral Art,* pp. 210-52, are more cognizant of irregularity.

45. Colie, *"My Ecchoing Song,"* p. 278. The choice is usually considered to be of action over contemplation. See Lord's essay, "From Contemplation to Action: Marvell's Poetical Career," in *Andrew Marvell,* pp. 55-73; also Wallace, *Destiny His Choice,* p. 255. I have no quarrel with this idea, but I feel that the choice is more inclusive. Isabel Rivers, in *The Poetry of Conservatism* (Cambridge: Rivers Press, 1973), p. 108. holds an opposing view: "In *Upon Appleton House* . . ., Marvell is not persuading or making a choice."

46. See G. R. Hibbard, "The Country House Poem of the Seventeenth Century," *JWCI* 29 (1956): 159-74.

47. See Matt. 11:30.

48. See Matt. 25:1-13, where there are two *sets* of virgins.

49. See 266-67.

50. See Legouis, *Andrew Marvell,* p. 73; Friedman, *Marvell's Pastoral Art,* pp. 221-24, 248.

51. It is not entirely clear which Fairfax planted the garden. See *P and L,* 1:284.

52. *The First Anniversary,* 244; see above, p. 68.

53. O'Loughlin, "This Sober Frame," in Lord, *Andrew Marvell,* p. 129. See also Dennis Davison, *The Poetry of Andrew Marvell* (London: E. Arnold, 1964), p. 56; Lord, "From Contemplation to Action," in *Andrew Marvell,* pp. 61-62; Berthoff, *The Resolved Soul,* p. 170.

54. Annabel Patterson offers some evidence, not all of it from reliable or impartial sources, that Fairfax's shortcomings could have occasioned ironic treatment by the officially admiring poet (see *Marvell and the Civic Crown,* pp. 95-110). I do not deny that Marvell may have possessed an ironic awareness. But he was neither so insightful himself nor so virtuous that he could justifiably wield the irony against Fairfax. I suspect that Marvell knew this, however much he was inclined to self-righteousness.

55. See *RT,* 2:248: "By conscience I understand Humane reason acting by the Rule of Scripture, in order to obedience to God. . . ." Was Fairfax's conscience "informed"? Since Marvell was perplexed himself, he could not very confidently deny that it was.

56. Compare *Lycidas,* 64-65.

57. See above, p. 73ff.

58. That is, the "tormenting" beauty of "Black Eyes, red Lips, and curled Hair." See the discussion of "The Gallery," above, p. 56.

59. P. 105.

60. See Seneca, *Epistles,* 108.11. "The willing soul Fate leads, but the unwilling drags along."

61. See Matt. 7:13-14; Luke 13:24.

62. See Lord, "From Contemplation to Action," in *Andrew Marvell,* p. 65; Coolidge, "Marvell and Horace," in *Andrew Marvell,* pp. 95-97.

63. See Coolidge, "Marvell and Horace," p. 96.

64. As Kierkegaard did not. See his ironical essay, "The Rotation Method," in *Either/Or* (Robert Bretall, ed., *A Kierkegaard Anthology* [New York: Modern Library, n.d.], pp. 21–33).

65. My reading of "The Garden" runs counter to many interpretations. It has affinites with Frank Kermode's reading ("The Argument of Marvell's *Garden*," *EC* 2 [1952]:225–41, in Carey, *Andrew Marvell,* pp. 250–65) in that I treat the philosophical utterances as "pseudo-statements" and find parody in the poem; with Renato Poggioli's reading ("The Pastoral of the Self," *Daedalus* 88 [1959]: 686–99) in that I recognize the speaker's solipsism—although Poggioli does not distinguish speaker from poet; with Joseph Summers's reading (chapter 5 of *The Heirs of Donne and Jonson*) in that I consider the speaker's claims for contemplative retirement purposely exaggerated by the poet.

66. As Margoliouth pointed out, the phrase "Annihilating . . . Thought" may also be taken to mean "considering the whole material world as of no value compared to a green thought" (*P and L,* 1:268). If this interpretation is valid, one still has to take the speaker's word that "green Thought," whatever it is, is so magnificent, and one has to judge the reliability of that word from evidence about the speaker's character elsewhere in the poem—not, as many critics do, solely from a consideration of hermetic and Neoplatonic doctrine.

67. See Kermode, "The Argument of Marvell's *Garden*," in Carey, *Andrew Marvell,* pp. 263–64.

68. "Marvell and the New Critics," *RES* 8 n.s. (1957), in Carey, *Andrew Marvell,* p. 271.

69. A "curious" peach is one produced with "care" (from *curare*). See Legouis, *Andrew Marvell,* p. 45.

70. See Legouis's note in *P and L,* 1:271. The "*Desunt multa*" which divides the Latin poem remains a mystery. Only an editor would insert it. But on what grounds? Did he read the English version and simply infer that much was missing in the other? Or was there some indication in Marvell's papers that the Latin poem was incomplete? Legouis felt that "the lack of connection" between the two parts proved the editorial notice to be more than a "guess." Was it while contemplating this gap that Marvell turned to the English version and changed the poem's tenor?

71. See *P and L,* 1:277; Legouis, *Andrew Marvell,* pp. 93–94.

72. I suggest in the next chapter how Marvell may have worked toward such a state of mind. See below, p. 131ff.

73. See above, p. 65ff.

74. "To his Noble Friend Mr. Richard Lovelace, upon his Poems," 13. This poem was written in 1647 or 1648. See *P and L,* 1:239.

75. See above, p. 68.

76. An admiration which seems even more personal in *A Poem upon the Death of O. C.,* especially 247ff.

77. See above, pp. 68–70.

78. Undatable, although Leishman (pp. 31–32) has found resemblances to *Paradise Lost* in "The Resolved Soul, and Created Pleasure." Compare *PL,* 5.482–87, with 14–16; *PL,* 9. 602–609, with 51–54. Legouis notes that Sir Walter Raleigh, in his *Milton,* had also observed the "spiritual affinity," but finds the "*rapprochement* . . . hardly decisive" (*P and L,* 1:242).

79. In Spenser's *Shepheardes Calender,* E. K.'s gloss for May states that "Great Pan is Christ." See Donno, *Complete Poems,* p. 222.

80. "The Coronet"'s psychological complexity, greater than that of the

other two poems, need not make it a truer witness to Marvell's real feelings. Intense feelings do not always issue in complex, or even successful, art.

81. See above, 2ff.

82. *Skepticism and Animal Faith* (New York: Scribners, 1923), p. 67.

83. *The Growth of Popery*, pp. 412–13.

84. *Pensées*, trans. W. F. Trotter (London: Dent, 1947), 3.233.

85. P. 189.

86. *Mr. Smirke*, pp. 67–69.

87. Ibid., p. 67. See Jeremy Taylor, *Ductor Dubitantium*, 1:56–57.

88. See *RT*, 2:325.

89. *Ductor Dubitantium*, 1.2.189.

90. Ibid., 1.5..232. See also 1.3.146: "If the reason on both sides seems equally probable, the will may determine by any of its proper motives that are honest; any prudent interest, any fair compliance, any custom, in case these happen to be on the right side." The last phrase seems to beg the question, but a concern for "safety" can lead one into cautious inconsistencies.

91. See above, p. 4.

92. There is a pun on "Eye" and "edge" (59–60) based on the Latin *acies*, both "eyesight" and "blade."

93. See Leishman, *The Art of Marvell's Poetry*, pp. 221–27, 268.

94. Warnke, "Play and Metamorphosis in Marvell's Poetry," in Keast, *Seventeenth-Century English Poetry*, p. 50.

95. "Andrew Marvell," in Carey, *Andrew Marvell*, p. 50.

96. See *RT*, 2:187. On humor as a conscious strategy in Marvell's satirical writing, see Patterson, *Marvell and the Civic Crown*, pp. 175–220. My sense is that Patterson portrays Marvell as more scrupulous about the proper "decorum" than he really was.

97. See above, p. 40ff.

98. "Society and Andrew Marvell," in Carey, *Andrew Marvell*, p. 77. Ann Berthoff has said that Marvell could "afford the comic" (*The Resolved Soul*, p. 166). I would say that for him the comic was indispensable.

99. As C. Day Lewis translates *sunt lacrimae rerum*, true to Virgil's spirit if not exactly to his syntax.

100. *P and L*, 2:311.

Chapter 5

1. Letter to Sir Edward Harley, 30 June 1677; *P and L*, 2:353.

2. The letter from which I quote above, by no means an atypical one, rushes to the following conclusion:

> People were at twelue a clock at night beating up the Hall doore to get in [to the King's Bench]. By foure in the morning there were no places left. It lasted debate from halfe an houre past seuen till Noone. [Shaftesbury] was remanded as committed by the Superior Court yet sitting with wch the Kings Bench had nothing to doe. Severall were carried out of the Court for dead. Shaftesbury himsefe [*sic*] had spoke

as well as Williams and Wallop his Counsell. The King has giuen my L: Salisbury two moneths more. D: of Buckingham last weeke had two days to see Cliueden and returned. Sr John King went sick from the Bar a week agoe and dyed yesterday. I do not belieue the Dutch fears that fourteen of our men of war are gone to intercept their East India Fleet: yet so they write. I am told de Boyes has a letter that twelue Papists are clappd up at Dublin hauing a Designe at the jollity & carelesnesse which should be at the D: of Ormonds Coming ouer to seize and fire Castle Magazine &c. at Dublin. He goes next moneth, D: Lauderdale next Tuesday. My lord Obrians Son married thise weeke to the Treasurers daughter. Some of Quality of which wisdome is not one pay not the Tax but upon Distresse. I am S^r your most affect. Servt.

As a satirist, Marvell tended to be, as Legouis has called him, a "political journalist in verse." See especially *The Last Instructions to a Painter,* which Legouis accurately describes as follows: "In it Marvell tells nine or ten months of the history of England, diplomatic negotiations, parliamentary debates, naval operations, intrigues of the bed chamber or lobby, and his narrative seems to be written day by day, as the events impress him immediately" (*Andrew Marvell,* p. 168).

3. See Legouis, ibid., p. 11.

4. Marvell's prose is filled with evidence of his extensive and often unconventional reading. His poetry is also learned, although some critics have tried to make it excessively so. "The Garden" for example, has, by Joseph Summers's reckoning, been connected with "Buddha and the Canticles and the Mass, Plato and Plotinus and 'Hermes Trismegistus,' St. Paul and the Kabbala, St. Bonaventura and St. Thomas Aquinas, Hugh of St. Victor and the *Ancrene Riwle,* Ficino and Leone Ebreo, Henry More and John Smith . . ." (*The Heirs of Donne and Jonson,* p. 137).

James E. Siemon's Stanford dissertation, *Andrew Marvell's School Learning* (1966), describes the reading prescribed by the curriculum. Biographers have caught glimpses of Marvell at a bookseller's shop and at the Bodleian (Legouis, *Andrew Marvell,* pp. 4, 136).

5. See above, chapter 2, n. 183.

6. Anthony à Wood, *Athenae Oxonienses,* 2 (1692), 619.

7. See Legouis, *Andrew Marvell,* p. 4.

8. See the life of Marvell which prefaces Thomas Cooke's edition of the *Works* (1726), 1:4, and Grosart, 1:xxvii–viii.

9. See "Introduction to Making a Choice of a Way of Life," after the "Twelfth Day of the Second Week" of the *Exercises.* I refer to the translation of Anthony Mottola (New York: Image Books, 1964).

That the Jesuits used the *Exercises* in their conversion of Englishmen is clear from the case of Robert Persons. See Ethelred Taunton, *The History of the Jesuits in England* (London: Methuen, 1901), p. 27.

10. "General Examination of Conscience," p. 50.

11. Pp. 203–204.

12. *P and L,* 2:311.

13. *The History of the Worthies of England,* ed. P. A. Nuttall, 3 vols. (London: Thomas Tegg, 1840), 1:240.

14. Milton published his poem at Cambridge in 1638 while Marvell was still

in residence there. The elegy seems to have left its mark on Marvell, for he can be found paraphrasing it years after its publication. Compare "Fleckno" (1645–46), 27–28:

Only this frail Ambition did remain,
The last distemper of the sober Brain,

with *Lycidas*, 70–71:

Fame is the spur that the clear spirit doth raise
(That last infirmity of Noble mind). . . .

Compare also *The First Anniversary* (1655), 218: "the Kingdom blest of Peace and Love," with *Lycidas*, 177: "the blest Kingdoms meek of joy and love"; *The First Anniversary*, 358: "And beaked Promontories sail'd from far," with *Lycidas*, 94: "That blows from off each beaked promontory." (See *P and L*, 1:293, 324, 328.) An echo of *Lycidas* in *Upon Appleton House* is noted below, p. 137.

It is possible, but not likely, that Marvell first read *Lycidas* in Milton's *Poems* of 1645. Marvell had by then probably been away from England for several years. Besides, he would while at Cambridge not have failed to read when first published the memorials to Edward King, who was in fact a fellow poet: their poems had appeared together in *Musarum Cantabrigiensium* (1637), a tribute to the Royal Family.

15. Donald Friedman has proposed that the opening lines of "The Death of Lord Hastings" are indebted to *Lycidas*. See *Marvell's Pastoral Art*, pp. 5, 34.

16. *P and L*, 2:312–13.

17. As Legouis has pointed out. Compare the first chorus of "The Resolved Soul":

Earth cannot shew so brave a Sight
As when a single Soul does fence
The Batteries of alluring Sense,
And Heaven views it with delight,

with *On Providence*, 2.9:

Ecce spectaculum dignum ad quod respiciat intentus operi suo deus, ecce par deo dignum, vir fortis cum fortuna mala compositus, utique si et provocavit. Non video, inquam, quid habet in terris Iuppiter pulchrius.

(Here is a spectacle worthy of the regard of God as he contemplates his works; lo! here a contest worthy of God,—a brave man matched against ill-forutne, and doubly so if his also was the challenge. I do not know, I say, what nobler sight the Lord of Heaven could find on earth.)

See Legouis, *André Marvell*, p. 83.

18. To which he refers in *The Last Instructions*, 447–48. See L. N. Wall's "Marvell and Seneca," *NQ* 8 n.s. (1961): 185–86.

19. See above, p. 23ff.

20. Odes, 1.2; see Marvell's "Ad Regem Carolum Parodia."

21. "Saepe Diespiter / Neglectus incesto addidit integrum" (*Odes*, 3.2.29–30).

22. *Defence of John Howe*, p. 169.

23. See *RT,* 2:282. Here Marvell refers to Gregory Nazianzen, Chrysostom, Nectarius, and other "Ecclesiastical Writers of that time" who wrote about or against Julian. Among the others would be Cyril of Alexandria, who wrote a polemic *Contra Julianum.* In Cyril's work is found the passage from *In Galilaeos* which I quoted earlier (p. 29), to which should be compared "Upon the Death of Lord Hastings," 19–24. See also Pierre Legouis, "Marvell and Julian," *NQ* 21 n.s. (1974): 102–3.

24. Historical Essay [*on*] *General Councils,* p. 136.

25. Legouis refers to Milton's letter to Bradshaw in 1652/3, which "says of Marvell: 'he hath spent four years abroad in Holland, France, Italy, and Spain to very good purpose . . . and the gaining of these four languages.'" Legouis then reasons:

Since [he] returned to England by 1649 certainly, by 1646 possibly, Marvell may have left as early as 1642, the year when the Civil War broke out. If so, did he deliberately shun the shedding of blood, including his own? Though Milton left "the labour of the camps to any ordinary man," he had at least decided from the first (so he says) to share the dangers of his countrymen; and Marvell himself was to praise magnificently the *Defensio Secunda* from which that personal statement is extracted, though he may have had some difficulty swallowing the epithet "*turpe*" there applied to conduct that had been his own [*Andrew Marvell,* p. 9].

26. *RT,* 1:42. And see above, p. 5.

27. See *P and L,* 1:293; Legouis, *André Marvell,* pp. 144–45. It should be said that "Fleckno" describes incidents that occurred in 1645 or 1646. The poem need not have been written around that time, but it is likely that such an "occasional" piece was composed under the impact of the original inspiration.

28. Most of "Thyrsis and Dorinda" was composed before 1645; a version which lacks (among others) lines 39 to the end is extant in the autograph of William Lawes, who died in that year (see *P and L,* 1:247–48). Dorinda's proposal of suicide begins in line 40 of the printed work and may have been added some time after the appearance of *Biathanatos* in 1647. Indeed, in a Bodleian manuscript (Rawl. poet. 199, f. 27v), an early version of the poem, minus Lawes's concluding couplet, is attributed to one "H. Ramsay." If this ascription is correct, Marvell may have appended to another poet's work the dialogue in which Dorinda longs for death (as she had done more ambiguously in Lawes's final couplet) and in which, more significantly, the paradoxically ethical shepherd is won over to her view. Compare Donne: "In some cases, we may without sinne wish Death; and that not onely for enjoying the sight of God . . . but even to be delivered from the encumbrances of this life" (p. 119).

In the copy of the 1648 edition of *Biathanatos* owned by the Union Theological Seminary Library, the name "William Popple" is signed on the title page. The name and hand are those of Marvell's nephew. (See the facsimile published by the Facsimile Text Society [New York, 1930] and British Library Add. MS 8888.) It seems that Marvell was in the habit of recommending books to Popple (see *P and L,* 2:346), and may have mentioned Donne's.

29. He summarized the piece in *RT,* 2, quoting liberally from it. See pp. 175–77. Marvell says that he had read Donne's poem "many years" earlier (p. 175).

30. Donne dutifully separates himself from "the curious Rebell," but here reveals his skeptical concerns in a kind of *praeteritio,* posing questions in the process of saying that they are not worthy to be asked. He is consciously ironical in the next stanza:

> But snatch mee heavenly Spirit from this vaine
> Reckoning their vanities, lesse is their gaine
> Then hazard still, to meditate on ill,
> Though with good minde; their reasons like those toyes
> Of glassie bubbles, which the gamesome boyes
> Stretch to so nice a thinnes through a quill
> That they themselves breake, doe themselves spill:
> Arguing is heretiques game, and Exercise
> As wrastlers, perfects them; Not liberties
>   Of speech, but silence; hands, not tongues, end heresies.

[111–20]

"Arguing" is Donne's game too, as he is well aware, and as the irreverent spirit of the rest of the poem makes clear. If he were perfectly intent on "silence," he would be silent. The high spirits and wit of *Metempsychosis* do not, of course, preclude a "fundamental moral seriousness" (see Helen Gardner, "'The Metempsychosis' of John Donne," *TLS,* 29 December 1972, 587). Questioning may be serious.

31. *RT,* 1:144.

32. On the question of the date, see *P and L,* 1:276–77.

33. See *P and L,* 1:276.

34. See above, pp. 67–8.

35. Even Marvell's later antagonist, Samuel Parker, knew to whom the work was to be attributed. See the excerpt from Parker's *History of His Own Time* given in Elizabeth Story Donno, *Andrew Marvell: The Critical Heritage,* pp. 85–86.

36. P. 79.

37. See James H. Elson, *John Hales of Eton* (New York: King's Crown Press, 1948), pp. 121, 65–84, and *passim.*

38. "Of the Sin Against the Holy Ghost," in *The Works of the Ever Memorable Mr. John Hales,* 3 vols. (Glasgow, 1765), 1:45–46. Compare Marvell's *Mr. Smirke:* "a man cannot force himself to believe" (p. 67).

39. See Elson, *John Hales, passim.*

40. "Concerning Schism and Schismatics," *Works,* 1:126–27. See also Jeremy Taylor, *The Liberty of Prophesying,* 2.10 (*Works,* 5:384–85); Milton, *Of True Religion, CW,* 6:168.

41. "The Severity of the Divine Judgments Vindicated"; *Works,* 3:171.

42. Ibid., p. 178. Hales advances some "reasons," but shows no great confidence in them.

43. See above, p. 123.

44. In *RT,* 1 (1672), Marvell quotes extensively from the "little Treatise of Schism," which he had read "many years ago," and which he had just come across again in a bookseller's stall (p. 79ff.). One might compare Hales's condemnation, in his *Tract,* of the Second Council of Nicaea (1:124) with Marvell's denunciation, in his *Historical Essay* [*on*] *General Councils,* of the First (p. 110ff.).

45. *Works,* 1:138.

46. Ibid., p. 115.

47. Ibid., p. 116.

48. "Peace, the Legacy of Christ"; *Works*, 3:4.

49. See the "Two Songs at the Marriage of the Lord Fauconberg and the Lady Mary Cromwell" and the references to Cromwell's "Eliza" in *A Poem Upon the Death of O. C.*

50. See Christopher Hill, *God's Englishman*, pp. 203, 95.

51. See Legouis, *Andrew Marvell*, p. 93.

52. Marvell professed to esteem the *Defensio Secunda* as a work of "the most compendious Scale, for so much, to the Height of the Roman eloquence." "When I consider," he said,

> how equally [the work] turnes and rises with so many figures, it seems to me a Trajans columne in whose winding ascent we see imboss'd the severall Monuments of your learned victoryes. And Salmatius and Morus make up as great a Triumph as That of Decebalus, whom too for ought I know you shall have forced as Trajan the other, to make themselves away out of a just Desperation [*P and L*, 2:306].

The letter in which this homage appears is an attempt by Marvell to soothe Milton's wounded vanity. Bradshaw had not reacted with ecstatic enthusiasm upon receiving a copy of the work in question.

Marvell was well aware, then, of Milton's limitations, but hardly persuaded by them to withhold his admiration for a man whose person he defended (as Edward Phillips claimed) in dangerous times and whose character and learning he publicly admired even when it was disadvantageous to do so (see *RT*, 2:311–12).

53. *P and L*, 2:306.

54. See *Upon Appleton House*, 591, 610, 642, 657–72; *Apology for Smectymnuus; YPW*, 1:930; *Lycidas*, 40, 104; *Nativity Ode*, 32ff., 64ff., 229ff. The parallels are noted in *P and L*, 1:290–91.

55. Compare *The First Anniversary*, 151–52, with *Nativity Ode*, 168–72; *The First Anniversary*, 218, 358, with *Lycidas*, 177, 94. See *P and L*, 1:323–24. Also J. M. French, *The Life Records of John Milton*, 4 vols. (New Brunswick, N.J.: Rutgers University Press, 1949–56), 3:444–45; and Judith Scherer Herz, "Milton and Marvell: The Poet as Fit Reader," *MLQ* 39 (1978): 239–63. For comparison of *The First Anniversary* with Milton's *Defensio Secunda*, see Annabel Patterson, "Against Polarization: Literature and Politics in Marvell's Cromwell Poems," 264ff.

56. *Areopagitica*; YPW, 2:555.

57. Legouis observes: "Cromwell's first Parliament had met in September 1654. If in December Marvell did not foresee its dismissal, he at least knew that ninety members had from the first been excluded for refusing to sign an engagement to be faithful to the Commonwealth *and* the Lord Protector" (*P and L*, 1:322).

58. *Areopagitica*; YPW, 2:557–58, 553.

59. *The Life of John Milton*, 6 vols. (London: Macmillan, 1859–80), 6:716.

60. Some of the political affinities have been discussed by Christopher Hill in "Milton and Marvell," in Patrides, *Approaches to Marvell*, pp. 1–30.

61. YPW, 2:526. As the Yale editor of *Areopagitica*, Ernest Sirluck, notes, Milton had not always been hostile to utopian theorizing. See *An Apology for Smectymnuus . . . (YPW*, 1:881): "That grave and noble invention which the greatest

and sublimest wits in sundry ages, *Plato in Critias,* and our two famous countrey-men, the one in his *Utopia,* the other in his *new Atlantis* chose . . . to display the largenesse of their spirits by teaching this our world better and exacter things, then were yet known."

On Marvell's relationship to the author of the utopian *Oceana,* James Harrington, see Legouis, *Andrew Marvell,* pp. 123-24, and Donal Smith, "The Political Beliefs of Andrew Marvell," *UTQ* 36 (1966): 57-59.

62. See *De Doctrina Christiana,* 2.17; *YPW,* 6:802ff. Also, *The History of Britain,* 6; *YPW,* 5:385.

63. On Milton's changing belief in "justification by success," see William Riley Parker, *Milton: A Biography,* 2 vols. (Oxford: Clarendon Press, 1968), *passim.* (A partial index to this topic as treated in the biography is given in 2:1457.)

64. *YPW,* 4:678-79.

65. *A Poem upon the Death of O. C.,* 221-22; *RT,* 1:111. On Milton's view of law as "force" in matters of conscience, see *De Doctrina Christiana,* 2.17; *YPW,* 6:797ff.

66. *Of True Religion, CW,* 6:168.

67. "Milton," from Lecture 10 of *The Literary Remains of Samuel Taylor Coleridge,* 4 vols., ed. Henry Nelson Coleridge (London: William Pickering, 1836), 1:178.

68. *RT,* 2:324. The quotation is from Bacon's *Resuscitatio* (1671 ed.), p. 129. See *RT,* p. 403.

69. Letter to William Popple, 15 July 1676; *P and L,* 2:346. "If you wish something more perfect, you should consult Cornelius Agrippa himself on the vanity of the sciences."

70. "On the Notoriousnesse of the Evil" (1667), in Stillingfleet's *Twelve Sermons Preached in Several Occasions,* 2 vols. (London, 1696), 1.2.51. Marvell sent a copy of this sermon to Lord Wharton in April of 1667. See *P and L,* 2:310.

71. "On the Notoriousnesse of the Evil," p. 64-66. In *The Rehearsal Transpros'd* Marvell said that Stillingfleet, "though yet living, deserves the honour to be already cited for good Authority" (2:295). It is, of course, possible that Marvell also read Stillingfleet's more systematic theodicy in *Orgines Sacrae: A Rational Account of the Christian Faith* (see the 3d ed. [1666], 3.iii), but more likely that his admiration for the doctor was occasioned by the case for toleration made in Stillingfleet's *Irenicon* (mentioned in *RT,* 2:295).

72. "On the Notoriousnesse of the Evil," pp. 82-84.

73. *RT,* 2:323; from Bacon's *Resuscitatio,* p. 129. This is not Bacon's full-fledged, philosophical fideism, but is a product of the habit of mind which produced the philosophy.

74. *RT,* 2:255. I stress that Marvell's problems were epistemological rather than metaphysical. I can agree, therefore, with Wallace (*Destiny His Choice,* p. 200), who finds that Harold Toliver misinterprets the warning against "hooking things up to Heaven." Toliver takes the phrase to mean that "Marvell was coming to accept as inevitable the separation of the providential universe from the naturalistic world of seventeenth-century philosophy and science" (*Marvell's Ironic Vision,* p. 191). On the other hand, as is clear from what follows, I find unacceptable Wallace's judgment that Marvell's political philosophy in *The Rehearsal Transpros'd* and in other Restoration statements "depends . . . on hitching the [earthly life and heaven] together as closely as any casuist had done during the civil war."

75. *RT,* 2:250.

76. Ibid., p. 232.

77. Ibid.

78. Ibid., p. 289.

79. *RT,* 1:15 and 2:231–32.

80. *RT,* 2:250.

81. Ibid., p. 240.

82. Ibid., p. 250.

83. *RT,* 1:111.

84. *Mr. Smirke,* p. 55.

85. Ibid., p. 50; *The Growth of Popery,* p. 281. See also the opening of the *Historical Essay [on] General Councils* (p. 91ff.) for Marvell's emphasis on the separation of Christ's kingdom from Caesar's.

86. See *RT,* 1:79, 83 and 2:295–96, 325. For a survey of these thinkers in the context of seventeenth-century intellectual history, see Herschel Baker, *The Wars of Truth* (Cambridge: Harvard University Press, 1952). And see W. K. Jordan, *The Development of Religious Toleration in England,* 4 vols. (Cambridge: Harvard University Press, 1932–40).

87. Within limits, of course. Marvell never advocated broadened toleration for Catholics. (The Declaration of Indulgence, however, to which he gave his approval in print, granted Catholics the right to worship in their own homes.) He had approved of Cromwell's restrictions upon the more radical Protestant sects (*The First Anniversary,* 293ff.); and although in the fervently latitudinarian days of the Restoration he worked for toleration of "Dissenters" generally, he did not take a clearly defined stand for or against comprehension.

88. *RT,* 2:251.

89. *The First Anniversary,* 125ff. See Marvell's estimate of Rome's strength and durability in *RT,* 1:15.

90. *RT,* 2:251: "All Laws . . . are but Probationers of time; and, though meant for perpetuity, yet, when unprofitable, do as they were made by common consent, so expire by universal neglect, and without Repeal grow Obsolete."

91. *The Last Instructions to a Painter,* 891ff.

92. Forty-nine of the sixty-nine Trinity House letters—dating from 1661 to 1678—are in the "Spurn Lights" file. See *P and L,* 2:247–303, 371.

93. See Legouis, *Andrew Marvell,* p. 129ff.

94. See the unpublished doctoral dissertation of Caroline Robbins, *A Critical Study of the Political Activity of Andrew Marvell* (University of London, 1926), appendix IV.

95. See Legouis, *Andrew Marvell,* pp. 153–54.

96. *P and L,* 2:315.

97. See Legouis, *Andrew Marvell,* pp. 142, 157–58, 176–77; *The Last Instructions to a Painter,* 285ff.

98. So John Wallace has suggested (*Destiny His Choice,* pp. 190–91). This may be a tenable mental distinction. But Marvell mentioned the Declaration by name—the "Gracious *Declaration of Indulgence,* of which I wish His Majesty and the Kingdom much joy" (p. 73). For Marvell to have withdrawn this specific approval without any explicit statement would have required of him a subtlety that would have been lost on his audience.

99. See pp. 279–80.

100. Wallace's attempt (pp. 146–47) to deny Marvell authorship of most of the

satires which vilify the king is not convincing. See Legouis, *Études Anglaises* 21 (1968):414–15; also the notes to the satires in *P and L*, 1.

101. See Patterson, *Marvell and the Civic Crown*, pp. 33–34; Kelliher, *Andrew Marvell*, pp. 84–86, 90.

102. See Legouis, *Andrew Marvell*, pp. 148–49.

103. Ibid., p. 117. See the two letters to the English diplomat George Downing in *P and L*, 2:307–8.

104. Swift, *Verses on the Death of Dr. Swift*, 213–14.

105. See Donal Smith, "The Political Beliefs of Andrew Marvell," 55–67.

106. See *Character* in *Halifax: Complete Works*, ed. J. P. Kenyon (Harmondsworth: Penguin, 1969), p. 85.

107. *History of My Own Time*, quoted in Kenyon, p. 35.

108. *Moral Thoughts and Reflections; Works*, p. 215.

109. *Character; Works*, p. 50.

110. Ibid., p. 63.

111. 2:232.

112. *Character; Works*, p. 102.

113. Ibid.

114. Ibid., p. 65.

115. For an opinion to the contrary, see Crutwell, *The Shakespearean Moment*, p. 123.

116. Legouis, *Andrew Marvell*, p. 128.

117. See *P and L*, 2:321–23, 357; Legouis, *Andrew Marvell*, p. 127. Since the *i* in *occidere* can be either long or short, the Latin can be construed in more than one way. Legouis translates: "I rather fear to kill than to be killed [and if I fear at all to die a violent death it is] not because I hold life of such a price but to avoid dying unprepared" (*P and L*, 2:396).

118. "Utility of Religion," p. 74.

Bibliography

Unless I indicate otherwise, all references to classical texts and translations are to the editions of the Loeb Classical Library. In quoting from Plato, however, I generally use Jowett's translation, and I generally cite W. D. Ross's translation of Aristotle's *Nicomachean Ethics*. I have taken the liberty of altering some translations—with acknowledgment—in light of the originals. Translations of non-classical texts are, except where noted, my own.

A. Primary Sources

Aubrey, John. *Brief Lives*. Edited by Oliver Lawson Dick. Ann Arbor: University of Michigan Press, 1962.

Aquinas, Thomas. *Summa Contra Gentiles*. 4 vols. Translated by the Fathers of the English Dominican Province. London: Burns, Oates, and Washbourne, 1924-29.

———. *Summa Theologica*. 22 vols. Translated by the Fathers of the English Dominican Province. London: Burns, Oates, and Washbourne, 1921-42.

Augustine. *Earlier Writings*. Translated by J. H. S. Burleigh. Philadelphia: The Westminster Press, 1953.

———. *Opera Omnia*. 12 vols. Edited by Monks of the Order of St. Benedict. Paris: J. P. Migne, 1841-77.

———. *The Works of Aurelius Augustine*. 15 vols. Edited by Marcus Dods. Edinburgh: T. and T. Clark, 1871-.

Bayle, Pierre. *The Dictionary Historical and Critical of Mr. Peter Bayle*. 5 vols. 2d ed. London: 1734-38.

———. *Dictionnaire historique et critique*. 4 vols. 3d ed. Rotterdam, 1720.

———. *Oeuvres diverses*. Reproduced in 4 vols. Hildesheim: Georg Olms, 1966.

Bruno, Giordano. *Giordano Bruno's The Heroic Frenzies*. Translated by P. E. Memmo, Jr. University of North Carolina Studies in the Romance Languages and Literatures, 50. Chapel Hill: University of North Carolina Press, 1964.

Calvin, John. *Commentary on Genesis*. Translated by John King. Edinburgh: Calvin Translation Society, 1847.

———. *Institutes of the Christian Religion*. 2 vols. Edited by John T. McNeill. Translated by F. L. Battles. London: S. C. M. Press; Philadelphia: The Westminster Press, 1961.

Castiglione, Baldasare. *The Book of the Courtier*. Translated by Charles S. Singleton. New York: Anchor Books, 1959.

Cleanthes. "Hymn to Zeus." Translated by James Adam. In *Stoic and Epicurean*, edited by R. D. Hicks, 14–16. New York: Scribner's, 1910.

Coleridge, Samuel Taylor. *The Literary Remains of Samuel Taylor Coleridge*. Edited by Henry Nelson Coleridge. 4 vols. London: William Pickering, 1836.

Cudworth, Ralph. *The True Intellectual System of the Universe*. 1678. 4 vols. London: R. Priestly, 1820.

Donne, John. *Biathanatos*. 1647. Facsimile edition of the Facsimile Text Society. New York, 1930.

———. *Devotions upon Emergent Occasions*. Edited by Anothony Raspa. Montreal and London: McGill-Queen's University Press, 1975.

———. *The Divine Poems*. Edited by Helen Gardner. 2d ed. Oxford: Clarendon Press, 1978.

———. *The Elegies and the Songs and Sonnets*. Edited by Helen Gardner. Oxford: The Clarendon Press: 1965.

———. *The Epithalamions, Anniversaries, and Epicedes*. Edited by W. Milgate. Oxford: Clarendon Press, 1978.

———. *The Satires, Epigrams, and Verse Letters*. Edited by W. Milgate. Oxford: Clarendon Press, 1967.

———. *Selected Prose*. Edited by Helen Gardner and Timothy Healy. Oxford: Clarendon Press, 1967.

———. *The Sermons of John Donne*. Edited by E. M. Simpson and G. R. Potter. 10 vols. Berkeley and Los Angeles: University of California Press, 1953–62.

Duns Scotus, John. *Opera Omnia*. Edited by Franciscan Fathers of the Strict Observance. 26 vols. Paris: L. Vivès, 1891–95.

Fuller, Thomas. *The History of the Worthies of England*. Edited by P. A. Nuttall. 3 vols. London: Thomas Tegg, 1840.

Goethe, Johann Wolfgang von. *Faust. Part I*. Translated by C. F. MacIntyre. New York: New Directions, 1949.

Greville, Fulke. *Poems and Dramas of Fulke Greville, First Lord Brooke*. Edited by Geoffrey Bullough. 2 vols. Edinburgh: Oliver and Boyd, 1939.

Hales, John. *The Works of the Ever Memorable Mr. John Hales*. 3 vols. Glasgow, 1765.

Herbert, George. *The Works of George Herbert.* Edited by F. E. Hutchinson. Oxford: Clarendon Press, 1941.

Hopkins, Gerard Manley. *Correspondence of Gerard Manley Hopkins and Richard Watson Dixon.* Edited by C. C. Abbott. London: Oxford University Press, 1935.

―――. *The Sermons and Devotional Writings of Gerard Manley Hopkins.* Edited by Christopher Devlin, S.J. London: Oxford University Press, 1959.

Howell, James. *The Vision: Or a Dialog Between the Soul and The Bodie.* London, 1651.

Hume, David. *Dialogues Concerning Natural Religion.* Edited by Norman Kemp Smith. 2d ed., 1947. Reprint. Indianapolis: Bobbs-Merrill, n.d.

Irenaeus. *Against Heresies.* Vol. 1 of *The Ante-Nicene Christian Library,* edited by A. Roberts and J. Donaldson. Edinburgh: T. and T. Clark, 1867-72.

―――. *Demonstration of the Apostolic Preaching.* Vol. 16 of *Ancient Christian Writers: The Works of the Fathers in Translation.* Westminster, Md.: Newman Press, 1946-.

James, William. *The Varieties of Religious Experience.* 1902. Reprint. New York: Collier, 1961.

Johnson, Samuel. *A Johnson Reader.* Edited by E. L. McAdam, Jr. and George Milne. New York: Modern Library, 1966.

Jonson, Benjamin. *Ben Jonson.* Edited by C. H. Herford and Percy and Evelyn Simpson. 11 vols. Oxford: Clarendon Press, 1925-52.

Kant, Immanuel. *Groundwork of the Metaphysic of Morals.* Translated by H. J. Paton. New York: Harper & Row, 1964.

Kierkegaard, Søren. *A Kierkegaard Anthology.* Edited by Robert Bretall. New York: Modern Library, n.d.

Lactantius. *On the Anger of God.* Vol. 7 of *The Writings of the Ante-Nicene Fathers.* Grand Rapids: William B. Eerdmans, 1951.

Lipsius, Justus. *Two Bookes of Constancie.* Translated by Sir John Stradling. 1594. Edited by Rudolf Kirk. New Brunswick, N. J.: Rutgers University Press, 1939.

Loyola, Ignatius. *The Spiritual Exercises of St. Ignatius.* Translated by Anthony Mottola. New York: Image Books, 1964.

Luther, Martin. *The Bondage of the Will.* Translated by J. I. Packer and O. R. Johnston. Westwood, N.J.: Revell Press, 1957.

Marvell, Andrew. *The Complete Poems.* Edited by Elizabeth Story Donno. Harmondsworth: Penguin Books, 1972.

―――. *Complete Poetry.* Edited by George deF. Lord. New York: Random House, 1968.

———. *The Complete Works of Andrew Marvell.* Edited by Alexander Grosart. 4 vols. London: Fuller Worthies' Library, 1875.

———. *The Latin Poetry of Andrew Marvell.* Translated by William A. McQueen and Kiffin A. Rockwell. University of North Carolina Studies in Comparative Literature, no. 34. Chapel Hill: University of North Carolina Press, 1964.

———. *The Poems and Letters of Andrew Marvell.* Edited by H. M. Margoliouth. Revised by Pierre Legouis with the collaboration of E. E. Duncan-Jones. 2 vols. 3d ed. Oxford: Clarendon Press, 1971.

———. *The Rehearsal Transpros'd and the Rehearsal Transpros'd, the Second Part.* Edited by D. I. B. Smith. Oxford: Clarendon Press, 1971.

———. *Selected Poetry.* Edited by Frank Kermode. New York: New American Library, 1967.

———. *The Works of Andrew Marvell, Esq.* Edited by Thomas Cooke. 2 vols. London, 1726.

Mill, John Stuart. *"Nature" and "Utility of Religion."* Edited by George Nakhnikian. Indianapolis: Bobbs-Merrill, 1958.

Milton, John. *Complete Poems and Major Prose.* Edited by Merritt Y. Hughes. Indianapolis and New York: Odyssey Press, 1957.

———. *Complete Prose Works.* Edited by Don M. Wolfe et al. 6 vols. New Haven: Yale University Press, 1953-.

———. *The Works of John Milton.* Edited by Frank Allen Patterson. 18 vols. New York: Columbia University Press, 1931-38.

More, Henry. *Divine Dialogues.* London, 1668.

———. *An Explanation of the Grand Mystery of Godliness.* London, 1660.

Newman, John Henry. *An Essay in Aid of a Grammar of Assent.* 1870. Reprint. New York: Image Books, 1955.

Origen. *Contra Celsum.* Translated by Henry Chadwick. Cambridge: Cambridge University Press, 1965.

Parker, Samuel. *A Free and Impartial Censure of the Platonick Philosophy.* 2d ed. London, 1667.

———. *A Reproof to the Rehearsal Transpros'd.* London, 1673.

Pascal, Blaise. *Entretien avec M. de Saci.* In *Pensées de Pascal.* Introduction et notes par Ch.-M. des Granges. Paris: Éditions Garnier Frères, 1964.

———. *Pensées.* Translated by W. F. Trotter. London: Dent, 1947.

Renan, Ernest. *Feuilles détachées.* Paris: Calmann Lévy, 1892.

Savile, George, marquess of Halifax. *Halifax: Complete Works.* Edited by J. P. Kenyon. Harmondsworth: Penguin, 1969.

Shakespeare, William. *The Riverside Shakespeare.* Edited by G. B. Evans et al. Boston: Houghton Mifflin, 1974.

Spenser, Edmund. *Poetical Works.* Edited by J. C. Smith and E. De Selincourt. London: Oxford University Press, 1912.

Stillingfleet, Edward. *Irenicum: A Weapon-salve.* London, 1661.

———. *Origines Sacrae: A Rational Account of the Grounds of the Christian Faith.* 3d ed. London, 1666.

———. *Twelve Sermons Preached in Several Occasions.* 2 vols. London, 1696.

Swift, Jonathan. *The Poems of Jonathan Swift.* Edited by Harold Williams. 3 vols. Oxford: Clarendon Press, 1937.

Sylvester, Joshua, translator. *Bartas his Devine Weekes and Workes.* London, 1605.

Taylor, Jeremy. *Ductor Dubitantium.* 1660. 2 vols. Edited by the Rev. Alexander Taylor. London: Longman, 1855.

Waller, Edmund. *The Poems of Edmund Waller.* Edited by G. Thorn Drury. 2 vols. London: G. Routledge and Sons, 1893.

Wood, Anthony à. *Athenae Oxonienses.* 2 vols. London, 1691-92.

Wyatt, Sir Thomas. *The Collected Poems of Sir Thomas Wyatt.* Edited by Kenneth Muir and Patricia Thompson. Liverpool: Liverpool University Press, 1969.

B. Studies

Abrams, M. H. *The Mirror and the Lamp.* New York: Norton, 1958.

———. *Natural Supernaturalism.* New York: Norton, 1971.

Alpers, Paul. "*Lycidas* and Modern Criticism." *ELH* 49 (1982): 468-96.

———. *The Singer of the Eclogues: A Study of Virgilian Pastoral.* Berkeley, Los Angeles, and London: University of California Press, 1979.

Alvarez, A. *The School of Donne.* 1961. Reprint. New York: Mentor Books, 1967.

Bagguley, Walter A., ed. *Andrew Marvell 1621-78: Tercentenary Tributes.* Oxford: Oxford University Press, 1922.

Baker, Herschel. *The Wars of Truth.* Cambridge: Harvard University Press, 1952.

Bald, R. C. *John Donne: A Life.* Oxford: Clarendon Press, 1970.

Barker, Arthur E., ed. *Milton: Modern Essays in Criticism.* London: Oxford University Press, 1965.

Baron, Hans. "'An Horatian Ode' and Machiavelli." *JHI* 21 (1960): 450-51.

Berthoff, Ann Evans. *The Resolved Soul: A Study of Marvell's Major Poems.* Princeton: Princeton University Press, 1970.

Billicsich, Friedrich. *Das Problem des Uebels in der Philosophie des Abendlandes.* 3 vols. Vienna: A. Sexl, 1936-59.

Bradbrook, M. and Lloyd-Thomas, M. G. *Andrew Marvell.* Cambridge: Cambridge University Press, 1940.

Brett, R. L., ed. *Andrew Marvell: Essays on the Tercentenary of his Death.* Oxford: Oxford University Press, 1979.

Buckley, George T. *Atheism in the English Renaissance.* Chicago: University of Chicago Press, 1932.

Bush, Douglas. "John Milton." In *English Institute Essays, 1946.* New York, 1947.

Carey, John, ed. *Andrew Marvell: A Critical Anthology.* Harmondsworth: Penguin Books, 1969.

The Catholic Encyclopedia. New York: R. Appleton, 1909.

Chernaik, Warren. "Politics and Literature in Marvell." *Renaissance and Modern Studies* 16 (1972): 25-36.

Colie, Rosalie. "Marvell's 'Bermudas' and the Puritan Paradise." *RN* 10 (1957): 75-79.

————. *"My Ecchoing Song": Andrew Marvell's Poetry of Criticism.* Princeton: Princeton University Press, 1970.

Copleston, Frederick, S. J. *A History of Philosophy.* 9 vols. 1946-. Reprint. New York: Image Books, 1962-.

Creaser, J. M. "Marvell's Effortless Superiority." *EC* 20 (1970): 403-23.

Crutwell, Patrick. *The Shakespearean Moment.* 1954. Reprint. New York: Modern Library, 1960.

Cullen, Patrick. *Spenser, Marvell, and Renaissance Pastoral.* Cambridge: Harvard University Press, 1970.

Cummings, R. M. "The Difficulty of Marvell's 'Bermudas.'" *MP* 67 (1969-70): 331-40.

Damon, Phillip, ed. *Literary Criticism and Historical Understanding: Collected Papers from the English Institute.* New York: Columbia University Press, 1967.

Danielson, Dennis. *Milton's Good God: A Study in Literary Theodicy.* Cambridge and New York: Cambridge University Press, 1982.

Davison, Dennis. *The Poetry of Andrew Marvell.* London: E. Arnold, 1964.

Donno, Elizabeth Story. *Andrew Marvell: The Critical Heritage.* Boston: Routledge & Kegan Paul, 1978.

Duncan-Jones, E. E. "Marvell His Own Critic." *NQ* 3 n.s. (1956): 383-84.

Edel, Leon. *Literary Biography.* 1957. Reprint. Bloomington, Indiana: Indiana University Press, 1973.

Ellrodt, Robert. *L'Inspiration personelle et l'esprit du temps chez les poètes métaphysiques anglais.* 2 vols. 3 parts. Paris: Corti, 1960.

Elson, James H. *John Hales of Eton.* New York: King's Crown Press, 1948.

Evans, J. Martin. *Paradise Lost and the Genesis Tradition.* Oxford: Clarendon Press, 1968.

Fizdale, Tay. "Irony in Marvell's 'Bermudas.'" *ELH* 42 (1975): 203-13.

French, J. M. *The Life Records of John Milton*. 4 vols. New Brunswick, N.J.: Rutgers University Press, 1949-56.

Friedenreich, Kenneth, ed. *Tercentenary Essays in Honor of Andrew Marvell*. Hamden, Conn.: Archon, 1977.

Friedman, Donald. *Marvell's Pastoral Art*. Berkeley and Los Angeles: University of California Press, 1970.

Gardner, Helen. *The Business of Criticism*. Oxford: Clarendon Press, 1959.

Gauthier, René-A. *La Morale d'Aristote*. Paris: Presses Universitaires de France, 1958.

Greene, William Chase. *Moira: Fate, Good, and Evil in Greek Thought*. Cambridge: Harvard University Press, 1948.

Grierson, H. J. C. *Metaphysical Lyrics and Poems of the Seventeenth Century*. Oxford: Clarendon Press, 1921.

Guild, Nicholas. "The Contexts of Marvell's Early 'Royalist' Poems." *SEL* 20 (1980): 125-36.

―――. "Marvell's 'The First Anniversary of the Government Under O. C.'" *Papers on Language and Literature* 11 (1975): 242-53.

Harris, Victor. *All Coherence Gone*. Chicago: University of Chicago Press, 1949.

Heilman, Robert. "Tragedy and Melodrama." *Texas Quarterly* 3 (1960): 36-50.

Herz, Judith Scherer. "Milton and Marvell: The Poet as Fit Reader." *MLQ* 39 (1978): 239-63.

Hibbard, G. R. "The Country House Poem of the Seventeenth Century." *JWCI* 29 (1956): 159-74.

Hick, John. *Evil and the God of Love*. London: Macmillan, 1966.

Hill, Christopher. *God's Englishman: Oliver Cromwell and The English Revolution*. 1970. Reprint. New York: Harper Torchbooks, 1972.

―――. *Puritanism and Revolution*. 1958. Reprint. New York: Schocken, 1964.

Hodge, R. I. V. *Foreshortened Time: Andrew Marvell and Seventeenth Century Revolutions*. Cambridge: D. S. Brewer, 1978.

Hyman, Lawrence. *Andrew Marvell*. New York: Twayne, 1964.

Jolivet, Régis. *Le Problème du mal d'après St. Augustin*. 2d ed. Paris: G. Beauchesne et fils, 1936.

Jordan, W. K. *The Development of Religious Toleration in England*. 4 vols. Cambridge: Harvard University Press, 1932-40.

Keast, William R, ed. *Seventeenth-Century English Poetry: Modern Essays in Criticism*. London and New York: Oxford University Press, 1971.

Kermode, Frank. "Marvell Transprosed." *Encounter* 27 (1966): 77-84.

Kelliher, Hilton. *Andrew Marvell*. London: The British Library, 1978.

King, Bruce. "In Search of Andrew Marvell." *REL* 8 (1967): 31-41.

Kittel, Gerhard, ed. *Theological Dictionary of the New Testament.* 10 vols. Translated by G. W. Bromiley. Grand Rapids: William B. Eerdmans, 1964-76.

Labrousse, Elizabeth. *Pierre Bayle.* 2 vols. The Hague: Nijhoff, 1963-64.

Legouis, Pierre. *André Marvell: poète, puritain, patriote, 1621-78.* Paris: Didier, 1928.

————. *Andrew Marvell: Poet, Puritan, Patriot.* 2nd ed. Oxford: Clarendon Press, 1968.

————. Review of *Destiny His Choice; The Loyalism of Andrew Marvell,* by John M. Wallace. *Études Anglaises* 21 (1968): 414-15.

Leishman, J. B. *The Art of Marvell's Poetry.* 2d ed. New York: Minerva Press, 1968.

————. *On Translating Horace.* Oxford: B. Cassirer, 1956.

Levin, Harry. *The Myth of the Golden Age in the Renaissance.* New York: Oxford University Press, 1969.

Lord, George deF., ed. *Andrew Marvell: A Collection of Critical Essays.* Englewood Cliffs, N.J.: Prentice-Hall, 1968.

Lovejoy, Arthur O. *Essays in the History of Ideas.* Baltimore: Johns Hopkins Press, 1948.

————. *The Great Chain of Being.* Cambridge: Harvard University Press, 1936.

————, and Boas, George. *A Documentary History of Primitivism and Related Ideas in Antiquity.* Baltimore: Johns Hopkins Press, 1935.

Mazzeo, J. A. "Cromwell as Machiavellian Prince in Marvell's 'Horatian Ode.'" *JHI* 21 (1960): 1-17.

————. *Reason and Imagination.* New York: Columbia University Press, 1962.

The New Catholic Encyclopedia. New York: McGraw-Hill, 1967.

Palmer, Paulina. "Marvell, Petrarchism and 'De gli eroici furori.'" *English Miscellany* 24 (1973-74): 19-57.

Parker, William Riley. *Milton: A Biography.* 2 vols. Oxford: Clarendon Press, 1968.

Patrides, C. A. "Adam's 'Happy Fault' and XVIIth-Century Apologetics." *Franciscan Studies* 23 (1963): 238-43.

————. *Approaches to Marvell. The York Tercentenary Lectures.* London: Routledge & Kegan Paul, 1978.

Patterson, Annabel. "Against Polarization: Literature and Politics in Marvell's Cromwell Poems." *ELR* 5 (1975): 251-72.

————. *Marvell and the Civic Crown.* Princeton: Princeton University Press, 1978.

Poggioli, Renato. "The Oaten Flute." *Harvard Library Bulletin* 11 (1957): 147-84.

―――. "The Pastoral of the Self." *Daedalus* 88 (1959): 686-99.

Press, John. *Andrew Marvell.* London: Longmans, 1958.

Richards, I. A. *Principles of Literary Criticism.* 1925. Reprint. New York: Harvest Books, n.d.

Ricoeur, Paul. *The Symbolism of Evil.* Translated by Emerson Buchanan. Boston: Beacon Press, 1967.

Rivers, Isabel. *The Poetry of Conservatism.* Cambridge: Rivers Press, 1973.

Robbins, Caroline. *A Critical Study of the Political Activity of Andrew Marvell.* Ph.D. Dissertation. University of London, 1926.

Røstvig, Maren-Sofie. *The Happy Man.* 2 vols. 2d ed. Oslo: Norwegian Universities Press, 1962.

Rose, H. J. *A Handbook of Greek Mythology.* 2d ed. London: Methuen, 1933.

Royce, Josiah. *Studies in Good and Evil.* New York: D. Appleton, 1898.

Sackville-West, Victoria. *Andrew Marvell.* London: Faber and Faber, 1929.

Santayana, George. *Skepticism and Animal Faith.* New York: Scribner's, 1929.

Schwartz, Richard B. *Samuel Johnson and the Problem of Evil.* Madison: University of Wisconsin Press, 1975.

Scoular, Kitty. *Natural Magic.* Oxford: Clarendon Press, 1965.

Sertillanges, A. D., O.P. *Le Problème du mal.* 2 vols. Paris: Aubier, 1948-51.

Siemon, James. *Andrew Marvell's School Learning.* Ph.D. Dissertation. Stanford University, 1966.

Smith, Donal. "The Political Beliefs of Andrew Marvell." *UTQ* 36 (1966): 55-67.

Steadman, John M. *Milton's Epic Characters.* Chapel Hill: University of North Carolina Press, 1968.

Summers, Joseph. *The Heirs of Donne and Jonson.* New York and London: Oxford University Press, 1970.

Taunton, Ethelred. *The History of the Jesuits in England.* London: Methuen, 1901.

Tayler, Edward. *Nature and Art in Renaissance Literature.* New York: Columbia University Press, 1964.

Toliver, Harold. *Marvell's Ironic Vision.* New Haven: Yale University Press, 1965.

Trilling, Lionel. *Sincerity and Authenticity.* Cambridge: Harvard University Press, 1972.

Wall, L. N. "Marvell and Seneca." *NQ* 8 n.s. (1961): 185-86.

Wallace, John M. *Destiny His Choice: The Loyalism of Andrew Marvell.* Cambridge: Cambridge University Press, 1968.

Wallerstein, Ruth. *Studies in Seventeenth-Century Poetic.* Madison: University of Wisconsin Press, 1950.

Warnke, Frank J. "Play and Metamorphosis in Marvell's Poetry." *SEL* 5 (1965): 23-30.

Weisinger, Herbert. *Tragedy and the Paradox of the Fortunate Fall.* London: Routledge & Kegan Paul, 1953.

Wellek, René and Warren, Austin. *Theory of Literature.* 3d ed. New York: Harcourt, Brace, and World, 1963.

Wilding, Michael, ed. *Marvell: Modern Judgements.* London: Macmillan, 1969.

Wiley, Margaret. *The Subtle Knot: Creative Skepticism in Seventeenth-Century England.* Cambridge: Harvard University Press, 1952.

Williams, N. P. *The Ideas of the Fall and of Original Sin.* London: Longmans, 1927.

Wilson, A. J. N. "Andrew Marvell's 'The First Anniversary.'" *MLR* 69 (1974): 254-73.

Zwicker, Stephen. "Models of Governance in Marvell's 'The First Anniversary.'" *Criticism* 16 (1974): 1-12.

Index

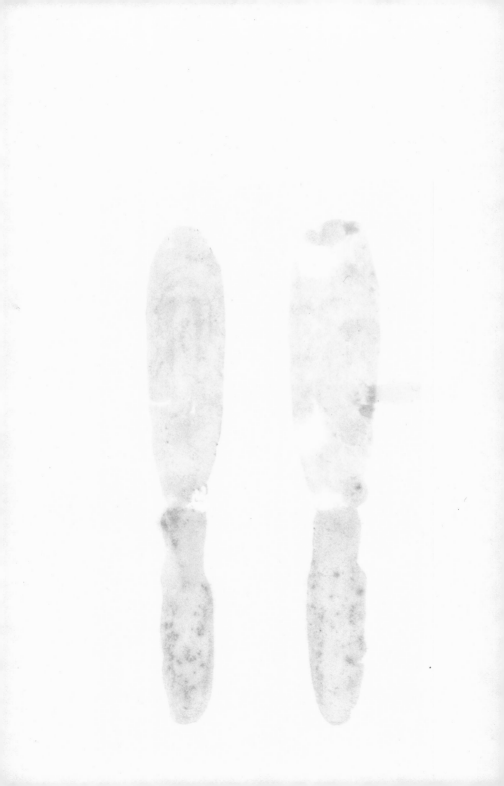